INTERNATIO
SOCIALISI

CW00515638

A quarterly journal of socialist theory

Summer 1998
Contents

Issue 79 of INTERNATIONAL SOCIALISM, quarterly journal of the Socialist Workers Party (Britain)

Published July 1998
Copyright © International Socialism
Distribution/subscriptions: International Socialism,
PO Box 82, London E3.
American distribution: B de Boer, 113 East Center St, Nutley,
New Jersey 07110.
Subscriptions and back copies: PO Box 16085, Chicago
Illinois 60616
Editorial and production: 0171-538 1626
Sales and subscriptions: 0171-538 5821
American sales: 773 665 7337

ISBN I 898876 39 8

Printed by BPC Wheatons Ltd, Exeter, England
Typeset by East End Offset, London E3
Cover by Sherborne Design Ltd

For details of back copies see the end pages of this book

Subscription rates for one year (four issues) are:

Britain and overseas (surface):	individual	£14.00 ($30)
	institutional	£25.00
Air speeded supplement:	North America	£3.00
	Europe/South America	£3.00
	elsewhere	£4.00

Note to contributors

The deadline for articles intended for issue 81 of *International Socialism* is 1 August 1998

All contributions should be double-spaced with wide margins. Please submit two copies. If you write your contribution using a computer, please also supply a disk, together with details of the computer and programme used.

INTERNATIONAL SOCIALISM ★

A quarterly journal of socialist theory

150 YEARS after its first publication there are 14 different editions of *The Communist Manifesto* now in print in Britain alone. Last year 80,000 copies of just one of these editions were sold. In an extended editorial John Rees examines the revival of interest in Marx among media pundits and academics and assesses what this means for the working class movement. The *Manifesto* was written during the revolutionary years of the 1840s, and in a major article Lindsey German examines these revolutions and explains the *Manifesto*'s continuing relevance for understanding and changing the world today. Judy Cox introduces Marx's concept of alienation, looking at the material basis for the dominance of ruling class ideas and how they can be undermined. Another central aspect of Marx's work was his explanation of why economic crises are endemic in capitalism. Judith Orr reviews a new account of this analysis and this quarter's Bookwatch focuses on Marxism and science with Phil Gasper's comprehensive survey of classic and contemporary books on the subject.

MODERN ART is ridiculed by the tabloids and yet the art world makes millions from it. John Molyneux gives a Marxist analysis of the controversies surrounding modern art in his review of the recent 'Sensation' exhibition at the Royal Academy. This year marks the 100th anniversary of the birth of Sergei Eisenstein, the acclaimed Russian film maker. Anna Chen puts Eisenstein In perspective examining his innovative techniques and his relationship to revolutionary politics.

A SELECTION of new books which examine the origins of and prospects for New Labour are reviewed by Megan Trudell. In his book review Jonathan Neale explores one legacy of the Vietnam War—the trauma experienced by US veterans.

Editor: John Rees. Assistant editors: Alex Callinicos, Chris Harman, John Molyneux, Lindsey German, Colin Sparks, Mike Gonzalez, Peter Morgan, Mike Haynes, Judy Cox, Megan Trudell, Mark O'Brien and Rob Hoveman.

The return of Marx?

JOHN REES

Suddenly, after years where the only words used about Marx in the main-stream media insisted on his irrelevance to contemporary events, there is a revival of interest in Marxism. Recently the *Independent on Sunday* devoted the three page cover story of its review section to an article titled 'Was He Right All Along?' touting Marx as 'the next big thinker' and insisting on the importance of his analysis of capitalism before con-cluding that 'despite his errors, he was a man for whom our economic system held few surprises. His books will be worth reading as long as capitalism endures'.[1] The *Financial Times* paid tribute to 'Marx's extra-ordinary impact on the last century and a half' and reminded its readers that 'Marx was not only the harbinger of revolutionary hatred, but a shrewd, subtle analyst of capitalist society'.[2] This was the second time in a week that the *Financial Times* praised Marx. A few days earlier colum-nist Edward Mortimer quoted *The Communist Manifesto* to prove that 'Marx and Engels described a world economy more like that of 1998 than 1848'.[3]

The 150th anniversary of *The Communist Manifesto* has been the occasion for many of these reappraisals of Marx. *The Guardian* ran a full page feature, half of which was an extract from Eric Hobsbawm's intro-duction to the new Verso edition of the *Manifesto*. The other half was an account of the 1848 revolutions.[4] BBC2's *Newsnight* chose to run the longest section of one evening's programme on an assessment of the *Manifesto*[5] and even Marx's daughter Eleanor gained some recognition in *The Independent* with an article commemorating the anniversary of her death.[6] This list, and it is not exhaustive, certainly testifies to a flurry of journalistic interest in Marx.[7] But is there anything more substantial to the revival of Marx than a passing fad among editors short of sensationalist copy?

In fact the rediscovery of Marx in the press was preceded for some years by a softening of attitudes towards Marx among some left academics. Throughout the 1980s and early 1990s postmodernism commanded an almost unqualified allegiance among left leaning academics. Marxism was rarely mentioned in anything but disparaging terms. Marx was said to be reductionist, determinist, authoritarian and worse. Any attempts at what Jean François Lyotard described as historical 'grand narratives' were said to be simply an attempt to project the subjective desires of the particular theorist onto a necessarily fragmented and atomised reality. The result of any attempt to act on such reductive theories could only be an authoritarian forcing of others to share in 'discourses' which were not their own. Such coercion would lead, ultimately, to the gulag.

A significant break in this theoretical anti-Marxist front came with the publication of postmodernist Jacques Derrida's *Specters of Marx* in 1994. The book itself, based on earlier lectures, is a rambling, discursive stream of consciousness from which little of substantive interest can be rescued. Its significance lay in the simple fact that, beneath the verbiage, it seemed to transmit a message that a prodigal was returning:

> ...*the Marxist inheritance was—and still remains, and so it will remain—absolutely and thoroughly determinate. One need not be a Marxist or a communist in order to accept this obvious fact. We all live in a world, some would say a culture, that still bears, at an incalculable depth, the mark of this inheritance...*[8]

And Derrida is not alone. In a recently published series of interviews conducted by Eva Corredor a number of prominent intellectuals reassess the influence of Marxism, particularly the Marxism of George Lukács, at the end of the 20th century.[9] Some are figures, like Terry Eagleton and Lukács's biographer Michael Lowy, who have never sought to distance themselves from the Marxist tradition. Others, like Etienne Balibar, co-author with Louis Althusser of *Reading Capital*, were among those whose critique of Marxism paved the way for the triumph of postmodernism in the 1980s. Balibar now seems not only to be rekindling his interest in Marxism, but also to have developed a partial critique of his own earlier work. Balibar remembers that 'in the sixties I would not read Lukács very much, mainly because of the influence of Althusser'.[10] He adds that:

> ...we were very opposed to any form of what we called a Hegelian interpreta-
> tion of history, and we would see [Lukács's work] as a form of return of
> Hegelianism into Marxism itself. Our idea, right or wrong, was that we should
> develop a critique or a new foundation of Marxism, not in that direction, but
> almost exactly in the opposite direction. So our great names were not Lukács
> and Korsch but Brecht, Levi-Strauss to some extent, and Freud above all.[11]

But Balibar, 'at the other end of my career', now records a significant
shift in focus:

> I am now and have for some time been in a process of re-evaluating the
> importance of Lukács in the intellectual history of the 20th century. To my
> own surprise, possibly because I was too ignorant, too naive, or too sec-
> tarian, I have now become aware of the fact that he is a very central figure, to
> say the least.[12]

Balibar's reappraisal does not run to embracing the crucial notion of the
working class as the subject of history, but it nevertheless marks a shift in
emphasis back towards the central concerns of the classical Marxist tradition, founded by Marx and Engels and developed by Lenin, Luxemburg,
Gramsci, Lukács and Trotsky. Other writers much further from this tradition than Balibar are also finding the 1990s to be a time in which it is
useful to recall Marx. Writer Cornel West describes himself both as 'a
black Christian' and as 'deeply indebted to the Marxist tradition'. George
Steiner, the model of an establishment intellectual, concludes an interview
full of admiration for Lukács, with these sentiments:

> If one has not read [Hegel's] **The Phenomenology of the Spirit**, one is not of
> our time. And really read it, not just little post-deconstructivist idiocies about
> it... The same is true of others. Not to have read **The Eighteenth Brumaire**,
> **The Condition of the Working Class in England** by Engels—very, very
> important—not to have read part of the **Grundrisse**, not to have read about
> the French Revolution, would be to deprive one of the masters of epic narra-
> tive and invectives, which is to have missed the turning point of modern
> history even while disagreeing totally.[13]

All this comes after a steady stream of books with titles like *Marx at
the Millennium, The Future of Socialism* and *Reinventing Socialism.*[14]
The Communist Manifesto anniversary has added to this current. Two of
the more interesting and substantial pieces are Eric Hobsbawm's introduction to the Verso edition and Colin Leys and Leo Panitch's

contribution to the special edition of the *Socialist Register* devoted to the *Manifesto*.[15]

The first sense in which these contributions are interesting is that they forcibly state one of the main reasons for the revival of interest in Marxism—the continued economic and political chaos of the global capitalist system in the late 20th century. Behind the ephemeral journalistic enthusiasms, the waning of postmodernist fashion and the convenient dual anniversaries of 1848 and 1968, lies the brute and inescapable fact of a world caught in the coils of instability first described in the *Manifesto*. This is the constantly repeated refrain in both media and academic commentary. *The Guardian*'s economics correspondent, Larry Elliott, even imagined, in an article called 'How the Next Depression Began', the possible effects of the next worldwide slump: 'Did anybody emerge with any credit from this debacle? Well...Karl Marx...won hundreds of millions of new followers among the huddled masses...'[16] But mostly commentators reserve their praise for Marx's ability to foresee the shape of the global economic crisis in advanced capitalism. Eric Hobsbawm expresses the common position:

> ...what will undoubtedly...strike the contemporary reader is the **Manifesto**'s remarkable diagnosis of the revolutionary character and impact of 'bourgeois society'. The point is not simply that Marx recognised and proclaimed the extraordinary achievements and dynamism of a society he detested—to the surprise of more than one later defender of capitalism against the red menace. It is that the world transformed by capitalism which he described in 1848, in passages of dark, laconic eloquence, is recognisably the world in which we live 150 years later.[17]

Leys and Panitch make the same point more directly:

> Journalists can no longer speak, as they did in the 1980s, of 'the business community', as if it were some benign college whose interests were more or less identical to those of the nation as a whole; simply to stay credible they must now talk about 'the corporate agenda' and the threat capitalism (no longer a taboo word) poses to the environment, and about the problems of poverty and homelessness it is creating, the erosion of social security and the negative impact of the standards of health and education.[18]

And so they argue:

> The tide of reaction is still flowing, but with diminishing confidence and force, while the counterflow of progressive feeling and ideas gathers strength but has yet to find effective political expression. As the contradictions of

unbridled neoliberalism become increasingly plain, fewer and fewer people any longer mistake its real character. 'Stubborn historical facts' are breaking through the illusions fostered by neoliberal rhetoric—and equally through the pseudo-left illusions of 'new times', 'radicalism of the centre' and all similar dreams of a capitalist world miraculously freed from alienation, immiseration and crises.[19]

This turn of the tide has been gathering force during the 1990s, fuelled by the failure of the New World Order in the Gulf War and subsequently everywhere from the Middle East through the Balkans to Somalia and Rwanda. The failure of the Asian Tiger economies and the revolution in Indonesia are merely the latest, if also some of the greatest, chapters in the unravelling story of capitalism's failure to live up to the bright future painted for it by its apologists in the wake of the collapse of the Stalinist states. The most important popular expression of this mood has been a series of mass strikes in many European countries, most importantly in France. Another has been the return, especially in Britain, of social democratic governments after many years of conservative dominace which has further raised hopes of a socialist revival.

The current 'return to Marx' is a product of these interlinked events. But, welcome as it is, this revival contains a number of crucial weaknesses which, if it is to be sustained and built upon, must be overcome. Firstly, the return to Marx is partial and selective. Marx's analysis of capitalism is praised, but his belief in the revolutionary potential of the working class is denigrated nearly everywhere. Hobsbawm again provides a summary of the common argument:

> *...if at the end of the millennium we must be struck by the acuteness of the manifesto's vision of the then remote future of massively globalised capitalism, the failure of another of its forecasts is equally striking. It is now evident that the bourgeoisie has not produced 'above all...its own gravediggers' in the proletariat.*[20]

It is not that Hobsbawm dismisses the working class as a political force altogether. He is willing to admit that the *Manifesto* was right in its 'prediction of the central role of the political movements based on the working class' and points out that 'descendants of the social-democratic parties of the Second International, sometimes under their original names, are parties of government in all except two European states (Spain and Germany), in both of which they have provided the government in the past, and are likely to do so again'.[21] Such optimism about the prospects for reformism is an unacknowledged change in Hobsbawm's analysis. He famously predicted in the 1980s, in the essay 'The Forward March of Labour Halted', that the erosion of the traditional working class would undermine the possibility of reformist parties repeating the electoral success they enjoyed before the Thatcher-Reagan era. That particular form of impressionism seems to have been dispelled by the electoral success of reformism in the 1990s.

Hobsbawm's criticism of Marx is now specifically directed at the claim that the working class is a potentially revolutionary class.[22] Both Derrida's rediscovery of Marx and Balibar's rediscovery of Lukács founder on the same rock. Indeed the only interviewee in the Corredor collection who will defend the proposition that the working class is the agent of social change is Terry Eagleton. The incredulity with which this idea is received by his interviewer speaks volumes for how academically unfashionable this notion remains.[23]

Yet the revolutionary potential of the working class is an indispensable central tenet of Marxism. Indeed it was the theoretical recognition of this fact which was the founding moment of Marx's distinctive analysis of capitalism. Many before Marx had pointed to the destructive nature of the capitalist system, not least the Utopian Socialists. And any number of social critics, radical sociologists and assorted reformers have done so since. What was and remains unique about Marx's approach was that it insisted that working class self emancipation could provide an alternative to the barbarity of capitalism. Almost alone among recent commentators Leys and Panitch have some sense that the working class movement is still, in the words of the *Manifesto*, 'the self-conscious, independent movement of the immense majority, in the interests of the immense majority':

> By the mid-1990s strikes in France, the USA and Canada once more occupied the front pages alongside reports of strikes in South Korea and 'IMF riots' throughout much of the Third World from Zimbabwe to Mexico. There was also a sharp rise in class awareness. Even the **Economist** noted, 'Many commentators think that class is dying, but ordinary people are not convinced. In fact class antagonisms may even be worsening—the proportion believing that there is a 'class struggle' in Britain rose from around 60 percent in the early 1960s to 81 percent in the mid-1990s, according to Gallup...[24]

The evidence for the vitality of the class struggle is, in fact, a good deal more substantial than this quotation suggests. There have, after all, been general strikes in Greece, Italy, Spain and Denmark in the mid-1990s. Moreover, there have been, on one calculation, mass political strikes in some 20 countries between 1994 and 1997.[26] Without a recognition of this fundamental revival in working class combativity and consciousness in recent years—notwithstanding all its continuing problems, weaknesses and limitations—it is difficult to see how those who are sympathetic to the revival of Marx can make any theoretical headway, let alone play any useful role in the development of the class struggle.

Secondly, the return to Marx is not a return to Marxism—that is, to the revolutionary Marxist tradition. Nothing exemplifies this more clearly than the very different fashions now affecting, on the one hand, Marx himself, and, on the other hand, the history of the Russian Revolution. The renewed interest in Marx may be a minority current even now. It may have important weaknesses. But it is, as we have seen, real enough. There is no such current, however shallow, willing to grant the same credence to the experience of the Russian Revolution or the work of Lenin. It is only sufficient to note that two of the most popular and widely praised historians of the Russian Revolution, both equally and violently anti-Bolshevik, are a former member of Ronald Reagan's National Security Council, Richard Pipes, and a former colonel in the propaganda department of the Russian army, Dmitri Volkogonov. There is virtually no counter-current on the left.[26]

But without the recognition that Marxism is a tradition, those who wish to see its revival will be hamstrung. However far-seeing Marx and Engels were, they could not foresee the series of problems which the further development of capitalism placed in the path of the working class movement. The development of imperialism, mass reformism, Third World nationalism and Stalinism, to mention only the most obvious issues, pose problems which are almost impossible for modern Marxists to resolve unless they regard the work of Lenin, Luxemburg, Trotsky and Gramsci as part of a live, coherent and, for all the differences between its various representatives, unitary tradition.

Finally, the revival of interest in Marx is hampered by its proponents' lack of any direct contact with the radicalised mood among the mass of workers. The renewed interest in Marx is still largely a phenomenon restricted to an older generation of intellectuals, often those first radicalised by 1968 and its aftermath. Although there are some signs of a younger generation keen to rediscover the Marxist tradition, they have yet to make a mark and often remain mired in the obscure modes of expression typical of an academic milieu much more cramped by ideological conservatism and funding restrictions than their predecessors. Previous generations of radicalised theorists mostly found their home in the various Communist Parties internationally or in one brand or other of left reformism. Both forces are much weaker now than they were 30, 20 or even ten years ago. Yet some organised connection will have to be remade with the working class struggle if the revival of Marxism is not to wither on the vine as a mere literary episode with no serious social consequences.

Yet it is on this issue that even the best of the current commentators on Marx are least certain. *Socialist Register* has always insisted that some sort of organised political link to the working class struggle is desirable, but has long argued that this could not take the form of a Leninist party. Leys and Panitch continue this tradition by paying tribute to the 'brilliantly argued' case of Sheila Rowbotham, Lynne Segal and Hillary Wainwright who, in the 1970s pamphlet *Beyond the Fragments*, criticised 'the defects of the old parties and their sectarian offshoots'.[27] In fact *Beyond the Fragments* was a conspicuous failure: it did not lead to any new socialist grouping but it did provide an intellectual justification for a layer of former revolutionaries to either rejoin the Labour Party, initially its Bennite wing but later currents further right, or to drop out of politics altogether. And the current issue of *Socialist Register* leads with an essay by Rowbotham which resurrects many of the old canards, principle among them being that Marx was insufficently feminist.

But Leys and Panitch, despite their praise of old allies, seem to sense that something more is now required by the revival of the workers' movement. While claiming that the 'original new left's critique' of Bolshevism 'pointed in the right direction', they explicitly cite 'the failure of the new left either to transform the existing Social Democratic and Communist parties or to found viable new ones'. Furthermore they acknowledge that this led 'a strong current of left wing opinion to give up on both socialism and the working class, in favour of a more diffuse, "decentred" conception of "radical democracy" ' and this 'swept under the carpet the irreconcilability of democracy with private property'.[28] In response to this failure, Leys and Panitch call for a different form of socialist organisation:

> What has always been missing—and this is now strongly felt by many social movement leaders themselves—is something that would be more than the sum of the parts, something which the Social Democratic and Communist parties did partly provide in their heyday... These include providing activists with a strategic, ideological and educational vehicle; a political home which is open to individuals to enter (rather than restricted, as today's social movement networking is, to representatives of groups); a political community which explicitly seeks to transcend particularistic identities while supporting and building on the struggles they generate.[29]

The problem with this description of socialist organisation, at least for people who reject Leninism, is that it could have been written by Lenin himself. Lenin's model of the party was precisely designed to give a strategic and educational direction to the militants who joined it; it was specifically built with the intention of providing solidarity with the struggles of the exploited and oppressed and at the same time overcoming their particularistic character. And, if the revival of Marx is to have any practical effect on the working class struggle which he was the first to properly comprehend, such a party is necessary to fuse the movement of the day with the prospect of transforming society.

Notes

1   J Cassidy, 'The Next Big Thinker', *Independent on Sunday*, 7 December 1997. This itself was a reprint of an article which originally appeared in *The New Yorker*.
2   P Aspden, 'The Place Where All Workers are United', *Financial Times*, 28-29 March 1998.
3   E Mortimer, 'Global Gloom', *Financial Times*, 25 March 1998.
4   '23 Pages that Shook the World', *The Guardian*, 28 February 1998. Verso claim some 125 newspaper stories in the US concerned with their edition of the *Manifesto* alone.
5   *Newsnight*, BBC2, 2 April 1998.
6   F Evans, 'The Daughter of Modern Socialism', *The Independent*, 1 April 1998— although the article itself was largely ill informed gossip about the domestic life of the Marx family.
7   Other pieces, for instance, by Charlotte Raven appeared in the *Modern Review*, and, by Barrie Clement in *The Independent*, 8 March 1998. The same paper returned to the theme a few weeks later insisting that it had never been more fashionable to be 'red' and that 'now, more than ever, revolution is the ecstasy of history.' Noting the waning of the postmodern fashion, Howard Byrom wrote, 'The very instant you get a grip on Barthes, the chattering classes have switched to discussions of dialectical materialism'. H Byrom, 'Commie des Garcons', *Independent on Sunday*, 29 March 1998.
8   J Derrida, *Specters of Marx* (Routledge, 1994), p14.
9   E L Corredor, *Lukács After Communism*, interviews with contemporary intellectuals (Duke University Press, 1997).
10 Balibar, ibid, p116.
11 Ibid, p114.
12 Ibid, p117.
13 G Steiner, ibid, p74.
14 C Smith, *Marx at the Millennium* (Pluto Press, 1996), W K Tabb (ed), *The Future of Socialism, Perspectives from the Left* (Monthly Review Press, 1990), H J Sherman, *Reinventing Socialism* (The Johns Hopkins University Press, 1995).
15 C Leys and L Panitch, 'The Political Legacy of the Manifesto', in L Panitch and C Leys (eds), *Socialist Register 1998* (Merlin Press, 1998).
16 L Elliott, 'How the Next Depression Began', *The Guardian*, 30 March 1998.
17 E Hobsbawm, Introduction to *The Communist Manifesto* (Verso, 1998), pp15-16.
18 C Leys and L Panitch, op cit, p19.
19 Ibid, p18.
20 E Hobsbawm, op cit, p18.
21 Ibid, p21.
22 Ibid.
23 E L Corredor, op cit, 142.
24 C Leys and L Panitch, op cit, p20.
25 K Moody, *Workers in a Lean World* (Verso, 1997), p10.
26 For an account, and refutation, of the left's capitulation to the right wing historiography of the Russian Revolution see J Rees et al, *In Defence of October* (Bookmarks, 1997). See also M Haynes, 'Social History and the Russian Revolution', in J Rees (ed,) *Essays on Historical Materialism* (Bookmarks, 1998).
27 C Leys and L Panitch, op cit, p22.
28 Ibid, p40.
29 Ibid, pp22-23.

Reflections on *The Communist Manifesto*

LINDSEY GERMAN

'The history of the *Manifesto* reflects to a great extent the history of the modern working class movement; at present it is undoubtedly the most widespread, the most international production of all socialist literature, the common platform acknowledged by millions of workingmen from Siberia to California'.[1] So wrote Frederick Engels towards the end of his life of the impact of *The Communist Manifesto*. The statement remains as true today, 150 years later. The impact of *The Communist Manifesto* has been remarkable. This small book has been translated into all the major languages and has remained an inspiration for generations of socialists. It has entered into working class consciousness in a way that few other political works have been able to do. It is often the first and perhaps even the only piece of writing by Marx and Engels that many workers read. It also has a dramatic and literary quality which makes it one of the great pieces of political writing. Its powerful arguments and its sense of providing a complete picture still overshadow most modern political work. The *Manifesto* must rank as one of the few pieces of writing whose opening and closing lines are well known in their own right. 'A spectre is haunting Europe, the spectre of communism,' and, 'The proletarians have nothing to lose but their chains. They have a world to win,' are phrases which have entered the language of international socialism. But reading *The Communist Manifesto* it is impossible not to recognise a number of other well known phrases which encapsulate some key Marxist formulations. 'All that is solid melts into air', the capitalists produce their 'own gravediggers', 'the workingmen have no country', 'the free development of each is the condition for the free development of all.'

The success of *The Communist Manifesto* lies in two huge strengths which the book possesses. It is the clearest short exposition of the ideas of revolutionary Marxism, and alongside its clarity of thought and language it is also a guide to action.

Marx and Engels had a sense of tremendous upheaval in the world around them during the 1840s. They viewed the capitalist development which had taken hold in England, Belgium and to a certain extent France as revolutionary. It could destroy the old feudal societies which still dominated much of Europe and it could lead to major social and economic advances for the mass of humanity. This new order with its completely new ways of organising production would come into conflict with the old. Marx and Engels saw revolutionary upheaval as an inevitable outcome of these clashes, especially in their native Germany, which was still made up of a large number of small states and principalities, although increasingly dominated by the militarised eastern state of Prussia.

The coming revolutions would be 'bourgeois revolutions', necessary to pave the way for full capitalist development by sweeping away the old political autocracies, which still based themselves on the feudal methods of production. But Marx and Engels recognised that they would have a significant working class component. Key to their theory was their understanding that the working class was the most powerful revolutionary class. Engels had direct experience of the English working class—he had gone to England at the end of 1842 in the aftermath of the general strike of that year and he was familiar with the politics of the Chartists. His experiences, on which he based his book *The Condition of the Working Class in England*, were of a capitalism which could create immense wealth and revolutionise work, but which also created immense human misery. The potential of the working class to change the world was a key part of the polemic in which both Marx and Engels engaged with those involved in socialist or democratic politics. The *Manifesto* summarised their analysis: the big battles between the feudal order and the bourgeoisie were imminent, but these would soon be replaced by the battles between the now powerful capitalist class and the emerging revolutionary working class.

In 1847 Marx and his family were living in Brussels and Engels in Paris. They were politically active mainly among other German émigrés in the Communist Correspondence Committees which existed in Paris, Brussels and London. They were also in contact with socialists organised in the League of the Just, a body which based its political support on German artisans living in London. Although the League's politics harked back to a world based on workshop rather than factory production, many of its members were also undergoing a period of ideological upheaval. In the summer of 1847 the League changed its name to the Communist League. Even before this date Marx and Engels were asked by one of its leaders, the watchmaker Joseph Moll, to join the League and to write its founding principles.

Engels first embarked on the project, writing his little book *Principles of Communism* which is sometimes described as a first draft of the *Manifesto* and which he called a communist catechism. In this book Engels attempted to answer many of the basic questions about communist ideas raised by potential supporters.[2] *Principles of Communism* starts with the development of the factory system and how this imposes a division of labour upon work, so that the labour needed for a particular task is broken down into a series of repetitive tasks capable of being performed by a machine. Thus the spread of machinery and the factory to every branch of industry led to the increased polarisation of society into two major classes: the bourgeoisie which owns the factories and raw materials; and the proletariat which is forced to sell its labour power as a commodity in order to live. However, the anarchy of the system means that the spread of capitalism into every area of life, without any plan or any thought about what should be produced, leads to a crisis of overproduction, where goods are left unsold, factories lie idle and workers are made unemployed. The capitalist organisation of industry and production is a barrier to further development and thus society can only advance when ownership of production becomes social and therefore fitted to the needs of the producers. This means the abolition of private property—something only possible under socialism—and with it the abolition of class society.

> So long as it is not possible to produce so much that not only is there enough for all, but also a surplus...So long must there always be a ruling class, disposing of the productive forces of society, and a poor, oppressed class. How these classes are composed will depend upon the stage of the development of production. In the Middle Ages which were dependent on agriculture, we find the lord and the serf; the towns of the later Middle Ages show us the master guildsman and the journeyman and day-labourer; the 17th century has the manufacturer and the manufacturing worker; the 19th century has the big factory owner and the proletarian. It is obvious that hitherto the productive forces had not yet been developed so far that enough could be produced for all or to make private property a fetter, a barrier to these productive forces.

With capitalism, however, the massive increase in the productive forces and the development of the two main contending classes meant that 'only now...has the abolition of private property become not only possible but even absolutely necessary'.[3]

The question and answer form of *Principles of Communism* was a starting point for a statement of aims, but it was only the bare bones of what became the *Manifesto*. Marx took some of its structure and arguments but built a much more substantial and engaging piece of writing from them. He did this because towards the end of 1847 a conference of the Communist League in London, which Marx attended, commissioned him to write a manifesto for the organisation which he set about doing after a number of disagreements over political issues. Marx's failure to produce a draft led to an irate letter at the end of January 1848 from the central committee of the League saying that, 'if the "Manifesto of the C Party", the writing of which he undertook at the last congress, has not arrived in London by Tuesday 1 February of this year, further measures will be taken against him'.[4] The warning did the trick and the draft was completed by early February and sent to London where it was published in February 1848.

What *The Communist Manifesto* says

'The history of all hitherto existing society is the history of class struggles.' The starting point of the *Manifesto* is also the starting point of the Marxist theory of history. In all previous societies there have been struggles between the classes which eventually proved decisive and which led either to the creation of a new way of organising work and living, a revolutionary change in society as a whole, or to the 'common ruin of the contending classes'.[5] If the outcome of the struggle between the classes was not decisive, if neither side could effectively break through, then rather than going forward, the whole of society could be pushed backwards. Such crucial struggles had marked the development of society in particular historical periods as it moved from one mode of production to another. Most recently, the great battles in England in the 1640s and France in the 1780s and 1790s represented the successful struggle of the bourgeoisie over the forces of feudalism. The bourgeois revolutions which would, Marx and Engels assumed, spread throughout other parts of Europe would usher in a period of rapid development of the forces of production which in turn would lead quite rapidly to working class or proletarian revolution. The *Manifesto* therefore starts its analysis by looking at the progress which capitalism represents compared to previous societies, and looks initially not at the emerging working class but at the revolutionary nature of the capitalist class itself.

The *Manifesto* creates a powerful and striking image of capitalism as a constantly changing and dynamic system which is altering almost before the authors' eyes. Perhaps unexpectedly it also conveys Marx and Engels' admiration for many of the achievements of capitalist development. If this is perhaps hard for us to imagine 150 years later—when in living memory there have been two world wars, numerous slumps, the Holocaust, and when genocide, famine and acute poverty are all facts of modern capitalist life—we have to bear in mind the background against which Marx and Engels wrote. The development of capitalism was for them a tremendous advance on what had gone before. German society in particular was held back by political and regional divisions, autocratic political systems, archaic laws and restrictive trading conditions. The dynamic elements of German society were hindered by these social relations which acted as fetters to prevent society from moving forward. By the 1840s there was already a clear division between the dynamism of some societies, driven forward on the basis of rapid capitalist development, and the stagnation of others.

Capitalism was in the process of destroying the old feudal order and establishing its own rule. This in turn, Marx and Engels argued, would create the preconditions for the struggle for socialism—in particular, it would create mass industrial production and a new revolutionary working class. The *Manifesto* gives a brilliant short portrait of the development of capitalism: the growth of the towns in the Middle Ages, the voyages of discovery which led to merchant capitalism, the growth of manufacture to meet the demands of the new markets:

> *The feudal system of industry, under which industrial production was monopolised by closed guilds, no longer sufficed for the growing wants of the new markets. The manufacturing system took its place. The guildmasters were pushed on one side by the manufacturing middle class; division of labour between the different corporate guilds vanished in the face of division of labour in each single workshop. Meantime the markets kept ever growing, the demand ever rising. Even manufacture no longer sufficed. Thereupon, steam and machinery revolutionised industrial production. The place of manufacture was taken by the giant modern industry, the place of the industrial middle class by industrial millionaires, the leaders of whole industrial armies, the modern bourgeois.*[6]

The system developed into a world system with the search for markets taking it into the corners of the globe and bringing with it cities, railways, modern communications. The bourgeoisie was a revolutionary class because it transformed production and destroyed ways of living and working which had often been in existence for hundreds of years:

> *The bourgeoisie cannot exist without constantly revolutionising the instru-*

ments of production, and thereby the relations of production, and with them, the whole relations of society. Conservation of the old modes of production ...was...the first condition of existence for all earlier industrial classes. Constant revolutionising of production, uninterrupted disturbance of all social conditions, everlasting certainty and agitation distinguish the bourgeois epoch from all earlier ones.[7]

This revolutionising of production has the same effect in every area of life. Old religions, beliefs or customs disappear, and men and women begin to think in dramatically different ways because they are living and working in different ways: 'All fixed, fast-frozen relations, with their chain of ancient and venerable prejudices and opinions, are swept away, all new-formed ones become antiquated before they can ossify. All that is solid melts into air, all that is holy is profaned, and man is at last compelled to face with sober sense, his real conditions of life, and his relations with his kind'.[8]

The development of commodity production—where all goods can be bought and sold on the market—also led to a market in wage labour. Old crafts and professions found that they could not compete with large scale industry. Jobs were transformed and performed by wage labourers. Artisans were propelled towards the proletariat. Capitalism, sweeping all before it, destroyed old societies, old jobs, whole communities, and established new ones. The dynamism of the system meant that, once it began to spread throughout the world, it had devastating effects: for example, destroying traditional ways of life such as those of the Native Americans, who found their methods of agriculture, nomadic life or even warfare no match for the machinery, railroads and telegraphs, and rifles which conquered a continent in a matter of decades. In India the indigenous cotton industry was destroyed by the import of cheap Lancashire cloth.

This spread of capitalist production spelt the end of many industries and societies, yet the awesome advances of the bourgeoisie are praised in the *Manifesto*: 'The bourgeoisie has subjected the country to the rule of the towns. It has created enormous cities, has greatly increased the urban population as compared with the rural, and has thus rescued a considerable part of the population from the idiocy of rural life.' Marx and Engels list achievements made by the capitalists in the space of around a century: 'Subjection of nature's forces to man, machinery, application of chemistry to industry and agriculture, steam navigation, railways, electric telegraphs, clearing of whole continents for cultivation, canalisation of rivers, whole populations conjured out of the ground—what earlier century had even a presentiment that such productive forces slumbered in the lap of social labour?'[9]

However, there is a fundamental failing in the system which leads Marx and Engels to compare capitalist society with the sorcerer who can no longer control the forces he has conjured up. The system is not logical or planned—its whole motor is capital accumulation for its own sake. It is therefore periodically prone to what the *Manifesto* describes as crises of overproduction which its authors describe in the most graphic terms: 'There is too much civilisation, too much means of subsistence, too much industry, too much commerce'.[10] The overproduction results from the unplanned nature of the system: production based on blind accumulation becomes an end in itself, the means of maintaining the capitalist's profit, rather than having any relationship to whether goods produced are needed.

Capitalist society—based on private commodity production and on the exploitation of wage labour—becomes a barrier to further production rather than a spur. Private property prevents the productive forces from being developed as they could be to supply the needs of the whole humanity. Instead capitalism's answer to the crisis is to destroy wealth. Factories close, workers are left unemployed, and those who could benefit from the goods produced in those factories have to go without.

So precisely the people who produce the wealth for the capitalists are not only denied any share in the riches of capitalism, they are also the victims in times of crisis when they lose their means to a livelihood. The solution to this deprivation, however, lies in their own hands.

The working class

The working class or the proletariat—meaning literally those without property—is the unique product of capitalism, which creates a class of wage labourers who have no means of subsistence other than to sell their labour power. The workers become slaves to machinery, their lives dominated by the process of exploitation. Marx and Engels describe the early development of the working class as a conscious class. Workers' struggles tend to be directed against the machinery which is destroying their old livelihoods. Their first political protests are not directed at the capitalists themselves but at the old order—'at this stage, therefore, the proletarians do not fight their enemies, but the enemies of their enemies, the remnants of absolute monarchy, the landowners, the non-industrial bourgeois, the petty-bourgeoisie'.[11] But as industry grows this tendency changes. The working class is organised in larger and larger numbers, the wages and conditions of different trades become more similar and the experience of factory work leads them towards collective organisation, trade unions and political organisations. The constant struggle between the classes, centred on production in the workplace, leads workers to co-operate and act together, and to develop ideas of collectivity and solidarity.

Marx and Engels describe the working class as the only really revolutionary class: workers' position as a class makes them uniquely placed to overthrow capitalist society. It does not matter, in the first instance, that they do not think of themselves as revolutionary. Their position in the workplace is key. Here they potentially have the power to run society because they produce the wealth and they are forced through their work experience to organise collectively. This means that they are the only class capable of leading a revolution. Whereas previous revolutions, even when they were victorious, resulted in one ruling class being replaced by another minority ruling class, acting in its own interests, such an outcome is not possible in a successful proletarian revolution. The working class can only make a revolution by abolishing the class society which creates its exploitation, thus emancipating all the dispossessed: 'All previous historical movements were movements of minorities, or in the interests of minorities. The proletarian movement is the self-conscious, independent movement of the immense majority, in the interest of the immense majority'.[12] The development of industry itself therefore creates the weapon for the destruction of the capitalist class and the establishment of a class whose collective power enables it to run society on an equitable basis—in the famous phrase, it creates the 'gravedigger' of capitalism.

Capitalism is marked by the increasing dominance of the proletariat and the bourgeoisie, the two major contending classes. The old classes tend to disappear in the face of capitalist development, the vast majority of their members being pushed towards the proletariat. 'The lower strata of the middle class—the small tradespeople, shopkeepers and retired tradesmen generally, the handicraftsmen and peasants—all these sink gradually into the proletariat, partly because their diminutive capital does not suffice for the scale on which modern industry is carried on. They are swamped in the competition with the large capitalists, partly because their specialised skill is rendered worthless by new methods of production'.[13] Greater numbers of people are forced to sell their labour power in order to make a living—a process which is still continuing at the end of the 20th century. Over recent decades, for example, peasants have moved from the land to the cities, migrants have crossed the world to work in the advanced industrial countries, and women in these countries have been drawn into the labour market in unprecedented numbers.

When workers do begin to organise collectively their struggles, if successful, usually lead to advances in society as a whole. Whereas the old classes when they fought tended to do so on a conservative basis, trying to preserve their threatened position inside capitalist society, the workers' struggle against the capitalists tended to lead to improvements in society and in the conditions of working people. In most capitalist societies today where workers have relatively high living standards and benefits, there is likely to be a relationship with high working class expectations, and often resulting from high levels of workers' organisation in the past or present.

Questions and answers

This first section of the *Manifesto* stands in opposition to those who claim that Marxism cannot address the modern world. It anticipates the speed and direction of actual capitalist development in countries such as the US and Germany by decades and explains a lot about 20th century capitalism, especially in many of the so called 'Third World' countries. The description of the growth of the proletariat, of capital accumulation and of the onset of crisis could all apply to the recent history of the Asian 'Tigers'. It is unsurprising therefore that a growing number of people are looking once again at the ideas of Marxism and socialism in trying to explain what is wrong with the world.

Marx and Engels were active revolutionaries who found an audience of potential socialists bitterly unhappy about what capitalism was doing to workers' lives and looking for an alternative. The second section of the *Manifesto* tries to deal with their arguments. It is in effect a series of questions and answers about socialism and communism and what it will achieve. Many are familiar to socialists today who find themselves faced with questions from those who are attracted to ideas of revolution but believe it will never take place. Take for example the question of private property. Central to Marx and Engels' view of communism is the need to abolish private property, since this is based on the exploitation of the vast majority. Yet they met an objection still commonly raised today—doesn't this mean you want to take away someone's personal possessions, and that you are denying them their personal means of choosing how to express themselves? What will be the incentive to work if people have no property of their own? The *Manifesto* explains that capital—or property—is not a personal but a social power: 'to be a capitalist is to have not only a purely personal but a social status in production'.[14]

Abolition of private property would not therefore result in every small item owned by a worker being taken away. Instead the social aspect of property would change: it would not be controlled by a tiny minority class and it would not form the basis of the oppression of everyone else. In fact 'communism deprives no man of the power to appropriate the products of society: all that it does is to deprive him of the power to subjugate the labour of others by means of such appropriation'.[15]

Complaints about property are in any case hypocritical coming from the capitalists. Capitalism has destroyed the property of the small peasantry, the artisans and small businessmen. Many of them have been forced to sell their labour power on the market; the wages of the labourers, which barely cover the costs of reproduction for them and their families, hardly allow the possession of very much individual property:

> *You are horrified at our intending to do away with private property. But in your existing society, private property is already done away with for nine-tenths of the population; its existence for the few is solely due to its non-existence in the hands of those nine-tenths. You reproach us, therefore, with intending to do away with a form of property, the necessary condition for whose existence is, the non-existence of any property for the immense majority of society. In one word, you reproach us with intending to do away with your property. Precisely so: that is just what we intend.*[16]

Despite talk of property-owning democracies in modern capitalism, the concentration of property among a tiny minority is still staggering, especially when housing—or debt in the form of mortgages—is excluded. For example, in Britain in the 1980s the share of marketable wealth for the richest 1 percent was 28 percent, while that of the richest 5 percent was 53 percent.[17] Another common objection to communism is that no one would work if there were no private property. Marx and Engels answer that if this were the case society would long ago have collapsed since 'those of its members who work acquire nothing, and those who acquire anything, do not work'.[18]

The *Manifesto* also points to a contradiction that while the forces of capitalism are turning the world upside down, destroying much of the fabric of the old societies, the capitalists themselves cling to the old customs, habits and ideas as though they spring from an eternal human nature. The capitalists can see clearly what was wrong with ancient or feudal society but not what is wrong with their own. They can see no other way of living and working. 'The selfish misconception that induces you to transform into eternal laws of nature and of reason, the social forms springing from your present mode of production and form of property, historical relations that rise and disappear in the progress of production—this misconception you share with every ruling class that has preceded you'.[19]

The *Manifesto* is completely scathing about some of the bourgeois horror stories of communism which arise from such attitudes. To accusations that they are out to abolish the family, Marx and Engels reply that the capitalist system has already destroyed communities, ripped working class families apart, enforced migration and pushed every member of the family, including small children, onto the labour market. This explains 'the practical absence of the family among the proletarians, and prostitution'.[20] The attitude of the bourgeoisie towards its own family and the sanctity of family life is hypocritical in the extreme. It bases its family on property, and its views on monogamy and sexual morality are based on inheritance and the idea of women as the property of men, to be bought and sold, either as wives or as prostitutes. Instead communism would free women from loveless and enforced sexual relations by taking away the economic constraints which dominated love and marriage under capitalism.

Underpinning these ideas—and Marx and Engels' equally radical ideas on nationality and religion—was the understanding that in the process of changing society and of moving from one mode of production (capitalism) to another (socialism) all the old ideas would be thrown into ferment and replaced with new forms of consciousness:

> *Does it require deep intuition to comprehend that man's ideas, views, and conceptions, in one word, man's consciousness, changes with every change in the conditions of his material existence, in his social relations and in his social life?*
>
> *What else does the history of ideas prove, than that intellectual production changes its character in proportion as material production is changed? The ruling ideas have ever been the ideas of its ruling class.*[21]

Any society based on the exploitation of one group by another, as class societies are, will develop ideas which justify the rule of its exploiters. It is not surprising that the ideas of the capitalists sanctify and protect property. The struggle for a new form of society which overcomes those class antagonisms means not just a material struggle against exploitation but an alternative ideological explanation of the world. The history of ideas has to be understood not as a series of disparate religions and thinkers, but as themselves being tied to the development of particular modes of production. The notion that there can be 'eternal truths' which transcend different societies and even different epochs does not stand up to historical scrutiny.

The radical social changes which Marx and Engels set out and the establishment of communism itself could only be achieved by sweeping away the old system of production, based on private property, which allowed a minority to accumulate wealth while the majority suffered. Only by ridding itself of these conditions can the working class begin to end the class antagonisms which the conditions produce. Eventually production for need based on workers themselves running society would lead to a classless society—communism—where 'the free development of each is the condition for the free development of all'.[22]

What sort of socialism?

The analysis of scientific socialism spelt out in the *Manifesto* was the first simple attempt by the authors to define their form of socialism and communism in relation to the various other sorts of socialism which had sprung up in England, France and Germany during the 1840s. They had direct experience of a number of these tendencies. Engels had been in contact both with the followers of Robert Owen and then with the Chartist movement when he first came to England in the early part of the decade. Marx had written his work *The Poverty of Philosophy* in response to the ideas of the French socialist Pierre Joseph Proudhon. Many of the German exiles in Paris, Brussels and London during the 1840s were influenced by the ideas of the German 'true socialists'.

The various forms of socialism on offer at the time tended to be backwards looking, towards a supposedly better society before the excesses of capitalism. Their proponents lacked any strategy for changing society except for appeals to representatives of the old classes themselves under attack from capitalism, or to the more liberal minded capitalists themselves, or to general but abstract appeals to 'truth' or 'justice'. Marx and Engels were fiercely critical of these various strands of socialism, as the final sections of the *Manifesto* explain in some detail. Having spelt out their theory of socialism, they engage in a polemic against those competing to win workers to different ideas. They consider the various sorts of socialism popularised in the years before the *Manifesto* was written, and start with a material analysis of why these sorts of socialism have found an audience. The different socialist theories express the various attempts by different classes and social forces to come to terms with the phenomenon of capitalism.

Many of the early forms of socialism were inspired, led and articulated by the representatives of those classes who had lost out the most in the transition from feudalism to capitalism and whose critique of the new system was based on the desire to preserve its old place in the social order. Even the aristocracy was prepared to attack the emerging bourgeoisie in words, although it was compromising with it in deeds and in sharing the spoils of wealth. The 'Young England' movement was not really a socialist movement at all but it had some following in the early 1840s. Disraeli, later to be a Tory prime minister, wrote two novels, *Sybil* and *Coningsby*, which 'can be read as textbooks of the [Young England] school… These Tory scions of the aristocracy had an idealistic aim: to counteract the rising bourgeoisie and regenerate the power of the aristocracy by appealing to the working classes of the factories and farms, not simply by social demagogy but by real amelioration of the workers' lot—exclusively at the expense of the rival ruling classes'.[23] These forces therefore represented divisions inside the ranks of the rulers and a real conflict of interests between different sections of the ruling class. However, they had no desire to see the working class acting in its own interests, since this would threaten the property and position of the landowners and the church as much as it would the factory owners. Their critique of capitalism, therefore, attracted the most compliant and least class conscious of the workers, those most likely to be deferential to their 'betters'.

The 'petty bourgeois' socialists also based their ideas on a class whose time had passed and which found its existence threatened by the creation of modern industry and the growth of the proletariat. Their social base lay among the peasantry, which was substantial in France and Germany, and the remnants of the old medieval producers. 'In its positive aims...this form of socialism aspires either to restoring the old means of production and of exchange, and with them the old property relations, and the old society, or to cramping the modern means of production and of exchange, within the framework of the old property relations that have been, and were bound to be, exploded by those means. In either case, it is both reactionary and utopian'.[24] An example of 'petty bourgeois' socialism was the German 'true socialism' which was influential before 1848. The 'true socialists' drew on the socialist ideas which had first come out of France but formulated them in such a way that they became totally distorted. They did not take into account the differences between the countries in terms of capitalist development and reduced socialist ideas to abstract philosophising rather than the product of a real struggle between the classes. 'True socialism' tried to straddle the basic conflict between the classes, and therefore identified with the status quo. It was popular in Germany in so far as it represented a rejection of the horrors of industrial capitalism, but 'true socialism' also stood for the preservation of petty bourgeois values and ideas against the rise of a new revolutionary working class. It placed store in eternal values such as 'truth' which supposedly transcended the limits of class society but in reality tried to ignore the fundamental class divisions. Put to the test by real events, 'true socialism' failed:

> *German socialism forgot in the nick of time, that the French criticism, whose silly echo it was, presupposed the existence of modern bourgeois society, with its corresponding economic conditions of existence, and the political constitution adapted there, to the very things whose attainment was the object of the pending struggle in Germany. To the absolute governments, with their following of parsons, professors, country squires and officials, it served as a welcome scarecrow against the threatening bourgeoisie.*[25]

The 'true socialists' epitomised reactionary interests in the German context and this came from their petty bourgeois class base; their attempts to preserve this class meant opposing revolution in Germany, since they feared the dominance of both the industrial bourgeoisie and the proletariat. Capitalist development in Germany would mean the petty bourgeoisie being completely squeezed, which is why despite the high sounding rhetoric of the 'true socialists' they presented no real challenge to the existing order.

Socialist and communist ideas had been in existence long before Marx and Engels started writing. However, all previous such theories started from a completely justified sense of moral revulsion at the outrages of the system but could not explain how these 'excesses' could be stopped and how society could be changed. Marx and Engels divided such socialists into two sorts: first were the conservative or bourgeois socialists, represented above all by Proudhon. These socialists denied the fundamental class antagonism of capitalist society and tried to appeal to 'progressive' sections of the bourgeoisie over 'humanitarian' issues. Some sections of the bourgeoisie did want limited reforms of the system because they felt that untrammelled capitalism was less likely to survive, its own existence being threatened by its excesses. They aimed to reform away the worst aspects of capitalism, thereby preserving the system. The *Manifesto* was completely scathing about such aims, which it classed as follows: 'To this section belong economists, philanthropists, humanitarians, improvers of the condition of the working class, organisers of charity, members of societies for the prevention of cruelty to animals, temperance fanatics, hole and corner reformers of every imaginable kind'.[26] Proudhon offered a 19th century version of market socialism—it's not the market itself which is the problem, but the market distorted by banks and monopolies.

The 'utopian socialists' were the other group considered by the *Manifesto*. Their ideas had heavily influenced Marx and Engels and they retained a degree of respect for the individuals and their ideas. But even the best of them, the French socialists Claude Henri de St Simon and Charles Fourier, and the English socialist Robert Owen, were subject to criticism in the *Manifesto*. A short while after 1848 Engels wrote of the 'three men who, in spite of all their fantastic notions and all their utopianism, have their place among the most eminent thinkers of all times, and whose genius anticipated innumerable things the correctness of which is now being scientifically proved by us'.[27] Years later Engels continued to repay the theoretical debt he owed to the utopian socialists when he praised them in *Socialism, Utopian and Scientific*.

The utopians developed their theories of socialism when the working class was in its infancy. This affected their view both of how capitalism could be changed and which forces could be the agency of change. Rather than seeing the working class in this role, they looked instead to great plans and schemes for building the new society. Their theories crystallised into some speculative and some actual social experiments—Fourier's 'phalansteries' or societal palaces or Owen's model workers' settlement in New Lanark—but there was a huge gulf between their visions of society and the means of achieving it. The utopians saw the working class as passive victims of exploitation, not agents of change in their own right. The grand visions of the utopians did not extend to the working class; instead they saw 'the spectacle of a class without any historical initiative or any independent political movement'.[28] So for the utopian socialists 'only from the point of view of being the most suffering class does the proletariat exist for them' and this led them, like all the other socialists whose methods Marx and Engels dismissed, to look to forces other than the working class to achieve socialism:

> *The undeveloped state of the class struggle...causes socialists of this kind to consider themselves far superior to all class antagonisms. They want to improve the condition of every member of society, even that of the most favoured. Hence, they habitually appeal to society at large, without distinction of class; nay, by preference, to the ruling class. For how can people, when once they understand their system, fail to see in it the best possible plan of the best possible state of society?*[29]

The value of the utopian socialists' critique of capitalism was further diminished by the growth of capitalist development and the corresponding growth of the working class. The followers of the great utopian socialist thinkers were incapable of relating to the real struggles of workers when they broke out. Marx and Engels pointed out that 'the Owenites in England, and the Fourierists in France, respectively oppose the Chartists and the "Reformistes".'[30] The latter day utopians became irrelevant sects who dreamed of setting up socialist colonies financed by the wealthy, of course. They had no impact on the class struggle and no relevance for workers. Indeed their politics led them in the opposite direction: forced to rely on the (limited) goodwill of the wealthy, they tried to smooth over class antagonisms and were opposed to independent workers' action. 'To realise all these castles in the air they are compelled to appeal to the feelings and purses of the bourgeois. By degrees they sink into the category of the reactionary conservative socialists'.[31]

The failure to recognise and act on the class antagonisms which formed the basis of capitalism led to a practice which has many parallels in the socialist movement today. The emphasis on 'humanism' and on appealing to 'the whole of society' is widespread in the ecological and Green movements, where appeals to moral decency are supposed to be enough to save the environment and where major capitalists such as

Anita Roddick (owner of the Body Shop and the seventh richest woman in Britain) can pose as eco-friendly. Parallels are also apparent in movements against nuclear weapons such as CND in the early 1980s, which consciously downplayed the class interests which led to the deployment of nuclear weapons in the first place. The history of the working class movement contains numerous examples of sects who have a formally socialist or even revolutionary programme but who refuse to engage in the day to day struggles of working people and who have found themselves doomed to extinction.

The final section of *The Communist Manifesto* disproves any idea that Marx and Engels played down building revolutionary organisation. In it they spell out their attitudes to existing organisations in various countries—for example, their support for the Chartists in England. They support all revolutionary movements against the existing order, but add two provisos: they always bring to the fore the question of property as the key class dividing line; and they publicly support revolution to overthrow all existing social conditions.[32] Earlier in the *Manifesto* they state, 'In what relation do the communists stand to the proletarians as a whole? The communists do not form a separate party opposed to other working class parties. They have no interests separate and apart from those of the proletariat as a whole'.[33] Does this mean that Marx and Engels were against building specific working class revolutionary organisation? Any brief acquaintance with their lives will show that is not the case. Although there were long periods when they were not members of any organisation or party, whenever the level of struggle or the needs of the working class movement enabled them to build organisation they were in the thick of it. This was true of the early communist organisations in the 1840s, and of Marx's central role in the building of the First International in the 1860s. Although Engels was not himself directly involved in the parties built around the Second International towards the end of the 19th century, he was central in discussing tactical and political questions relating to those parties with some of their leading participants.

The use of the word 'party' has to be seen in a different light from its meaning today. Its meaning in 1848 was much closer to the idea of a political current or to a set of ideas. When Marx and Engels argued that the communists do not form a separate party, they meant that their ideas and the interests of the proletariat coincided and they did not put up artificial barriers between the two. At the same time, their fierce criticism of the other forms of socialism are not simply an academic exercise: they are part of a polemic in favour of building the Communist League. They also emphasise the importance of theoretical clarity: 'The communists, therefore, are on the one hand, practically, the most advanced and resolute section of the working class parties of every country, that section which pushes forward all others; on the other hand, theoretically, they have over the great mass of the proletariat the advantage of clearly understanding the line of march, the conditions, and the ultimate general results of the proletarian movement'.[34] This description of the role of the communists suggests a commitment to building an active and politically developed body of people united by a set of ideas and a commitment to activity—very close to the modern version of a party.

Background to revolution

The *Manifesto*'s publication in February 1848 coincided almost exactly with the outbreak of revolution throughout Europe. Signs of discontent had been there much earlier. The old rulers throughout Europe were incapable of delivering the most basic democratic reforms or of guaranteeing decent living standards. In Italy and Germany, still not unified as nations but comprising numbers of small states, and in much of the Austrian Empire which included dozens of nationalities, the feeling for national liberation was paramount, as it was in Poland and the Russian Empire. Everywhere there were calls for an end to autocracy and the absolute powers of monarchs and princes. Political protests reflected the mood for constituent assemblies, for parliaments and for legal reforms. Demands for reform reflected the clash between the old way of organising the world and the new. As Marx and Engels had already predicted, the spread of capitalist development was making its impact felt socially and politically as well as economically. The new towns and cities and the new industries and professions tended to form centres of opposition to feudalism, which was based on the Catholic church, the monarchy and aristocracy, and the landowners. Pitted against these conservative forces were the emerging capitalist class of factory owners, the small businessmen, the lawyers, students, the poor peasants and the growing numbers of workers. The authors of the *Manifesto* believed that a coalition of these various classes and groups would form the basis of the democratic revolution which was to come.

Enthusiasm for revolution in Europe could only be enhanced by the terrible social and economic conditions in which many found themselves in the late 1840s. There was famine in Europe, most notoriously in Ireland but also in Belgium. In spring 1847 there were disorders relating to food shortages in Scotland, south west England, Brussels, Berlin, Ulm, Vienna and in the Italian areas of Genoa, Tuscany, Romagna and Lombardy.[35] The depression of 1847 exacerbated the problems with millions suffering wage cuts, unemployment and business failures.

Revolution first broke out in a leading bastion of reaction in Europe, the Kingdom of the Two Sicilies, which incorporated Sicily and most of

present day southern Italy. A revolt against the monarchy in the Sicilian
capital of Palermo led to the king in Naples granting a constitution on 10
February 1848. The big explosion took place in France, however. In the
second half of 1847 discontent had been growing with the regime of the
'bourgeois monarch' Louis Philippe and there was clamour for electoral
and parliamentary reform. Thousands took part in 'reform banquets'
around the country. The aim of much of the middle class opposition was
to win moderate reforms without having to take to the streets. A huge
reform banquet was planned for 22 February 1848 in Paris. This would
have been the 71st such banquet but it was banned by the government.
Crowds gathered and over the next two days there were demonstrations
and barricades were thrown up. Louis Philippe abdicated and the Second
Republic was declared. The new government included radicals and
socialists and its programme was influenced by the radicalism which had
swept the monarchy from power. 'From 25 February to 2 March the government lived in constant fear of being swept away, either by the crowds
massed before the Hotel de Ville which, according to the latest rumours,
either acclaimed or booed it, or by the delegations which invested it and
demanded an immediate hearing'.[36]

The year 1848 was one of the great years when revolution seems both
desirable and possible. It spread throughout Europe, affecting both
Austria and Germany by March. As uprisings broke out clashes between
the feudal order and the emerging capitalist class were played out in the
streets of Vienna and Berlin. The sense of euphoria was everywhere in
the early months of 1848. It seemed that the old world of a tiny parasitic
and dictatorial class ruling over a poor peasantry was coming to an end.
Nowhere was this more true than in Germany. Its fragmentation was a
significant political and economic barrier to capitalist development. The
demand for national unification was therefore central for many of the
democrats. Marx and Engels took the view that they were on the extreme
left of the democracy movement and that they supported demands which
they felt would lead inevitably to unification. Bourgeois revolution in
Germany would, they believed, lead very rapidly to working class revolution. 'The communists turn their attention chiefly to Germany, because
that country is on the eve of a bourgeois revolution, that is bound to be
carried out under more advanced conditions of European civilisation,
and with a much more developed proletariat than that of England was in
the 17th, and of France in the 18th century, and because the bourgeois
revolution in Germany will be but the prelude to an immediately following proletarian revolution'.[37]

The bourgeois revolution was necessary in order to free German
society from the fetters of feudalism, thereby allowing the development
of capitalism and the creation of a working class which in turn had the

potential to make its own revolution. However, the commitment of Marx and Engels to the democratic movement went far beyond calls for the suffrage or the establishment of parliaments. These very important demands were preconditions for political organisation in many countries but political democracy on its own meant little without economic freedom. Most sections of society in Germany wanted to achieve the freedoms which had been won in revolutionary France after 1789. The middle classes and the intelligentsia were acutely conscious that over half a century later most German states had still not achieved the legal, social and political freedoms taken for granted in France. At the same time, however, there was a crucial difference between the revolutionary movements of 1789 and 1848: by the middle of the 19th century the working class was a real force in a number of European countries—in Britain especially but also in Belgium and France—and even in the countries with a less developed capitalism, the growing importance of the working class was clear. In Germany the working class was fully behind the demands of the bourgeois revolution. But it also increasingly wanted to go further and raise its own economic and social demands.

In France the bourgeois revolution had taken place long before 1848 and the working class was relatively well developed, so it was here that class polarisation was most acute—and the fate of the French Revolution of 1848 determined the outcome of revolution throughout Europe. The dramatic nature of France's February Revolution led the new radical and republican government to make a number of concessions to working class demands, most notably that of the right to work, with the establishment of national workshops to ensure work for the unemployed. However, these were soon vociferously opposed by some of those who had initially supported the February Revolution. Once the questions of economics and who controlled wealth came to the fore, the tensions between the different classes which had made the revolution became apparent. By April the left and the revolutionaries had lost the initiative. By June the class divisions had come into the open and the workers were once again forced to the barricades to defend themselves, this time not against the monarchy but against the bourgeois forces which ruled the new republic. After four days of street fighting in Paris the workers were cruelly defeated by the National Guard and the process of counter-revolution began in France—a process which was to lead within a few years to the dictatorship of Louis Napoleon.

Marx and Engels, along with many other exiled revolutionaries, decided to return to Germany once the revolution had broken out. Marx went to Cologne, part of the most progressive region of Germany, the Rhineland, which was still under the legal code enacted during French rule under Napoleon. This constitution allowed more possibilities for agitation and political discussion than were available in Prussia. Although the members of the Communist League returned to different parts of Germany merely as individuals, their impact was substantial in the months of upheaval during the spring and summer of 1848. As Marx's biographer Franz Mehring put it, 'Wherever the revolutionary movement in Germany showed any signs of vigorous development the members of the League were seen to be the driving force behind it: Schapper in Nassau, Wolff in Breslau, Stephan Born in Berlin and other members elsewhere. Born hit the nail on the head when he wrote to Marx: "The League has ceased to exist and yet it exists everywhere".'[38]

In Cologne Marx and Engels raised the money to launch a newspaper which Marx edited. The first edition of the *Neue Rheinische Zeitung* appeared on 1 June. It was devoted to spreading the revolution and to arguing the case for the most left wing revolutionary course. Almost immediately Marx was faced with the task of analysing the June days in France: 'The plebeians are tortured with hunger, reviled by the press, abandoned by doctors, abused by honest men as thieves, incendiaries, galley-slaves, their women and children thrown into still deeper misery, their best sons deported overseas: it is the privilege, it is the right of the democratic press to wind the laurels around their stern and threatening brows'.[39]

The paper had already lost a number of its well heeled backers who found the first issue too left wing for their tastes. Now, Mehring pointed out, this article 'cost the *Neue Rheinische Zeitung* the greater number of those shareholders who still remained'.[40] The dilemma which Marx and Engels faced was symbolic of the German Revolution itself. The backwardness of economic development in Germany meant that the bourgeoisie was from the outset hesitant and timid in making the revolution. At every stage it would rather compromise with the old order than align itself with more radical forces to take the revolution forward. This was particularly true in Berlin where 'on 18 March the revolution overthrew the Prussian government, but in the given historical situation the fruits of victory fell first into the lap of the bourgeoisie, and the latter hurried to betray the revolution,' according to Mehring.[41] The new Prussian government decided in April that a constitution would be drawn up in agreement with the crown. The national assembly held in Frankfurt in May, supposedly the prelude to unification, remained nothing more than a talking shop.

The old order was therefore able to survive the wave of revolutions in Germany, if not in every respect then in all the fundamentals. The June events in France made the bourgeoisie even more scared and ineffective and after the defeat of the Austrian Revolution in October 1848, counterrevolution was on the agenda everywhere. The revolutionary movement was destroyed within the next few months and the revolutionaries were forced into exile, Marx and Engels among them. Writing in December

1848 Marx summed up the nature of the German capitalists:

> *Whereas 1648 and 1789 had the infinite self confidence that springs from standing at the summit of creativity, it was Berlin's ambition in 1848 to form an anachronism. Its light was like the light of those stars which first reaches the earth when the bodies which radiated it have been extinct for a hundred thousand years. The Prussian March Revolution was such a star for Europe—only on a small scale, just as it was everything on a small scale. Its light was light from the corpse of a society long since putrefied.*
>
> *The German bourgeoisie had developed so sluggishly, so pusillanimously and so slowly, that it saw itself threateningly confronted by the proletariat, and all those sections of the urban population related to the proletariat in interests and ideas, at the very moment of its own threatening confrontation with feudalism and absolutism. And as well as having this class behind it, it saw in front of it the enmity of all Europe.*[42]

So the great revolutionary year ended in defeat for those who wanted a working class revolution. It was also a defeat for those who wanted the complete overthrow of feudalism. In Germany reaction triumphed and unification was completed not by a bourgeois government but by the conservative Bismarck. Both there and in Italy it took over 20 more years until this process was complete. The revolutions were the first major tests of Marx and Engels' political ideas. So how did the analysis put forward in the *Manifesto* measure up to the events of 1848 and how far did it provide an explanation for the development of capitalism in Europe after their defeat?

The impact of the *Manifesto* after 1848

The *Manifesto* had little direct impact on the revolutions themselves in 1848. They had already effectively broken out when the book was published and events in France had a much greater impact in spreading the revolution to Germany the following month than any single publication could have done. However, the revolutionaries did their utmost to ensure a wide readership for the *Manifesto* which was into its second edition by April. So 100 copies were shipped to German workers in Amsterdam in March, then 1,000 were sent to Paris. Early in April the communists in Paris gave *Manifesto*s to 3,000 or 4,000 German émigrés returning home to join the revolution. In March 1848 the émigré newspaper the *Deutsche Londoner Zeitung* serialised the book. When Marx and his allies returned to Cologne they distributed the *Manifesto* there, and in early 1849 it was serialised in the left wing paper *Die Hornisse*. Plans for translations into other languages were ambitious and not quickly realised. Despite claims in the

Manifesto itself there was no published French translation until after the Paris Commune of 1871. The only certain translation in 1848 was into Swedish. The first English translation was serialised in the left Chartist paper *Red Republican* in November 1850 and was translated by the Burnley socialist Helen Macfarlane; its opening line (later translated as, 'A spectre is haunting Europe') stated, 'A frightful hobgoblin stalks throughout Europe'.[44] The decline of the left wing and radical movement following the defeat of the 1848 revolutions did not create the conditions for further translations. As Engels put it, 'The manifesto has had a history of its own…it was soon forced into the background by the reaction that began with the defeat of the Paris workers in June 1848… With the disappearance from the public scene of the workers' movement that had begun with the February Revolution, the manifesto too passed into the background'.[45] It was only with the revival of the socialist movement internationally from the 1880s onwards that significant translations were undertaken, including the French one by Marx's daughter Laura Lafargue and the 'authorised' English translation by Sam Moore, which clearly had Engels' hand in it.[46]

The fate of the *Manifesto* was bound up with the political situation. It was ahead of its time in, for example, the description of the development of industry. 'Modern industry has converted the little workshop of the patriarchal master into the great factory of the industrial capitalist. Masses of labourers, crowded into the factory, are organised like soldiers…they are daily and hourly enslaved by the machine, by the overlookers, and, above all, by the individual bourgeois manufacturer himself'.[47] This was still not the picture in most parts of the world when they wrote it; it became the reality within the next half century, and then only in Germany, the US and France as well as in Britain.

The revolutions of 1848 taught Marx and Engels a great deal. Lenin wrote in 1907:

> In the activities of Marx and Engels themselves, the period of their participation in the mass revolutionary struggle of 1848-1849 stands out as the central point. This was their point of departure when determining the future pattern of the workers' movement and democracy in different countries. It was to this point that they always returned in order to determine the essential nature of the different classes and their tendencies in the most striking and purest form. It was from the standpoint of the revolutionary period of that time that they always judged the later, lesser, political formations and organisations, political aims and political conflicts.[48]

In addition to serving as a school of revolutionary tactics and strategy, the experience of 1848 also showed them the real nature of the capitalist class. The *Manifesto* based its revolutionary scenario on previous bourgeois revolutions, notably the English and French, which had produced leaders in Cromwell and Robespierre who understood the need to act decisively and courageously to further the aims of the revolution and destroy the old order. The bourgeoisie in 1848 had shown itself incapable of providing such decisive leadership. Only the embryonic workers' movement—led in parts of Germany by the communists—was capable of doing so. The root of the cowardice of the bourgeoisie was fear of raising a serious political challenge which might threaten property itself. So from the beginning it compromised and wheedled round the old absolutist forces and joined with them in defence of law, order and property against fundamental change. Before the revolution Marx and Engels had feared this would happen. Engels wrote just before the events of 1848 erupted that the bourgeoisie would only have a short period of rule following a successful bourgeois revolution. 'The hangman stands at the door,' he said, quoting the poet Heinrich Heine— the working class would soon usurp the rule of the capitalists.[49]

However, in the *Manifesto* it appears also that in spite of itself the bourgeoisie would be forced to act much more decisively than it might want. But in the course of 1848 it became increasingly obvious just how little could be expected. The June Days in Paris when the working class was defeated marked, as Marx wrote afterwards, 'the first great battle... between the two great classes which divide modern society. It was a fight for the preservation or destruction of the bourgeois order'.[50] The implications were not lost on anyone engaged in the revolution in Germany. By autumn the situation became increasingly polarised when insurrection in Frankfurt and the threat of it in Cologne were met by state repression, including the temporary banning of the *Neue Rheinische Zeitung*. In Vienna in October there was an insurrection in protest at military intervention against Hungary. It was successful for three weeks but was put down by the generals Jellacic and Windischgratz. Marx had already warned that the Vienna Revolution was 'in danger, if not of being wrecked, at least of being obstructed in its development, by the bourgeoisie's mistrust of the working class'.[51]

The Prussian monarchy took advantage of this counter-revolutionary move to appoint the reactionary Brandenburg ministry in Berlin. Marx's response to this was increasing bitterness against the bourgeoisie. By December he was absolutely clear that the bourgeoisie lacked the strength of purpose or inclination to make the revolution and that any revolution would have to be made without it. However much the working class held back its demands or tried to compromise, its very existence was enough to terrify the bourgeoisie into compromise with absolutism. So it is no surprise that Marx put more and more emphasis in his writings in the aftermath of the defeated revolutions of 1848-1849 on the independent role of the working class. He repeatedly refers to the 'revolution in permanence' or 'permanent revolution' meaning revolution which continues or is ongoing. This was a shift of politics from the 'springtime of revolution' to the stark reality of class warfare under capitalism—1848 marked a real turning point in this respect.

Marx did not make the mistake of believing that a relatively weak working class could have made a proletarian revolution immediately in the backward Germany of 1848, but he understood that any revolutionary role in leading mass struggles against the oppressive structures in society could no longer be expected from the bourgeoisie and would pass increasingly to the working class. Writing to the central committee of the Communist League from London in 1850 he stressed that German workers would have to go through a period of development as a revolutionary class before they could make a revolution but also argued that they could not put their trust in the 'democracy' as was possible before 1848: 'They themselves must contribute most to their final victory, by informing themselves of their own class interests, by taking up their independent political position as soon as possible, by not allowing themselves to be misled by the hypocritical phrases of the democratic petty bourgeoisie into doubting for one minute the necessity of an independently organised party of the proletariat. Their battle cry must be: The Permanent Revolution'.[52]

The defeat of the revolution meant coming to terms with other questions. Marx and Engels were forced to leave Germany and ended up in England. London was full of German émigrés most of whom, including Marx and Engels, believed that the resurgence of revolution in Europe was imminent. Marx's eventual conclusion was that it was not, and that revolutionaries would have to operate under the difficult circumstances of capitalist stability and expansion against a background of working class defeats. This led him to breaking politically with many of his colleagues from 1848 and Marx remained in political isolation for many years. Engels was based in Manchester where he worked in the family firm and supported Marx morally and financially. Marx spent his time studying for his eventual writing of *Capital*. The popular assessment of Marx as an academic, a dry student of socialism, dates from this period. The direct revolutionary experience which both Marx and Engels gained in 1848 belies this view, as do many of Marx's later actions. His assessment of the likelihood of political upheaval was cautious but his enthusiasm for left wing causes was undiminished. For example, he supported the continued battle for Polish independence. He also followed the American Civil War, which broke out in 1861, very closely and was a strong partisan of Northern victory and the abolition of slavery. He saw the outcome of this struggle as central to the future of capitalism and therefore to future prospects of revolution.

There are, of course, many issues of contemporary politics which *The Communist Manifesto* does not address. Some of these became much clearer during the remainder of Marx's lifetime. This is most obviously true of Marx's views following the defeat of the Paris Commune, which demonstrated that any attempt to win democracy and control of society by the working class will be crushed by the bourgeoisie because it threatens private property. His conclusion from this experience was that workers have to smash the state machine of the bourgeoisie and create their own democratic instruments of working class rule. Just as he had nailed his revolutionary colours to the mast in 1848, so Marx in 1871 was openly supportive of the Communards, even though this meant a political break with some of those he had worked with previously in the First International.

However, there were many issues that only arose after Marx's death in 1883. The growth of reformism as a current within the working class movement, the role of the large working class parties and of the trade unions with their bureaucracies were only just becoming apparent around the time of Engels' death in 1895. The full nature of imperialism and capitalism's tendency towards monopoly were also only apparent after Marx's death. So it was left to the generation of socialists involved in the revolutionary upheavals which emerged from the First World War to build on the experience and ideas of Marx. The Russian revolutionary Leon Trotsky developed the theory of permanent revolution. The failure of the 1905 Russian Revolution, whose defeat left Tsarism weakened but still intact, led him to argue that in the Russian situation the bourgeoisie was so weak and cowardly that it was utterly incapable of leading any kind of revolution. The revolution against Tsarism would have to be a working class revolution, despite the relative weakness numerically and organisationally of the Russian working class, and despite the economic backwardness of Russian society. This scenario proved to be the case in 1917. Similarly, events from 1914 through to 1919 clarified a number of vital issues: the need to build soviets or workers' councils rather than rely on changing society through parliament, the necessity of building independent working class parties based on working class power, the impossibility of taking over and running the existing state machine. In developing these theories socialists like Lenin, Trotsky and Luxemburg built on the ideas of Marx and Engels but also had to apply the actual experience of the growing workers' movement to new circumstances.

The relevance of the *Manifesto* today

A cheap paperback edition of the *Manifesto* published in 1996 sold tens of thousands of copies. Articles towards the end of 1997 in magazines as diverse as the *New Yorker* and the *Modern Review* have praised the insights of Marx. A new generation is beginning to look to Marxist ideas again and the *Manifesto* is often the first port of call. The *Manifesto*'s durability is partly due to its sweeping style. It provides a broad brush picture of capitalist development and of the nature of the bourgeoisie and the proletariat. It extrapolated from trends in the mid-19th century to present a clear and definite view of the future and because it pointed to tendencies in capitalism it is still able to help us comprehend a global system where capital's tentacles stretch into every corner of the world, and where the traditional ways of doing things are destroyed by the impact of commodity production. The spread of global capital and the revolution in technology have made this analysis even more relevant. People now buy exotic fruits from all over the world by just going to Sainsbury's. Clothes come from the Philippines or Malaysia, electrical goods from Korea. Migrant labour travels the world and international communications are instantaneous. Events taking place around the world can be beamed onto our television screens via satellite as they happen. But this global spread of capital has done little to overcome the inequalities of capitalism. Indeed industrial production or agricultural products designed for supermarkets in the advanced capitalist countries have often destroyed livelihoods, not enhanced them. Millions are denied the benefits of global production, and agricultural innovations have not touched many parts of the world. In China textile mills operate similarly to those Engels wrote of in Manchester in the 1840s. The combined and uneven development of capitalism portrays capitalism's strength and power but also its fundamental failings. In many parts of the world ox carts can exist alongside designer trainers, washing wells beside mobile phones.

Nor is global capital free from crisis, as recent events in the Far East have shown. The crisis of overproduction has hit countries such as South Korea, Indonesia and China, leading to waste and misery for millions who had expected the supposedly new era of 'crisis free' capitalism to deliver for them. Ruling classes everywhere have used the latest period of global expansion to attack jobs, hold down wages and generally increase the rate of exploitation. Even in the richest countries workers have found their lives becoming more miserable and constrained. The welfare cushion which was introduced in these countries during the long post-war boom is under sustained attack, with further devastating consequences to the social wage. Those who argued that capitalism could slowly and gradually reform and improve itself have been shown to be wrong.

Meanwhile, the *Manifesto*'s predictions about the growth of the working class have been borne out beyond any expectation. Everywhere in the world the gravedigger of capitalism, the working class, is bigger, more organised and more powerful than at any time before. Clerical workers, nurses, teachers, bank workers, have all joined transport workers and post office workers as part of the new working class. Countries from Brazil to South Africa have seen the development of new generations of workers with more power than ever before.

The whole point of the *Manifesto* was to make the case for working class revolution. It even states that the fall of the bourgeoisie and the victory of the proletariat are both equally inevitable.[53] Subsequent events have shown this to be wrong. Capitalism is still with us 150 years later and the working class has not permanently and successfully conquered power—even the most successful workers' revolution lasted barely ten years before the rise of Stalinism. Many critics take this phrase to mean that Marx and Engels based their materialist theory of revolution on a historical inevitability, that they believed socialism would come automatically. However, the refutation for this idea exists within *The Communist Manifesto* itself, when it argues that there is no guaranteed transition from one mode of production to another. Either society can go forward or the failure of one side to win decisively can lead to the 'common ruin of the contending classes'.[54] There was nothing preordained about revolution happening or being successful: the wheels of history did not move automatically. Changes in history depended on the objective clash between the different social forces but also on the subjective actions of men and women.

With the benefit of hindsight we can see that the role of the capitalist state, of the reformist working class parties, and the refusal by a number of those parties to engage in united work against the common capitalist enemy, have all been crucial at certain times in defusing or defeating revolutionary upsurges. The need to learn from and understand the lessons of history, and to organise around the strategy and tactics of an independent revolutionary workers' party was one of the crucial developments of revolutionary Marxism contributed after Marx and Engels' deaths, most notably by Lenin. In developing these ideas, however, the groundwork provided by *The Communist Manifesto* was invaluable in providing a unique introduction to Marxist politics and to the theory of revolution. It remains one of the great political texts which still inspires new generations of socialists and it can still serve as a guide to action.

Notes

1   Engels' preface to the English edition of 1888, quoted in H Draper, *The Adventures of the Communist Manifesto* (Berkeley, 1994), pp79-80.
2   F Engels, *Principles of Communism* in Collected Works vol 6 (London, 1976), pp341-357.
3   Ibid, p349.
4   See H Draper, op cit, p10.

5   *The Communist Manifesto* in H Draper, op cit, p107.
6   Ibid, p109.
7   Ibid, p113.
8   Ibid, p113.
9   Ibid, p117.
10   Ibid, p121.
11   Ibid, p127.
12   Ibid, p133.
13   Ibid, p125.
14   Ibid, p141.
15   Ibid, p145.
16   Ibid, p143.
17   J Westergaard, *Who Gets What?* (Cambridge, 1995), p124.
18   *The Communist Manifesto* in H Draper, op cit, p145
19   Ibid, p147.
20   Ibid, p147.
21   Ibid, p151.
22   Ibid, p157.
23   H Draper, *Karl Marx's Theory of Revolution* vol IV (New York, 1990), p183.
24   *The Communist Manifesto* in H Draper, *The Adventures...*op cit, p165.
25   Ibid, pp169-171.
26   Ibid, p173.
27   Quoted in H Draper, *Karl Marx's Theory...*vol IV, op cit, p3.
28   *The Communist Manifesto* in H Draper, *The Adventures...* op cit, p177.
29   Ibid, p179.
30   Ibid, p181.
31   Ibid, p181.
32   Ibid, p185.
33   Ibid, p137.
34   Ibid, p137.
35   See J Sigmann, *1848 (*London, 1970), p183.
36   Ibid, p219.
37   See H Draper, *The Adventures...*, op cit, p185.
38   F Mehring, *Karl Marx* (Harvester, 1981), p155.
39   K Marx, *The Revolutions of 1848*, (ed) D Fernbach (Harmondsworth, 1973), p134.
40   F Mehring, op cit, p159.
41   Ibid, p157.
42   K Marx, *The Revolutions...*, op cit , p193.
43   H Draper, *The Adventures...*, op cit, pp21-22.
44   Ibid, p104.
45   F Engels, 'Preface to German edition' 1890, quoted ibid, p32.
46   H Draper, *The Adventures...*, op cit, pp75-80.
47   Ibid, p123.
48   V I Lenin, *Collected Works* 13 (Moscow,??), p37.
49   K Marx and F Engels, *Collected Works* (London, 1976), vol 6, p529.
50   K Marx, 'The Class Struggles in France', in D Fembach (ed), *Surveys from Exile* (Harmondsworth, 1973), pp58-59.
51   K Marx, *The Revolutions...*, op cit, p165.
52   Ibid, p330.
53   H Draper, *The Adventures...*, op cit, p135.
54   Ibid, p107.

An introduction to Marx's theory of alienation

JUDY COX

We live in a world where technological achievements unimaginable in previous societies are within our grasp: this is the age of space travel, of the internet, of genetic engineering. Yet never before have we felt so helpless in the face of the forces we ourselves have created. Never before have the fruits of our labour threatened our very existence: this is also the age of nuclear disasters, global warming, and the arms race. For the first time in history we can produce enough to satisfy the needs of everyone on the planet. Yet millions of lives are stunted by poverty and destroyed by disease. Despite our power to control the natural world, our society is dominated by insecurity, as economic recession and military conflict devastate lives with the apparently irresistible power of natural disasters. The more densely populated our cities become, the more our lives are characterised by feelings of isolation and loneliness. To Karl Marx these contradictions were apparent when the system was still young. He noted that:

> On the one hand, there have started into life industrial and scientific forces, which no epoch of the former human history had ever suspected. On the other hand, there exist symptoms of decay, far surpassing the horrors of the Roman Empire. In our days everything seems pregnant with its contrary. Machinery, gifted with the wonderful power of shortening and fructifying human labour, we behold starving and overworking it. The new-fangled sources of wealth, by some strange weird spell, are turned into sources of want. The victories of art seem bought by loss of character.[1]

Marx developed his theory of alienation to reveal the human activity that lies behind the seemingly impersonal forces dominating society. He showed how, although aspects of the society we live in appear natural and independent of us, they are the results of past human actions. For Hungarian Marxist Georg Lukács Marx's theory 'dissolves the rigid, unhistorical, natural appearance of social institutions; it reveals their historical origins and shows therefore that they are subject to history in every respect including historical decline'.[2] Marx showed not only that human action in the past created the modern world, but also that human action could shape a future world free from the contradictions of capitalism. Marx developed a materialist theory of how human beings were shaped by the society they lived in, but also how they could act to change that society, how people are both 'world determined' and 'world producing'. For Marx, alienation was not rooted in the mind or in religion, as it was for his predessesors Hegel and Feuerbach. Instead Marx understood alienation as something rooted in the material world. Alienation meant loss of control, specifically the loss of control over labour. To understand why labour played such a central role in Marx's theory of alienation, we have to look first at Marx's ideas about human nature.[3]

What is human nature?

Marx opposed the common sense idea that humans have a fixed nature which exists independently of the society they live in. He demonstrated that many of the features attributed to unchanging human nature in fact vary enormously in different societies. However, Marx did not reject the idea of human nature itself. He argued that the need to labour on nature to satisfy human needs was the only consistent feature of all human societies, the 'ever lasting nature-imposed condition of human existence'.[4] Human beings, like all other animals, must work on nature to survive. The labour of humans, however, was distinguished from that of animals because human beings developed consciousness. Marx gave a famous description of this at the beginning of *Capital*:

> *A spider conducts operations that resemble those of a weaver, and a bee puts to shame many an architect in the construction of her cells. But what distinguishes the worst architect from the best of bees is this, that the architect raises his structure in imagination before he erects it in reality. At the end of every labour-process, we get a result that already existed in the imagination of the labourer at its commencement.*[5]

In a useful introduction to Marx's ideas, *How to Read Karl Marx*, Ernst Fischer also described what is unique about human labour. He explained how, because we act on nature consciously, we build on our successes and develop new ways of producing the things we need. This means that we have a history, whereas animals do not: 'The species-nature of animal is an eternal repetition, that of man is transformation, development and change'.[6]

Working on nature alters not only the natural world, but also the labourer himself. Marx frequently reinforced this idea, as in the following quote from *Capital*: 'By thus acting on the external world and changing it, he at the same time changes his own nature. He develops his slumbering powers and compels them to act in obedience to his sway.' Thus labour is a dynamic process through which the labourer shapes and moulds the world he lives in and stimulates himself to create and innovate. Marx called our capacity for conscious labour our 'species being'.

Our species being is also a social being, as Marx explained in the *Economic and Philosophical Manuscripts* (1844): 'The individual is the social being.' People have to enter into relationships with each other regardless of their personal preferences because they need to work together to get what they need to live. In the *Grundrisse*, Marx emphasised the point: 'Society does not consist of individuals; it expresses the sum of connections and relationships in which individuals find themselves.' Humanity relates to the physical world through labour; through labour humanity itself develops and labour is the source of human beings' relationships with each other. What happens to the process of work, therefore, has a decisive influence on the whole of society.

Our ability to work, to improve how we work and build on our successes, has tended to result in the cumulative development of the productive forces. One such development gave rise to class society. When society became capable of producing a surplus, it also became possible for a class to emerge which was liberated from the need to directly produce and could live from its control over the labour of others. This process was necessary in order to develop and direct the productive forces, but it also meant that the majority of society, the producers, lost control of their labour. Thus, the alienation of labour arose with class society, and Ernst Fischer has given a brilliant description of how it reversed the limitless potential of labour:

The first tool contains within it all the potential future ones. The first recognition of the fact that the world can be changed by conscious activity contains all future, as yet unknown, but inevitable change. A living being which has once begun to make nature his own through the work of his hands, his intellect, and his imagination, will never stop. Every achievement opens the door to unconquered territory... But when labour is destructive, not creative, when it is undertaken under coercion and not as the free play of forces, when it means the withering, not the flowering, of man's physical and intellectual potential, then labour is a denial of its own principle and therefore of the principle of man.[7]

The emergence of class divisions in which one class had control over the means of producing what society needed, led to a further division between individuals and the society to which they belonged. Certain forms of social life 'drive a wedge between the two dimensions of the self, the individual and the communal',[8] producing a separation between individuals' interests and those of society as a whole. However, alienation is not an unalterable human condition which exists unchanged in every class society.

Alienation and capitalism: all in a day's work

In feudal society humans had not yet developed the means to control the natural world, or to produce enough to be free from famine, or to cure diseases. All social relationships were 'conditioned by a low stage of development of the productive powers of labour and correspondingly limited relations between men within the process of creating and reproducing their material life, hence also limited relations between man and nature'.[9] Land was the source of production, and it so dominated the feudal-manorial system that men saw themselves not as individuals but in relation to the land. Marx described this in the *Economic and Philosophical Manuscripts*:

> *In feudal landownership we already find the domination of the earth as of an alien power over men. The serf is an appurtenance of the land. Similarly the heir through primogeniture, the first born son, belongs to the land. It inherits him. The rule of private property begins with property in land which is its basis.*[10]

Ownership of land was dependent on inheritance and blood lines: your 'birth' determined your destiny. In an early work Marx described how 'the aristocracy's pride in their blood, their descent, in short the genealogy of the body...has its appropriate science in heraldry. The secret of the aristocracy is zoology'.[11] It was this zoology which determined your life and your relationships with others. On the one hand, the low level of the productive forces meant constant labour for the peasants, while on the other, the feudal lords and the church officials took what they wanted from the peasants by force.

Thus alienation arose from the low level of the productive forces, from human subordination to the land and from the domination of the feudal ruling class. However, there were limits to these forms of alienation. The peasants worked their own land and produced most of the things they needed in their own independent family units. 'If a person was tied to the land, then the land was also tied to the people... The peasant, and even the serf of the middle ages, remained in possession of at least 50 percent, sometimes 60 and 70 percent, of the output of their labour'.[12] The social relationships in feudal society were relationships of domination and subordination, but they were obviously *social* relationships between individuals. In *Capital* Marx described how 'the social relations between individuals in the performance of their labour appear at all events as their own mutual personal relations, and are not disguised under the shape of social relations between the products of labour'.[13]

However, the constraints of feudalism were very different from the dynamic of capitalism. The bourgeoisie wanted a society in which everything could be bought and sold for money: 'Selling is the practice of alienation'.[14] The creation of such a society depended on the brutal enclosures of the common land. This meant that, for the first time, the majority in society were denied direct access to the means of production and subsistence, thus creating a class of landless labourers who had to submit to a new form of exploitation, wage labour, in order to survive. Capitalism involved 'a fundamental change in the relations between men, instruments of production and the materials of production'.[15] These fundamental changes meant that every aspect of life was transformed. Even the concept of time was radically altered so that watches, which were toys in the 17th century, became a measure of labour time or a means of quantifying idleness, because of the 'importance of an abstract measure of minutes and hours to the work ethic and to the habit of punctuality required by industrial discipline'.[16]

Men no longer enjoyed the right to dispose of what they produced how they chose: they became separated from the product of their labour. Peter Linebaugh in his history of 18th century London, *The London Hanged*, explained that workers considered themselves masters of what they produced. It took great repression, a 'judicial onslaught', in the late 18th century to convince them that what they produced belonged exclusively to the capitalists who owned the factories. During the 18th century most workers were not paid exclusively in money. 'This was true of Russian serf labour, American slave labour, Irish agricultural labour and the metropolitan labour in London trades'.[17] By the 19th century, however, wage labour had replaced all other forms of payment. This meant labour was now a commodity, sold on the market. Capitalists and workers were formally independent of each other, but in reality inextricably connected. Production no longer took place in the home, but in factories where new systems of discipline operated. The mechanisation of labour in the factories transformed people's relationship with machines, 'those remarkable products of human ingenuity, became a

source of tyranny against the worker'.[18] In *Capital* Marx compared the
work of craftsmen and artisans to that of the factory worker:

> In handicrafts and manufacture, the workman makes use of a tool, in the
> factory, the machine makes use of him. There the movements of the instrument
> of labour proceed from him, here it is the movements of the machines that he
> must follow. In manufacture the workmen are parts of a living mechanism. In
> the factory we have a lifeless mechanism independent of the workman, who
> becomes a mere living appendage.[19]

One of the most important, and devastating, features of factory production was the division of labour. Prior to capitalism there had been a
social division of labour, with different people involved in different
branches of production or crafts. With capitalism there arose the detailed
division of labour within each branch of production. This division of
labour meant that workers had to specialise in particular tasks, a series of
atomised activities, which realised only one or two aspects of their
human powers at the expense of all the others. Harry Braverman pointed
out the consequences of this division: 'While the social division of
labour subdivides *society*, the detailed division of labour subdivides
humans, and while the subdivision of society may enhance the individual
and the species, the subdivision of the individual, when carried on
without regard to human capabilities and needs, is a crime against the
person and humanity'.[20] John Ruskin, the 19th century critic of industri-
alisation, made a similar point when he wrote that the division of labour
is a false term because it is the men who are divided.

In this system workers become increasingly dependent on the capitalists who own the means of production. Just as the worker 'is depressed,
therefore, both intellectually and physically, to the level of a machine,
and from being a man becomes an abstract activity and a stomach, so he
also becomes more and dependent on every fluctuation in the market
price, in the investment of capital and on the whims of the wealthy'.[21] It
became impossible for workers to live independently of capitalism: to
work meant to be reduced to a human machine; to be deprived of work
meant living death. Without work, if capital ceases to exist for him, Marx
argued the worker might as well bury himself alive: 'The existence of
capital is his existence, his life, for it determines the content of his life in
a manner indifferent to him'.[22] There is no choice involved—work is a
matter of survival. Therefore labour became forced labour; you could not
choose not to work, you could not choose what you made, and you could
not choose how you made it. Marx noted:

> The fact that labour is external to the worker, does not belong to his essential

being; that he therefore does not confirm himself in his work, but denies himself, feels miserable and not happy, does not develop free mental and physical energy, but mortifies his flesh and ruins his mind. Hence the worker feels himself only when he is not working; when he is working he does not feel himself. He is at home when he is not working, and not at home when he is working. His labour is therefore not voluntary but forced, it is forced labour. It is therefore not the satisfaction of a need, but a mere means to satisfy need outside itself. Its alien character is clearly demonstrated by the fact that as soon as no physical or other compulsion exists it is shunned like the plague.[23]

There was another side to the fragmentation of labour in the factory system. The creation of the 'detail labourer who performed fractional work in the workshop meant that the value-producing class became collective, since no worker produced a whole commodity'.[24] This collectivity expressed itself in constant struggle against capitalist forms of production and frequent attempts by workers to assert their right to control machines rather than be controlled by them, most famously in the Luddite Rebellion of the early 19th century, a revolt so widespread that more troops were deployed to crush it than were sent to fight with Wellington at Waterloo.

Four aspects of alienation

The development of capitalism proved irresistible and it brought alienation on a scale previously unimaginable. In his *Economic and Philosophical Manuscripts* (also known as the *1844*, or *Paris Manuscripts*) Marx identified four specific ways in which alienation pervades capitalist society.

The product of labour: The worker is alienated from the object he produces because it is owned and disposed of by another, the capitalist. In all societies people use their creative abilities to produce objects which they use, exchange or sell. Under capitalism, however, this becomes an alienated activity because 'the worker cannot use the things he produces to keep alive or to engage in further productive activity... The worker's needs, no matter how desperate, do not give him a licence to lay hands on what these same hands have produced, for all his products are the property of another'.[25] Thus workers produce cash crops for the market when they are malnourished, build houses in which they will never live, make cars they can never buy, produce shoes they cannot afford to wear, and so on.

Marx argued that the alienation of the worker from what he produces is intensified because the products of labour actually begin to dominate the labourer. In his brilliant *Essays on Marx's Theory of Value*, I I Rubin outlines a quantitative and a qualitative aspect to the production of commodities. Firstly, the worker is paid less than the value he creates. A proportion of what he produces is appropriated by his boss; the worker is, therefore, exploited. Qualitatively, he also puts creative labour into the object he produces, but he cannot be given creative labour to replace it. As Rubin explains, 'In exchange for his creative power the worker receives a wage or a salary, namely a sum of money, and in exchange for this money he can purchase products of labour, but he cannot purchase creative power. In exchange for his creative power, the worker gets things'.[26] This creativity is lost to the worker forever, which is why under capitalism work does not stimulate or invigorate us and 'open the door to unconquered territory', but rather burns up our energies and leaves us feeling exhausted.

This domination of dead labour over living labour lies behind Marx's assertion in the *Manuscripts* that 'the alienation of the worker means not only that his labour becomes an object, an external existence, but that it exists outside him, independently of him and alien to him, and begins to confront him as an autonomous power; that the life which he has bestowed on the object confronts him as hostile and alien'.[27] For Marx this state of affairs was unique to capitalism. In previous societies those who work harder could usually be expected to have more to consume. Under capitalism, those who work harder increase the power of a hostile system over them. They themselves, and their inner worlds, become poorer. 'The worker becomes an ever cheaper commodity the more goods he creates. The devaluation of the human world increases in direct relation with the increase in value of the world of things'.[28]

The labour process: The second element of alienation Marx identified is a lack of control over the process of production. We have no say over the conditions in which we work and how our work is organised, and how it affects us physically and mentally. This lack of control over the work process transforms our capacity to work creatively into its opposite, so the worker experiences 'activity as passivity, power as impotence, procreation as emasculation, the worker's own physical and mental energy, his personal life—for what is life but activity?—as an activity directed against himself, which is independent of him and does not belong to him'.[29] The process of work is not only beyond the control of the workers, it is in the control of forces hostile to them because capitalists and their managers are driven to make us work harder, faster and for longer stints. In addition, as Harry Braverman points out, 'in a society based upon the purchase and sale of labour power, dividing the craft cheapens its individual parts',[30] so the bosses also have an interest in breaking down the labour process into smaller and smaller parts. The resulting rigidly repetitive process buries the individual talents or skills of the worker, as Marx described:

> Factory work exhausts the nervous system to the uttermost, it does away with
> the many-sided play of the muscles, and confiscates every atom of freedom,
> both in bodily and intellectual activity... The special skill of each individual
> insignificant factory operative vanishes as an infinitesimal quantity before the
> science, the gigantic physical forces, and mass of labour that are embodied in
> the factory mechanism and, together, with that mechanism, constitute the
> power of the master.[31]

Modern methods of production have increased the fragmentation of
the labour process since Marx's day. The organisation of modern production is still based on the methods of the assembly line. Scientific
research is used to break the production process down into its component
parts. This has led, firstly, to the deskilling of white collar jobs and to a
situation where managers have a monopoly of control over the production process: 'The unity of thought and action, conception and execution,
hand and mind, which capitalism threatened from it beginnings, is now
attacked by a systematic dissolution employing all the resources of
science and the various engineering disciplines based upon it'.[32]
Conditions of work, from the length of the working day to the space we
occupy, are predetermined: 'The entire work operation, down to it
smallest motion, is conceptualised by the management and engineering
staff, laid out, measured, fitted with training and performance standards—all entirely in advance'.[33] Workers are treated as machines, with
the aim of transforming the subjective element of labour into objective,
measurable, controlled processes. In some brilliant passages in *History
and Class Consciousness*, Lukács describes how the increasingly rationalised and mechanised process of work affects our consciousness. As
the following extract shows, his analysis was prophetic and gives a strik-
ingly accurate picture of today's white collar work:

> In consequence of the rationalisation of the work-process the human qualities
> and idiosyncrasies of the worker appear increasingly as mere sources of
> error when contrasted with these abstract special laws functioning according
> to rational predictions. Neither objectively nor in his relation to his work
> does man appear as the authentic master of this process; on the contrary, he
> is a mechanical part incorporated into a mechanical system. He finds it
> already pre-existing and self-sufficient, it functions independently of him and
> he has to conform to its laws whether he likes it or not.[34]

Our fellow human beings: Thirdly, we are alienated from our fellow
human beings. This alienation arises in part because of the antagonisms

which inevitably arise from the class structure of society. We are alien-ated from those who exploit our labour and control the things we produce. As Marx put it:

> If his activity is a torment for him, it must provide pleasure and enjoyment for someone else... If therefore he regards the product of his labour, his objecti-fied labour, as an alien, hostile and powerful object which is independent of him, then his relationship to that object is such that another man—alien, hostile, powerful and independent of him—is its master. If he relates to his own activity an unfree activity, then he relates to it as activity in the service, under the rule, coercion and yoke of another man.[35]

In addition, we are connected to others through the buying and selling of the commodities we produce. Our lives are touched by thousands of people every day, people whose labour has made our clothes, food, home, etc. But we only know them through the objects we buy and consume. Ernst Fischer pointed out that because of this we do not see each other 'as fellow-men having equal rights, but as superiors or subor-dinates, as holders of a rank, as a small or large unit of power'.[36] We are related to each other not as individuals but as representatives of different relations of production, the personification of capital, or land or labour. As Bertell Ollman wrote, 'We do not know each other as individuals, but as extensions of capitalism: "In bourgeois society capital is independent and has individuality, while the living person is dependent and has no individuality".'[37] The commodities of each individual producer appear in depersonalised form, regardless of who produced them, where, or in what specific conditions. Commodity production means that everyone 'appropriates the produce of others, by alienating that of their own labour'.[38]

Marx described how mass commodity production continually seeks to create new needs, not to develop our human powers but to exploit them for profit:

> Each attempts to establish over the other an alien power, in the hope of thereby achieving satisfaction of his own selfish needs...becomes the inven-tive and ever calculating slave of inhuman, refined, unnatural and imaginary appetites. He places himself at the disposal of his neighbour's most depraved fancies, panders to his needs, excites unhealthy appetites in him, and pounces on every weakness, so that he can then demand the money for his labour of love.[39]

We see other people through the lens of profit and loss. Our abilities and needs are converted into means of making money and so we consider other human beings as competitors, as inferiors or superiors.[40]

Our human nature: The fourth element is our alienation from what Marx called our species being. What makes us human is our ability to consciously shape the world around us. However, under capitalism our labour is coerced, forced labour. Work bears no relationship to our personal inclinations or our collective interests. The capitalist division of labour massively increased our ability to produce, but those who create the wealth are deprived of its benefits. Marx's descriptions of this process in the *Manuscripts* are extremely powerful indictments of the system:

> *It is true that labour produces marvels for the rich, but it produces privation for the worker. It produces palaces, but hovels for the worker. It procures beauty, but deformity for the worker. It replaces labour by machines, but it casts some of the workers back into barbarous forms of labour and turns others into machines. It produces intelligence, but it produces idiocy and cretinism for the worker.*[41]

Human beings are social beings. We have the ability to act collectively to further our interests. However, under capitalism that ability is submerged under private ownership and the class divisions it produces. We have the ability to consciously plan our production, to match what we produce with the developing needs of society. But under capitalism that ability is reversed by the anarchic drive for profits. Thus, rather than consciously shaping nature, we cannot control, or even foresee, the consequences of our actions. For example, new, cheaper techniques of production may, when repeated across industry, produce acid rain or gases which destroy the ozone layer.

Similarly, when one capitalist improves production in his factory, he is unwittingly contributing to the slowing up of the rate of profits for his class as a whole by lowering the rate of profit.[42] One firm can produce to fulfil a particularly sharp demand, only to find when the goods hit the market that other firms got there first. Instead of simply meeting demand, there is a glut in the market. This means that we produce more but what we produce is unwanted. All previous societies suffered from shortages, famines and the failure of crops. Under capitalism recessions mean that workers 'consume less because they produce too much. And they consume less, not because their labour is inadequately productive, but because their labour is too productive'.[43] There is nothing natural about the economic crises we face: it is our social organisation which prevents us enjoying the potential of our ability to produce.

What is commodity fetishism?

The domination of commodities in our society is so pervasive that it seems to be an inevitable, natural state of affairs. All our achievements, everything we produce, appear as commodities, as Marx noted: 'The wealth of societies in which the capitalist mode of production prevails appears as an immense collection of commodities'.[44] Capitalism is the first system of generalised commodity production, in which the commodity has become 'a universal category of society as a whole'.[45] The dominance of commodity production has implications for how we experience the world we have created.

The mysterious commodity: In every society human beings have laboured to created objects which help them fulfil their needs. So Marx began his analysis of commodities under capitalism by asserting that 'a commodity is an external object, a thing which through its qualities satisfies human needs of whatever kind', regardless of whether that need comes from stomach or the imagination.[46] Commodities must have a use value, but they also have an exchange value. In capitalist society our many different human needs can only be met through the purchase of commodities: to eat we have to buy food in a shop, to travel we have to buy a car or a bus ticket, to have access to knowledge we have to buy books, TVs or computers. Yet the usefulness of all these commodities is overwhelmed by their exchange value and the satisfaction of human needs becomes inseparable from the workings of the market.[47]

The circulation of commodities on the market is even more cloaked in mystery than the process of their production, where workers have some direct relationship with the commodity they produce. This relationship is lost when commodities are sent to market and exchanged for money, which, in turn, is exchanged for other commodities. As Marx wrote, 'The actual process of production, as a unity of the direct production process and the circulation process, gives rise to new formations, in which the vein of internal connections is increasingly lost, the production relations are rendered independent of one another, and the component values become ossified into forms independent of one another'.[48] Marx explained how the circulation of commodities transforms relationships between individual producers into relationships between the commodities they produce. They are divided from each other, yet utterly dependent on each other's commodities:

> *The owners of commodities find out that the division of labour which turns them into independent private producers also makes the social process of production and the relations of the individual producers to each other within that process independent of the producers themselves; they also find out that*

the independence of the individuals from each other has its counterpart and supplement a system of all-round material dependence.[49]

In the capitalist system individuals have to possess certain things—labour power, or materials of production, for example—in order to enter into productive relationships with each other. As a consequence, 'it seems as if the thing itself possesses the ability, the virtue, to establish production relations', rather than the individuals themselves.[50] Commodities acquire social characteristics because individuals enter the productive process only as the owners of commodities. Marx described this process: 'To the producers, therefore, the social relations between their private labours...do not appear as direct social relations between persons in their work, but rather as *material* relations between persons and *social* relations between things'.[51] Thus it appears as if the market itself causes the rise and fall of prices, and pushes workers into one branch of production or out of another, independent of human agency. 'The impact of society on the individual is carried out through the social form of things'.[52] This adds another dimension to alienated relationships because, as Marx argued, 'the characters who appear on the economic stage are merely personifications of economic relations; it is as the bearers of these economic relations that they come into contact with each other'.[53]

Marx described the whole process of the reification of human relationships, the attribution of human powers to inanimate objects, and the way in which social organisation appears as independent of human will as commodity fetishism. Commodity fetishism has increased with the growth of capitalism, in which 'the capitalist mode of production takes over the totality of individual, family, and social needs and, in subordinating them to the market, also reshapes them to serve the needs of capital'.[54] Today there is a market for everything, for sex and art, for labour itself, as well as for TVs and cars. As Ernst Fischer wrote, 'We have become so accustomed to living in a world of commodities, where nature is perhaps only a poster for a holiday resort and man only an advertisement for a new product, we exist in such a turmoil of alienated objects offered cheaply for sale, that we hardly ask ourselves any longer what it is that magically transforms objects of necessity (or fashion) into commodities, and what is the true nature of the witches' Sabbath, ablaze with neon moons and synthetic constellations, that has become our day to day reality'.[55]

Money: the 'universal pimp': The creation of exchange values and the circulation of commodities requires a commodity which can represent all other commodities, through which all other commodities can be compared. Marx described how the development of capitalism brought with

it the problem of how to evaluate different commodities and simultaneously created the solution in the form of money, the universal
commodity. Physical objects, gold or silver become the 'direct incarna-
tion of all human labour'. With the development of money people's
relationship to their production assumes a material shape which is independent of their control and their conscious action: 'This situation is
manifested first by the fact that the products of men's labour universally
take on the form of commodities. The riddle of the money fetish is therefore the riddle of the commodity fetish, now become visible and dazzling
to our eyes'.[56]

Marx called money the 'universal pimp', mediating between men and
their desires. The value of money, the metals in which it was originally
embodied, have long since been discarded in favour of intrinsically
worthless alloy metal coins or paper money. And yet money can buy
everything—it is the most powerful commodity in existence: 'Money is
all other commodities divested of their shape, the product of their universal alienation'.[57] The role of money in the circulation of commodities
shapes the consciousness of human beings involved in that process.
Money takes on the value of the objects it represents, it appears to be the
force which can create value itself. As Meszaros explains:

> Money is taken to possess these colossal powers as natural attributes.
> People's attitude toward money is, undoubtedly, the outstanding instance of
> capitalist fetishism, reaching its height in interest bearing capital. Here,
> people think they see money creating more money, self-expanding value...
> workers, machines, raw materials—all the factors of production—are down-
> graded to mere aids, and money itself is made the producer of wealth.[58]

Thus money acquires great abilities, but on the other side of the coin,
all our human desires and abilities contract into what Marx called a sense
of having: 'Private property has made us so stupid and one-sided that an
object is only ours when we have it, when it exists for us as capital or
when we directly possess, eat, drink, wear, inhabit it, etc, in short, when
we use it'.[59] Marx also described how this desire for possession is both
stimulated and denied: 'The worker is only permitted to have enough for
him to live, and he is only permitted to live in order to have'.[60] In a particularly perceptive passage from the *Manuscripts*, Marx explains how
money submerges our personalities. It is a brilliant rejoinder to those
who argue that capitalism allows our individuality to flourish:

> That which exists for me through the medium of money, that whic... can pay
> for, ie which money can buy, that am I, the possessor of the money. The
> stronger the power of my money, the stronger I am. The properties of money

are my, the possessors', properties and essential powers. Therefore what I am and what I can do is by no means determined by my individuality. I am ugly, but I can buy the most beautiful women. Which means to say that I am not ugly, for the effect of ugliness, its repelling power, is destroyed by money. As an individual I am lame, but money procures me 24 legs. Consequently, I am not lame. I am a wicked, dishonest, unscrupulous individual, but money is respected, and so also is its owner...through money I can have anything the human heart desires. Do I not therefore possess all human abilities? Does not money therefore transform all my incapacities into their opposite?[61]

Commodity fetishism and class: Alienation and commodity fetishism shape all relationships in society. Those who possess wealth also inhabit a world beyond their control, in which relationships are reified. Their individuality is submerged by the dictates of capitalism—as Marx wrote, the instinct to enrich himself, which 'in a miser is a mere idiosyncrasy, is, in the capitalist, the effect of the social mechanism, of which he is but one of the wheels'.[62] The huge productive forces owned by the ruling class may bring them riches beyond our imaginings, but they cannot control the vast economic forces of the system or even plan any section of it accurately. The capitalists are caught in a contradiction, that 'capital is a social force, but it is privately, rather than collectively, owned so its movements are determined by individual owners necessarily indifferent to all the social implications of their activities'.[63] The capitalist has constantly to compete in order to keep up with his competitors and while his actions may be perfectly sensible for the individual firm, when generalised across society they cause the economic recessions which can destroy many firms. Economic crises are irrefutable proof that the system is more powerful than any individual capitalist. This explains why crises are such a massive blow to the confidence and ideology of the ruling class. The capitalist may like to believe that his daring, entrepreneurial spirit creates his wealth, but in reality he 'rides a wave another has created'.[64] The class struggle, which he cannot prevent, brings home forcibly how dependent he is on the labour of his employees, and, like economic crises, is a wounding blow to the outlook of the ruling class.

In *The Holy Family* Marx gives a brilliant description of the situation of the ruling class:

The possessing class and the class of the proletariat present the same human self-alienation. But the former class feels at home in this self-alienation, it finds confirmation of itself and recognises in alienation its own power; it has in it a semblance of human existence, while the class of the proletariat feels annihilated in its self-alienation; it sees therein its own powerlessness and the reality of an inhuman existence.[65]

Thus, no matter how deeply alienation affects them, the ruling class will always be driven to defend the system that creates their alienation with all the power and brutality at their disposal because of their material position within it. In addition to this, Lukács argued that the ruling class can never rise above the commodity fetishism of capitalism. The bourgeoisie can never recognise the real nature of capitalism without confronting their own role as exploiters and upholders of the system. Therefore the capitalists do not want to recognise the real social relationships which underlie the institutions of capitalist society. They prefer to continue believing that the relations of production are natural and inevitable. In contrast, Lukács argued that workers, though also shaped by commodity fetishism, were not permanently blinded to the reality of capitalism. Rather he argued that the working class is in a unique position to be able to tear the veil of reification from capitalism because its struggle against capitalism reveals its real own role in producing the wealth of society. Class struggle means that workers no longer see themselves as isolated individuals. It means that they can become conscious of the social character of labour. Lukács suggests that when workers glimpse the reality behind commodity fetishism it can help them to realise the need for a revolutionary transformation of society: 'This enables us to understand why it is only in the proletariat that the process by which a man's achievement is split off from his total personality and becomes a commodity leads to a revolutionary consciousness'.[66]

The uses and abuses of Marx's theory

The concept of alienation is a central but controversial aspect of Marxism. When Marx's key work on alienation, *The Economic and Philosophical Manuscripts*, was eventually published in 1932, it had a dramatic impact on the tradition known as 'Western Marxism', which included writers like Herbert Marcuse and John Paul Sartre.[67] However, in the hands of the Western Marxists, the theory of alienation became intermingled with idealist theories, which explained alienation in terms of psychology rather than the organisation of society. The New Left which emerged in the late 1950s reacted against the theory and practice of Stalinism, but some of the writers associated with the New Left threw the Marxist baby out with the Stalinist bathwater. They abandoned some central aspects of Marxism, such as the central role of the economic structure in shaping the rest of society and the objective class antagonisms at the heart of capitalism. As Perry Anderson wrote, 'The most striking single trait of Western Marxism as a common tradition is thus perhaps the constant presence and influence on it of successive types of European idealism'.[68] Alienation was seized upon to explain the miseries of modern life, and the 'lonely crowd', 'those aggregations of atomised city dwellers who feel crushed and benumbed by the weight of a social system in which they have neither significant purpose nor decision-making power'.[69] Alienation came to refer predominately to a state of mind, rather than an understanding of how social organisation affected human beings.

Typical of the confused ideas about alienation fashionable in some quarters at this time is a book edited by Eric and Mary Josephson, *Man Alone: Alienation in Modern Society*, first published in 1962 and reprinted eight times before 1968. For the Josephsons, alienation describes 'the untold lives of quiet desperation that mark our age', and the long list of those suffering from alienation includes such diverse group as women, immigrants, sexual deviants, drug addicts, young people and artists.[70] But the editors understand alienation exclusively as a psychological state, 'referring to an extraordinary variety of psycho-social disorders, including loss of field, anxiety states, anomie, despair, depersonalisation, rootlessness, apathy, social disorganisation, loneliness, atomisation, powerlessness, meaninglessness, isolation, pessimism, and the loss of beliefs and values'.[71] If alienation is only a specific psychological problem, then it follows that the solution to alienation must be sought exclusively in the individual consciousness. If alienation is predominantly a state of mind, there is an implication that it can be cured without fundamentally changing the organisation of society. As Eric Fromm suggested, forms of alienation were 'chains of illusion' which can be broken within the context of capitalist society, because they arise from 'stereotyped alternatives of thinking'.[72]

However, Marx's writings on alienation, from the *Manuscripts* to the *Grundrisse* and *Capital*, demonstrate that for him alienation was not merely a state of mind. The roots of the individual psyche were to be located in how society as a whole is organised. As one Marxist described it, 'The life activity of the alienated individual is qualitatively of a kind. His actions in religion, family affairs, politics and so on, are as distorted and brutalised as his productive activity... There is no sphere of human activity that lies outside these prison walls'.[73] Marx's theory offers us an indispensable method of understanding how the production process shapes the whole of society. There are two areas of activity which are particularly controversial in relation to alienation. This first is the place of intellectual, or mental labour, and creativity in alienated production.

The division of labour described in this article leads to a sharp division between work and creativity. Work is regimented, broken down into separate tasks. The creative elements in each process are dispersed into a million fragments. Labour itself is a commodity and its value is determined by the labour time which went into its creation, for example, the

amount spent on training or educating a worker. A highly skilled techni-
cian or engineer will therefore be paid more than an unskilled labourer. As
Braverman wrote, 'In this way, a structure is given to all labour process
that at its extremes polarises those whose time is infinitely valuable and
those whose time is worth almost nothing'.[74] However, this does not mean
that the intellectual whose time is valuable escapes from the general
pattern of alienation. On the contrary, one of the features of modern capitalism is the commercialisation of knowledge.[75] The design of a microchip
or computer software is just as much the property of the capitalist as a tin
of beans or a car. Capitalists enrich themselves through the appropriation
of mental labour in the same way as they do through material labour.

The social division of labour undermines the potential of intellectuals
to discover new truths about society. As Franz Jakubowski wrote,

> The social division of labour creates a series of sub-spheres, not only in the
> economy but in the whole of social life and thought. These develop their own
> autonomous sets of laws. As a result of specialisation, each individual sphere
> develops according to the logic of its own specific object.[76]

Intellectual activity takes place within these limitations, in isolation
from society as a whole. In the end, the individual sciences 'cannot
understand either the method of the principle of even their own concrete
substratum of reality'.[77] All the potential we have to develop new techniques and methods is subordinated to competition. The very structure of
capitalist society condemns our intellectual developments to the chase of
facts in blind isolation from the real movements of society. This does not
mean that nothing useful can be developed, rather that research takes
place within a framework which constrains and limits its development.

The same processes are at work in the production and consumption of
art in capitalist society. As Eugene Lunn explained in his excellent book
Marxism and Modernism, bourgeois society offers artistic freedom on
one hand and snatches it back with the other: 'Bourgeois society—with
all its progressive advance over "feudal" constrictions—is also inimical
to many forms of art, for example because of division of labour, the
mechanisation of many forms of human activity, and the predominance
of quantitative over qualitative concerns'.[78] Marx argued that artists, like
scientists and intellectuals, could not escape from the general conversion
of all human creativity into commodities. Firstly this is because artists,
like all other workers, are dependent on their ability to make money:
'The bourgeoisie has stripped of its halo every occupation hitherto honoured and looked up to with reverent awe. It has converted the physician,
the lawyers, the priest, the poet, the man of science, into its paid wage
labourers'.[79] Secondly, Lunn points out how commodity production

shapes art. The fact that works of art are sold on the market shapes every level of their conception and production. Marx gave one example of this in his critique of the novels of Eugene Sue, in which he 'stresses the influence upon the author of the ethical and political assumptions of its intended bourgeois public'.[80] Neither can art escape commodity fetishism: 'If one form of spiritualising mystification has been eroded by expansion of commerce—the romantic apotheosis of the arts as soaring above material reality—a new fetishism has replaced it: the fetishism of commodities'.[81] This also points to how new, challenging cultural developments are rapidly incorporated into the system as mere commodities.

This does not mean that works of art can be reduced to exactly the same status as a tin of beans. Art stimulates our imagination and emotions. It enriches our understanding of society and can reveal something of the contradictions behind reified appearances: 'It can pierce through the ideological clouds which enshroud social realities.' Some artists devote their energies to attempting to reach beyond capitalism, while others choose to celebrate the system as it exists, but even then the art they produce can penetrate the reified appearance of capitalism. As Lunn wrote:

> We cannot reduce art to exchange rates reflecting the pervasive alienation. Even with its halo removed, art was capable of diagnosing, and pointing beyond alienating social and economic conditions... All art has the capacity to create a need for aesthetic enjoyment and education which capitalism cannot satisfy. Although coming increasingly under the influence of the marketplace, art is produced and consumed in relative autonomy and is not identical to factory work or to a pure commodity.[82]

The second controversial application of Marx's theory of alienation is in the formulation of an analysis of other activities outside the sphere of work, which we undertake through choice rather than necessity. The more the world of work confronts us as hostile, exhausting and miserable, the more people pour their energies into their lives outside work. As the system develops new markets are constantly being carved out of our needs and wishes. For example, consider the multimillion pound industries which have developed around commodities which are said to make us look thin or young, our desire to play games, to experience nature or enjoy art. The very fact that we have the 'leisure industry' and the 'entertainment industry' points to the fact that the separation of work from leisure has left a void in our free hours: 'Thus filling time away from the job also becomes dependent upon the market, which develops to an enormous degree those passive amusements, entertainments, and spectacles that suit the restricted circumstances of the city and are offered as substitutes for life itself'.[83]

The retreat into the privatised world of the individual and the family is a pronounced feature of life in the 1990s. Adopting particular lifestyles seems to offer the only real chance of personal fulfilment. Hence the increasing fascination for TV programmes and magazines about fashion, cooking, holidays and gardening and the boom in the Do-It-Yourself market. The family and the home have become leisure activities in and of themselves; they have also become subject to the priorities of the market. All the commodities which could increase our free time simply reinforce the family as a unit of consumption not an emotional haven: 'As the advances of modern household and service industries lighten the family labour, they increase the futility of family life; as they remove the burden of personal relations, they strip away its affections; as they create an intricate social life, they rob it of every vestige of community and leave in its place the cash nexus'.[84]

In addition, Meszaros describes how the retreat into private life simply increases the power of capitalism over us: 'The cult of privacy and of individual autonomy thus fulfils the dual function of objectively protecting the established order against challenge by the rabble, and subjectively providing a spurious fulfilment in an escapist withdrawal to the isolated and powerless individual who is mystified by the mechanisms of capitalist society which manipulate him'.[85] Meszaros also makes the point that alienation has deprived us of our ability to have genuinely human relationships. We are forced to seek compensation for the loss of our humanity in the limited area of our privatised personal lives, yet this merely reinforces our alienation from each other: 'To seek the remedy in autonomy is to be on the wrong track. Our troubles are not due to a lack of autonomy but, on the contrary, to a social structure—a mode of production—that forces on men a cult of it, isolating them from each other'.[86]

Our attempts to express the creativity of which capitalism has deprived us cannot negate the totality of alienation. The eradication of alienation depends on the transformation of society as a whole. However we organise our personal lives and leisure time, we cannot individually fulfil our collective ability to shape the natural world we live in. Lifestyles and leisure activities cannot liberate us from alienation, or even create little islands of freedom in an ocean of alienation. As alienation is rooted in capitalist society, only the collective struggle against that society carries the potential to eradicate alienation, to bring our vast, developing powers under our conscious control and reinstitute work as the central aspect of life. As Marx wrote in *Capital*, 'The veil is not removed from the countenance of the social life process, ie the process of material production, until it becomes production by freely associated men and stands under their conscious and planned control'.[87]

Notes

1 K Marx, 'Speech at the Anniversary of the Peoples' Paper' quoted in E Lunn, *Marxism and Modernism* (University of California Press, 1984), p31.
2 G Lukacs, *History and Class Consciousness* (Merlin, 1971), p47.
3 Marx was not the first to develop an analysis of human alienation. Marx's philosophical predecessor, Hegel, saw alienation as part of the development of the human mind. Ludwig Feuerbach put forward a materialist analysis of alienation, pointing out how men transfer the power to change the world to imaginary gods, but he believed that religious alienation could be eradicated through rational argument alone. Marx broke from both Hegel's idealist concept of alienation and the ahistorical materialism of Feuerbach. For an introduction to Marx's theorectical background, see A Callinicos, *The Revolutionary Ideas of Karl Marx* (Bookmarks, 1996), ch 3.
4 Quoted in E Fischer, *How to Read Karl Marx* (Monthly Review Press, 1996), p53.
5 Ibid, p52.
6 Ibid, p51.
7 Ibid, p54.
8 T Eagleton, *Marx* (Phoenix, 1997), p27.
9 K Marx, *Capital*, vol 1 (Penguin, 1976), p173.
10 K Marx, *Early Writings* (Penguin, 1975), p318.
11 Quoted in P Walton and A Gamble, *From Alienation to Surplus Value* (Sheed and Ward, 1972), p20.
12 E Mandel and G Novak, *The Marxist Theory of Alienation* (Pathfinder, 1970), p20.
13 *Capital*, op cit, p170.
14 K Marx quoted in I Meszaros, *Marx's Theory of Alienation* (Merlin Press, 1986), p35.
15 P Linebaugh, *The London Hanged* (Penguin, 1993), p396.
16 Ibid, p225.
17 Ibid, p374.
18 Ibid, p24.
19 *Capital*, op cit, p460
20 H Braverman, *Labour and Monopoly Capitalism* (Monthly Review Press, 1974), p73.
21 K Marx, *Early Writings*, op cit, p285.
22 Ibid, p335.
23 Ibid, p326.
24 P Linebaugh, op cit, p225.
25 B Ollman, *Alienation* (Cambridge University Press, 1996), p143.
26 I I Rubin, *Essays on Marx's Theory of Value* (Black Rose Books, 1975), pxxv.
27 K Marx, *Early Writings*, p324.
28 E Fischer, op cit, p67.
29 Ibid, p327.
30 H Braverman, *Labour and Monopoly Capitalism* (Monthly Review Press, 1974), p80.
31 E Fischer, op cit, pp58-9.
32 H Braverman, op cit, p171.
33 Ibid, p180.
34 G Lukács, op cit, p89.
35 K Marx, *Early Writings*, op cit, p331.
36 E Fischer, op cit, p63.
37 B Ollman, op cit, p144.
38 Rubin, op cit, p15.

39   K Marx, *Early Writings,* op cit, p359.
40   There is a brilliant description of one facet of this experience in C Caudwell, *The Concept of Freedom* (Lawrence and Wishart, 1977), p49.
41   K Marx, *Early Writings,* op cit, p325.
42   See C Harman, *Economics of the Madhouse* (Bookmarks, 1995).
43   E Mandel, op cit, p22.
44   K Marx, *Capital,* op cit, p125.
45   Ibid, p125.
46   Ibid, p1.
47   See ibid, p165.
48   Quoted in B Ollman, op cit, p187.
49   K Marx, *Capital,* op cit, pp202-203.
50   Ibid, p21.
51   Ibid, pp165-165.
52   Ibid, p24.
53   Ibid, p179.
54   H Braverman, op cit, p271.
55   E Fischer, op cit, p68.
56   Ibid, p187.
57   Ibid, p205.
58   I Meszaros, op cit, p197.
59   K Marx, *Early Writings,* op cit, p351.
60   Ibid, p361.
61   Ibid, p377.
62   K Marx, quoted in G Lukács, op cit, p133.
63   Ibid, p63.
64   B Ollman, op cit, p154.
65   K Marx, *The Holy Family,* quoted in F Jakubowski, *Ideology and Superstructure in Historical Materialism* (Pluto, 1990), p87.
66   G Lukács, op cit, p171.
67   P Anderson, *Considerations on Western Marxism* (New Left Books, 1976), pp50-51.
68   Ibid, p56.
69   E Mandel, op cit, p6.
70   E and M Josephson, *Man Alone: Alienation in Modern Society* (Dell Publishing Co, 1968), p12.
71   Ibid, p13.
72   Ibid, ch 1.
73   B Ollman, op cit, p202.
74   H Braverman, op cit, p83.
75   See, for instance, G Carchedi, *Frontiers of Political Economy* (Verso, 1991), p18.
76   F Jakubowski, op cit, p96.
77   Ibid, p96.
78   E Lunn, op cit, p15.
79   Ibid, p16.
80   Ibid, p12.
81   Ibid, p16.
82   Ibid, pp15-16.
83   H Braverman, op cit, p278,
84   Ibid, p282.
85   I Meszaros, op cit, p26.
86   Ibid, p267.
87   K Marx, *Capital,* op cit, p173.

Making a comeback: the Marxist theory of crisis

A review of Simon Clarke, **Marx's Theory of Crisis** (St Martin's Press, 1994), £15.99

JUDITH ORR

> *The alternation of boom and slump, the coexistence of overwork and unem-*
> *ployment, of staggering wealth alongside devastating poverty, of*
> *concentrations of power alongside hopeless impotence is as much a feature of*
> *capitalism today as it was a century and more ago. The sense of a world*
> *beyond human control, of a world driven to destruction by alien forces, is*
> *stronger today than it has ever been. The gulf between the bland assurances*
> *of the bourgeois economist and the reality of life for the mass of the world's*
> *population has never been wider.*[1]

The dramatic collapse of the Tiger economies has made Simon Clarke's description of modern capitalism even more apt than when it was written. So recently used as evidence that crises could be eradicated, the erstwhile miracles of South East Asia are now the best examples of Marx's assertion that such an eradication is impossible. As a result it's not uncommon now to see columnists in *The Guardian* or the *Financial Times* pointing out with surprise just how relevant Marx is for explaining the vagaries of the system. Clarke's book is therefore worth examining, for if even bourgeois commentators are admitting that Marx had a point then it is important that we are clear about what Marx actually said. Also, as the quote above indicates, Clarke writes as a Marxist wanting to further understanding of Marx's theory while raising at the same time a number of traditional criticisms to Marx which it is important to answer.

Clarke provides a useful account of what socialists after Marx have had to say on the subject of crisis and the debates that have taken place amongst Marxists at different times when the system has seemed to defy the basic theory. Although Clarke sees himself as part of the Marxist tradition, there is not much left of Marxist theory once he has finished. His main theme is that much of what Marx had to say about crisis and the system was valid but that ultimately Marx did not have a single theory of crisis but at least three:

> ...within the Marxist tradition three quite distinct theories of crisis have been proposed, based on rather different specifications of the underlying contradiction. These are underconsumptionist theory, which dominated the Marxism of the Second International, disproportionality theories, which became popular in the early twentieth century, and theories which associate crises with the falling tendency of the rate of profit, which have come to dominate contemporary Marxism...in the **Grundrisse**, as in Marx's later works, we apparently find all three theories coexisting... Is this simply an indication of the undeveloped character of Marx's theorising, or of his undoubted confusion when he comes onto discussion of these matters?[2]

Clarke goes on to answer his own question:

> There is no doubt that Marx's theorising is undeveloped, and that his discussion is often inconsistent and confused... His theory of crisis undoubtedly contains elements of underconsumptionist, disproportionality and falling rate of profit theories, but it is not a confused or an eclectic combination of all three. There is a conceptual unity and coherence running through his discussions.[3]

Apart from the fact that this assessment is itself contradictory, on the one hand criticising Marx for being confused and on the other pointing to a 'conceptual unity and coherence' in his work, even at its most generous it does Marx a disservice. For although Marx did write about the various elements at play in any economic crisis, for him the key factor was that crises were *endemic* to the system because the contradictions from which they emerged were *rooted in the central process of production*. He wrote, 'The progressive tendency for the general rate of profit to fall is thus simply the expression, peculiar to the capitalist mode of production, of the progressive development of the social productivity of labour. This does not mean the rate of profit may not fall temporarily for other reasons as well, but it does prove that it is a self evident necessity, deriving from the nature of the capitalist mode of production itself...'[4] The endemic nature of crises is equally emphasised in Marx's famous saying, 'The true barrier to capitalist production is capital itself'.[5]

Clarke takes us through how the ideas of Marx and later Engels have been debated historically in a chapter which begins with the words:

The failure of Marxism in the 1980s was essentially the failure of the Leninist tradition which had dominated Marxism since the 1930s... The triumph of Leninism led to the dismissal of the Social Democratic tradition of Marxism, yet this was a tradition which, for all its failures and defeats, had been forged in the experience of the crisis-riven and struggle torn development of the capitalist mode of production, by intellectuals who were neither academics nor state functionaries but were the builders of a mass movement.[6]

Yet Leninism was formed in the same circumstances, by individuals who were also builders of a mass movement but with one crucial difference; the Leninists led a successful revolution, while those who maintained the social democracy of the Second International became apologists for a savage imperialist war and in Germany allowed, and even participated in, the murder of their revolution.[7]

Despite the initial endorsement of revisionism Clarke does acknowledge and discuss problems with the analysis associated with the period writing that 'the political weakness of the Marxism of the Second International lay primarily in the growing divergence between its analysis of the historical tendencies of historical capitalist accumulation and its political programme for the transition to socialism'.[8] The discussions and theoretical developments of the Second International are covered by Clarke in detail. He also initially sketches, and later covers in more depth, subsequent developments in the theory of crisis in the Marxist tradition right up to the 1970s.

Falling rate of profit

More interesting, however, are Clarke's passages on Marx's economics. He devotes a whole chapter to his critique of the theory of the tendency of the rate of profit to fall, which Marx saw as pivotal to the theory of crisis but which Clarke believes to be flawed. It flows from the theory that labour creates value. As a result commodities exchange according to the average labour time required to produce them with average technology and work intensity—Marx called this the socially necessary labour time. Like all other commodities produced under capitalism, labour is bought and sold on the 'labour market'. And, as with other commodities, the price of labour is determined by the cost of sheltering, feeding, clothing and educating, in other words reproducing, each worker so they are fit to work. Under capitalism workers' wages amount to less than the value that they create in the production of commodities, leaving the capitalist to accrue the surplus. This is because labour is a unique commodity. Machinery can only pass on the value that went into creating it. Workers, however, can create enough value to cover the cost of their own reproduction and then carry on working and create surplus value.

This is the picture inside each unit of capital. But, of course, in the real economy there are many units of capital. No capitalist acts in a vacuum. Each is constantly forced to compete with other capitalists. So the accumulated surplus is continually invested into new labour saving machinery and technology to try and produce commodities more cheaply, ie with less labour involved in them than the next factory. Because commodities exchange according to the socially necessary labour time and not according to what labour time or technology actually went into making that specific product, the first capitalist has an incentive to make them with less labour:

> At first he can sell them above their price of production... He pockets the difference between their costs of production and the market price of other commodities, which are produced at higher production costs. This is possible because the average socially necessary labour time required to produce the latter commodities is greater than the labour time required with the new method of production. His production procedure is ahead of the social average.[9]

Initially any capitalist can make good profits in this way—undercutting those making the product in a more labour intensive way—but when all capitalists get the same or even better technology there's no advantage. In fact quite the opposite. Competition drives individual capitalists to this continual investment in new machinery designed to cut labour costs. Yet they face a contradiction because they are cutting back on the only element of production from which they can extract surplus value—labour, that is the activity of the workers. Without human intervention machines don't create value, they themselves are the product of past labour, or as Marx called it, crystallized labour. On their own they are incapable of creating any new value for the capitalist. So the drive to increase profits leads to a tendency for the ratio of machinery (dead labour) to increase in proportion to that of living labour—the source of surplus value. Marx referred to this process as the increase in the organic composition of capital. This contradiction at the heart of production is what leads to the tendency for the rate of profit to decline. So what is beneficial for the individual capitalist in the short term, actually starts to undermine the ability of the whole capitalist class to accrue surplus labour in the longer term.

The tendency for the rate of profit to fall underlies and intensifies the cycle of boom and slump, sometimes referred to as the 'business cycle'.

Clarke refers to the business cycle but puts it all in the pot together with other aspects of crises without showing how it can form a part of an integrated theory of crisis. As production under capitalism is driven by the need to maximise profits, not to produce what might be useful, so crises may result from, for the first time in history, an *overproduction* of commodities, a flooding of the market. This is because with no planning every capitalist in a certain industry will try provide enough goods to fulfil any increase in demand for any commodity. So a 50 percent increase in demand for jeans, for example, will not be equally shared across all the companies which produce jeans. Instead each will try and produce all the 50 percent extra and battle in the market place to sell them. Of course there will then be far more jeans on the market than there is demand for. Some will go unsold, or some may be sold at a loss, perhaps leaving the smaller jeans companies in particular at risk of collapsing if they cannot carry the subsequent loss in return for their investment. As some companies go bust investment in the industry slows as profits decline and so the cycle of investment and expansion turns downwards into slump. Workers are left unemployed and even less able to buy commodities, which serves to increase the decline across the whole system.

This 'underconsumption' on the part of the consumers—workers, who may want or need the commodities but are unable to afford to buy them—has been interpreted by some as the cause of crisis. Clarke implies that Marx himself saw it as a cause. But such lack of consumption occurred long before the existence of economic crises and it is not unique to capitalism; rather than being a cause of crises it is one of the possible features of crisis. As Engels writes in *Anti-Dühring*, 'The underconsumption of the masses is not a new phenomenon. It has existed as long as there have been exploiting and exploited classes...while...the general shrinkage of the market which breaks out in crises as the result of a surplus of production is a phenomenon only of the last 50 years'.[10]

As well as assessing different elements in Marx's theory of crisis, Clarke points to some common criticisms of Marx's analysis.[11] The first is that the process which results in the cheapening of commodities also cheapens the machinery which produces them, as it in turn will have had less and less labour used in its production. In terms of value, therefore, 'we cannot assume that the composition of capital in value terms will necessarily rise'. While it is true that new technology does decrease in price as new ways of producing it are developed, it is not true that every capitalist benefits from this. Each capitalist has to make enough profits to cover the cost of what he or she actually spent on the machinery in their factory, not on what the same machinery might currently cost. So the first capitalist to make cars using robotic technology will still have to pay back the bank, for instance, the full amount plus interest paid out for the original machinery, regardless of the fact that two years later the same machinery can be bought at half the price. In fact it can intensify the drive to extract surplus value from the workers he still employs as he tries to recoup his original larger investment when the socially necessary labour time for the production of cars lessens with every new development.

This leads to the second criticism, that 'Marx ignores the fact that the rise in the rate of exploitation may perfectly well be sufficient to counteract any increase in the composition of capital, so that the rate of profit might well rise'. Firstly it is of course true that increased investment in new means of production leads to an increase in the rate of exploitation in workers. Each worker is producing more than they did previously with the older machinery and so even if the length of the working day and wages remain the same each worker is making more surplus for the capitalist. In addition it is also true that capitalists will always try to maintain or increase their profit levels by increasing exploitation through direct attacks on workers' pay and conditions. This can be done by imposing longer hours, lower wages or more intense labour, but this process does not have unlimited potential for increasing the extraction of surplus value. Clarke shows that Marx himself addressed this question, explaining that there is, for instance, a physical limit on how many hours a day workers can labour. There has to be time for workers to have at least some sleep and their wages have to be at least sufficient to provide for enough food to be fit enough for work. (Although to help out capitalists trying to squeeze the maximum surplus value out of their workers governments have been found willing to 'top up' the wages of those who don't actually earn enough to live on. In Britain at the moment benefits such as Family Credit act as a subsidy for employers paying less than a living wage.)

The third and equally long standing objection is one which rejects Marx's characterisation of the system as being inherently irrational— 'Marx ignores the fact that the capitalist will only introduce a new method of production if it provides an increased rate of profit so that faced with such a fall capitalists will continue to use the old method of production and earn the old rate of profit.' But, as has been already been pointed out, what is profitable for an individual capitalist may not be beneficial for the system as a whole. Capitalists are not in control, they are 'like the sorcerer, who is no longer able to control the powers of the nether world whom he has called up by his spells'.[12] They are driven to invest and act in a certain way because survival depends on making more profits than your competitors and if they are producing, for example, pocket calculators at half the cost you can, then they can continually undercut you until you sell at a loss or go bust: 'those capitalists who operate under the old conditions of production must sell their product below its full price of production; the value of this product has fallen, so that they need more labour time to produce it than is socially necessary. In short, and this appears as the effect of competition, they must also introduce the new mode of production which reduces the ratio of variable capital to constant'.[13] This is a point Clarke makes himself elsewhere in the book: 'The tendency to expand production without limit is not just a matter of the subjective motivation of the capitalist, since it is imposed on every capitalist by the pressure of competition.' There's no room for a boss to decide, 'I don't want to get involved in all those new fangled computers, I'm happy with my profits so I'll just stick to hot metal printing.' It is clear that such a capitalist would not last long.

Clarke implies that he is vindicated in his criticisms of the tendency of the rate of profit to fall when he points out that Marx did not see it as a mechanical law.[14] But this is hardly an insight; Marx saw capitalism as a dynamic system and he referred to the *tendency* of the rate of profit to decline and acknowledged 'counteracting influences must be at work, checking and cancelling the effect of the general law, and give it merely the characteristic of a tendency'.[15] These counteracting tendencies include, of course, crises themselves which serve to wipe out chunks of constant capital, thus temporarily reversing the increase in the organic composition of capital—'Crises are never more than momentary, violent solutions for the existing contradictions, violent eruptions that re-establish the disturbed balance for the time being'.[16] If the tendency for the rate of profit to fall was a mechanical law then the system would have long since spiralled into a final collapse, much as some socialists such as Kautsky in the early 20th century said it would. Instead there is a tension and a contradiction in the system between the need for and the dangers of expansion. The way in which these contradictions are played out is not predestined. In some cases the capitalist class wins out, maintaining profits and riding out crises. This is often not just at the expense of workers but also of smaller, weaker sections of their own class.

At other times workers may refuse to accept longer hours and pay cuts, or state intervention may hold up failing capitals (though this sometimes only postpones the problem for, as has already been pointed out, the destruction of some capital can enable the system to return to profitability). But, as history has shown, as long as the system exists the underlying fault that threatens its whole basis remains. In the end Clarke renders all this discussion, and by implication his own book, irrelevant, writing:

> *The debate that has dominated Marxism between disproportionality theories, underconsumptionist theories and falling rate of profit theories has really been a red herring. A crisis arises when capitalists face a fall in their realised*

profit which can arise for all manner of reasons, but the precipitating cause of any crisis is inconsequential...the underlying cause of all crises remains the fundamental contradiction on which the capitalist mode of production is based.[17]

Such a flippant conclusion is of no use to readers who are looking to understand Marx to explain what appears an ever more irrational world system.[18] It is crucial to socialists who see theory as a guide to action to investigate what Clarke regards as a 'red herring'. For identifiying the precipitating causes of any crisis is essential if we are to show up the impossibility of reformists' claims to be able to tinker with the system to make it stable. But then this book is content to remain in the realms of the abstract rather than measure its ideas against the real world, historical or contemporary. Clarke has examined every scrap of paper that Marx ever wrote on the subject, seemingly with the aim of showing him to be confused, contradictory or just plain wrong. Anyone spurred into wanting to find out more about what Marx had to say on the subject should be advised to skip Clarke and go back to the writings of the man himself.

Notes

1   S Clarke, *Marx's Theory of Crisis* (St Martin's Press, 1994), p8.
2   Ibid, p137.
3   Ibid, p138.
4   K Marx, *Capital* vol 3 (Penguin, 1981), p 319.
5   Ibid, p358.
6   Ibid, p14.
7   For the best account of this period, C Harman, *The Lost Revolution: Germany 1918-1923* , 2nd edn (Bookmarks, 1997).
8   S Clarke, op cit, p15.
9   K Marx, op cit, p375.
10   F Engels, *Anti-Dühring* (Lawrence & Wishart, 1955), p397.
11   Ibid, p213.
12   K Marx and F Engels, *The Communist Manifesto* (Progress, 1971), p41.
13   K Marx, op cit, p374.
14   S Clarke, op cit, p241.
15   K Marx, op cit, p339.
16   Ibid, p 357.
17   S Clarke, op cit, p285.
18   Such readers will find Marx's theory of crisis clearly explained in C Harman, *Economics of the Madhouse* (Bookmarks, 1995), C Harman, *Explaining the Crisis* (Bookmarks, 1987), A Callinicos, *The Revolutionary Ideas of Karl Marx* (Bookmarks, 1987), L Huberman, *Man's Worldly Goods* (Monthly Review, New York, 1968) pp280-283.

New Labour, old conflicts: the story so far

A review of D Draper, **Blair's Hundred Days** *(Faber & Faber, 1997),*
£7.99; D Butler and D Kavanagh, **The British General Election of 1997**
(Macmillan, 1997), £17.50; P Anderson and N Mann, **Safety First: The**
Making of New Labour *(Granta, 1997), £9.99; L Panitch and C Leys,*
The End of Parliamentary Socialism: From New Left to New Labour
(Verso, 1997), £15

MEGAN TRUDELL

The weekend after the general election in May 1997 *The Observer* newspaper was emblazoned with the words 'The paper for the new era'. For
many liberal commentators, as for virtually everyone who voted for
Labour in May, the end of 18 years of Tory government seemed to herald
a change in priorities from a government whose policies slavishly bowed
to market forces to a government with a social conscience which would
improve people's lives. Yet only five months later *The Observer*'s editor,
Will Hutton, wrote that those who think the market should not be left to
devastate lives unchecked face 'the growing realisation...that we may
soon not be able to look to the Labour Party to represent what we
believe'.[1] John Edmonds, general secretary of the GMB, wrote in
January 1998, 'Working people should be looking forward to 1998 as the
best year in two decades...Yet, as I go around the country, what I find is
not joyous expectation but a mood of gloomy cynicism'.[2]

This shift in the popular conception of Labour comes too late to be
included in the various books on Blair's project and the general election
that were published in the summer of 1997, but they nonetheless provide
important insights into the development of Blairism and the potential
problems the Labour government might face. The books range from
Derek Draper's uncritical eulogy of the Blair project, through Butler and
Kavanagh's examination of the election campaign, to the much more
critical and useful books by Anderson and Mann, and Panitch and Leys.
These last two attempt to deal with several fundamental questions: why

Labour has shifted to the right; Labour's relationship with business and with the unions; and the possibility of a left revival should Labour fail to deliver.

To take the least first, Derek Draper has written a glowing account of the first 100 days of the Blair government. His book, offering a 'behind the scenes' look at the reality at Millbank, is interesting gossip, but it carries very little in the way of criticism, which is what one would expect from someone who used to be an adviser to Peter Mandelson. This is not to say that the book is entirely without merit. Despite himself he occasionally provides real insights, as when he describes how the size of Labour's majority sent expectations for change snowballing: 'We were elected on a cautious programme but the size of the mandate leads people to want bigger and bolder change. They expect that a 179 majority at the end of four years will mean the education system, the NHS, crime and the state of society will have radically improved'.[3] And he argues that welfare 'reform' will not go down well: 'In the short term, sticking plaster and good faith will do the trick; in the long term more money must be found. Or a crisis in the NHS could end up being Labour's ERM'.[4] If the sheer authoritarianism and cult of the personality that Blair has established is still in question, Draper removes any last doubts. It is perhaps not surprising to learn that Blair responded to questions from the new intake of MPs by replying, 'It is not your job to tell us what to do,' but it is confirmation of the tight rein MPs are on. Similarly, the reactionary nature of much of Blairite ideology—as pushed by an assorted team of advisers—is pretty breathtaking, like campaign 'wonk' Peter Hyman's inspired but rejected slogan, 'Young thugs will be caged'. Draper gives us a fairly unpleasant insight into those who govern us but his book is too full of approval to probe beneath the surface of Blairism.

The other three books are much more satisfying in this respect. Butler and Kavanagh have written the latest book in a series on national elections, tracing the last months of the Major government, the road to New Labour, the election campaign, and providing an analysis of the results. *The British General Election of 1997* is by definition concerned with the business of parliament and elections and it therefore provides masses of detail without much reference to the outside world. The analysis is standard psephological fare, but for statistics and opinion polls the book is invaluable.

Both *Safety First* and *The End of Parliamentary Socialism* have wider remits. In *Safety First* Anderson and Mann have written a very good account of the main players in the Labour administration and their road to the cabinet. In doing so they trace the history of the Labour Party from the Second World War in an accessible and informative way. Both authors write for *Tribune* and their critique of Blairism from the left is refreshing. The book by Panitch and Leys is a more academically written account, concentrating on the project of the 'new left' and Bennism. It is concerned primarily with the efforts during the late 1970s and early 1980s to democratise the Labour Party and, as such, often descends into the minutiae of conference resolutions and by-election details. Nonetheless, it is by far the most critical of the Blair project, and—especially read in conjunction with *Safety First*—provides a coherent account of Labour's development since the early 1970s and a welcome call for socialist organisation. I have criticisms of both *Safety First* and *The End of Parliamentary Socialism*, but it is to their credit that they both attempt to discuss some fundamental questions about the New Labour government. Why did Blair shift to the right to such an extent and what form did that shift take? What is Labour's relationship with business and the unions? And what possibility is there for left revival should Labour fail to match voters' expectations?

The 'modernisation' of Labour

None of these books disagree on the impact the fourth election defeat in a row had on Labour in 1992. In looking at the modernisation project Anderson and Mann cite Blair, quoted in the aftermath of Kinnock's defeat, drawing the lesson that Labour must 'continue and intensify the process of change...at the level of both ideas and organisation'.[5] They are clear that while Labour undoubtedly became 'dramatically more pro-business, even keener on flexible labour markets and more resigned than ever before to the powerlessness of the state in the face of market forces...if political leadership is to be judged in terms of policy rather than tone, Blair must be seen as a beneficiary of his predecessors' efforts'.[6]

Blair's ideological position, which he shared with the Labour right throughout the 1980s, was critical of Labour's dependence on the working class and asserted the need for its policies and structures to be changed to take account of the impact of Thatcherism. Implicit in this is the belief that Thatcher had changed the face of British politics and that voters were more conservative and could only be won to Labour if its policies reflected this shift.[7] Labour's 'modernisation' was an acceptance of the ideas that winning elections depended on appealing to 'Middle England', and that policies of renationalisation or 'tax and spend' would alienate Labour from the electorate. In other words, as increasing numbers of people were moving away from the Tories and rejecting their policies, Labour was embracing privatisation, low taxation and the free market. As Panitch and Leys point out, 'The electorally crucial ideas were those of voters who must be won back to Labour, not those of voters who had suffered most under Conservative rule, most of whom would vote Labour in any case'.[8] However, as Butler and Kavanagh's analysis of the general election shows, Labour is still dependent on the working class to get elected. In 'working class' seats in London the Tory vote fell by 16.5 percent, in the rest of the south east by 13.6 percent and elsewhere by 12.1 percent. In 'middle class' seats—ie those in which at least 19 percent of households include employers or managers—the respective figures were 15 percent, 13.1 percent and 11.4 percent.[9] They conclude, 'There is little evidence to support the view that voters in predominantly middle class constituencies were more inclined to swing to New Labour than working class voters'.[10]

Nonetheless, Blair's beliefs held sway in a party desperate for victory and in the run up to the election:

> Across the fields of social and economy policy the party shifted towards acceptance of much that the [Major] government was doing. The Welfare to Work scheme aimed to shift the long term young unemployed into work and make receipt of benefits conditional on seeking work or receiving training. The 1992 election promises to upgrade child benefit and pensions, and to link future pension increases to rises in prices or earnings—whichever was higher—were abandoned.[11]

Restructuring the party itself fitted in with this view. Anderson and Mann, in discussing the moves to the greater centralisation of the party, cite the controversial 1995 strategy document from adviser Philip Gould, which called for a new 'command structure' involving 'less but better people, a new culture and a new building', with the leader as the 'sole ultimate source of authority'.[12] Hence the move to Millbank, the establishment of the 'rapid rebuttal unit', the clique around Blair and the attacks on party democracy outlined in the 'Labour Into Power' document.

The modernisers' obsession with the media and its power to win or lose elections for Labour is also well illustrated in all three books. New Labour actively cultivated the tabloids and Blair met with News International executives prior to the election, and in the minds of the Blairites such moves bore fruit when *The Sun* declared for Labour in the election. In the spirit of quid pro quo, Labour dropped both its proposed ban on cross-media ownership and any talk of taking Rupert Murdoch before a Monopolies and Mergers Commission inquiry. For Blair '*The Sun* really did make a difference'.[13] Yet, as Butler and Kavanagh point out, Labour's support increased in 1997 among readers of every national newspaper, and they argue convincingly that, 'even if *The Sun*'s switch did impinge on its readers to a small extent, this effect was trivial in the overall context of the forces shaping Labour's election victory…like the rest of the press, *The Sun* was following opinion more than creating it'.[14] Labour's 'War Book' is more honest about the real reasons for Labour's success than the modernisers are in public: 'People still believe that the Conservatives do not deserve to be re-elected. Rejection of the Conservatives is so ingrained as to be almost visceral. People believe the country needs change'.[15]

Nonetheless, the overriding message from these accounts is that Blair and the modernisers in New Labour are convinced that the key job of government is to stay in power. Their belief in their own spin, that it was 'Middle England' who voted and mattered, and that 'it was New Labour wot won it', or as Mandelson rather ludicrously put it, 'Without New Labour the Conservatives could have won again',[16] shapes the political choices they make and the intellectual justifications for them. Blair, speaking in 1994 just after his election as party leader, bends theory to fit practice quite breathtakingly: 'The socialism of Marx, of centralised state control of industry and production, is dead... By contrast, socialism as defined by certain key values and beliefs is not merely alive, it has an historic opportunity now to give leadership... Once being radical is defined as having a central vision, based around principle but liberated from particular policy prescriptions that have become confused with principle, then being radical is the route to electability'.[17] Or, as one adviser put it rather more directly, 'In the mass media age, policy is there to win elections'.[18]

New Labour and the economy

For New Labour the policies that win elections appear to be those which continue the Thatcher project, and Blair's admiration of Thatcher is well documented. According to Draper, the now infamous meeting between the two on 22 May at Downing Street was about more than the impending European summit, 'spending most time on the issue of welfare reform, particularly for single mothers'. Blair explained the relationship saying that 'New Labour is not about turning the clock back but about taking forward Thatcher's record based on New Labour's distinct principles'.[19] This 'taking forward' of Thatcherism underlies much of the Blairite rhetoric. For instance, he is quoted as aiming for the sort of consensus politics that emerged during the 1945-1951 Attlee government: 'The ways of achieving [a different vision of society] must change. Those should and will cross the old boundaries between left and right, progressive and conservative'.[20]

The difficulty is, as Panitch and Leys put it, ' "New Labour" lacked at least two crucial assets which the government of 1945 possessed: a coherent project for social reform, distilled by several generations of socialist thinkers...and endorsed by a large majority of the public as a result of bitter experience; and a world trade and investment regime of the kind laid down at Bretton Woods'.[21] They touch on an important truth: that the British economy is not entering a period of long boom. They suggest that, however much a large majority of the public want real reform, it is difficult to realise without eating into the profits of business. The consensus Blair is looking for is far more likely to be one based on the Thatcherite ethic of the free market than one based on substantial government spending—which doesn't offer much in the way of a different vision.

New Labour makes no secret of its inclination towards complete deregulation of the market. In January 1997 Brown committed Labour to the Tories' spending plans for two years and ruled out any increase in the top rate of tax: 'Our first budget will not reopen overall spending allocations for the 1997-8 financial year...' New Labour was to stick to 'already announced departmental budgets...reordered to meet Labour's priorities'.[22] Brown's acceptance of Tory spending limits and income tax rates in 1997 are an extension of the rejection of the tax and spending commitments in the 1992 election manifesto and exemplify Labour's categoric abandonment of Keynesian economics.

It is important to understand the context of this ideological shift: The post-war consensus on Keynesianism had crumbled in the mid-1970s with the onset of stagflation (and therefore the theory's failure to offset rising inflation by lowering unemployment). The early 1970s had seen increased public spending leading to increased growth, but when recession bit—exacerbated by the 1973 oil price rises—and unemployment rose, the same policies led to a rise in inflation. By 1976 the Labour government was forced to apply to the IMF for loans and the 1976 Labour conference saw Callaghan formally accept monetarism. However, the centrality of Keynesianism to Labour's economics revived after the 1979 election defeat. Labour's 1983 manifesto adhered to policies of expanded public ownership and a return to government intervention in the economy.

But Labour's defeat in the 1983 general election meant this strategy was never pursued, and it is probable that it never would have been. In defeat, Labour began the ten year process of ditching any mention of widespread nationalisation and significant increases in public spending to reduce unemployment. The dominance of monetarist theory and policy under the Tories—given added impetus by the collapse of state capitalism in the Eastern bloc and by the idea that globalisation precluded government intervention even if it were desirable—became reflected, by the aftermath of the 1992 defeat, in Labour theory and policy.

Thus Brown stated in 1995 that in line with the 'golden rule' of balancing the budget over the economic cycle, 'Brown's law is that the government will only borrow to invest, public debt will remain stable and the cost effectiveness of public spending must be proved...nobody should doubt my iron resolve for stability and fiscal prudence'.[23] In other words, government debt will not be allowed to rise in response to short term factors, like unemployment rising or the pound staying strong. The potential impact of 'Brown's law' on the working class is, in the area of social security, a move away from universal provision towards a 'safety net' for the very worst off, couched in language that plays to prejudices over fraud and over rising welfare costs while paying lip service to protecting the poor.

Labour justifies cutting social security by arguing that welfare leads to poverty, and that spiralling welfare bills make Britain less competitive. Will Hutton has argued against this view:

Britain has simultaneously one of the highest proportions of people living in poverty and high labour market participation rates. Mr Blair is ill-advised to argue that the explanation of widespread poverty is a high non-working population; this is factually wrong. Nor is social security spending high and out of control. After 18 years of Conservative governments it is low and increasing below the average rate of economic growth.[24]

In fact Britain spends less on social security as a proportion of GDP—a mere 13 percent—than other EU states. And the projected nominal increase in that spending is slightly more than 1 percent a year for the next five years, which represents a cut in real terms. And 'Britain's state spending on old-age cash benefits, accounting for nearly half the total social security budget, is towards the bottom for the developed world'.[25] In the area of unemployment legislation the impact of limiting public expenditure to investment in reality means limiting measures to cheap 'flexible' labour, training, and minimal rights for workers in place of real job creation.

There is wealth in the economy now. The context within which 'Brown's law' was established was that of a British economy expanding by almost 4 percent a year—higher than the long term average of around 2.25 percent. It seems likely that when the economy does enter recession workers will be asked to pay a higher and higher price for Labour's cuts in public spending. In spring 1998 the British economy faced a squeeze on exports due to the strength of the pound—likely to be further hit by the shrinking East Asian markets—as well as high interest rates. The economy slowed down in the first 3 months of 1998. The *Financial Times* reported that the January-March growth was the slowest for a quarter since April-June 1995 at 4 percent; trimming the annual rate to 2.8 percent.[26] The TUC in April 1998 predicted the loss of

200,000 jobs by the end of 1999, and an independent forecast by the Centre for Economics and Business Research said that Britain was heading for a 'mini-recession'. The centre's report said that the strength of the pound was 'having a major impact on competitivencss' and estimated unemployment would rise by 350,000 by 2000, 'wiping out any gains from Welfare to Work measures in the budget'.[27]

The question then is, what happens to New Labour's balancing act of claiming that fairness to all in society is also efficient economically within the constraints of Tory spending limits? As one writer has asked:

> *What if, in the short run, deflation means a rise in unemployment? What if objectives conflict...in the real world, when the crunch comes, as it so often does soon after a Labour government takes office, it will, like its forbears, have to confront the problem of how best to deploy scarce resources among competing ends... In such circumstances and with no clearly articulated priorities and with the crucial levers of power in the hands of others, the danger is that it will move along the line of least resistance, the deflationary line which provokes least resistance from the City, the IMF, the US Federal Reserve and the US Treasury.*[28]

New Labour, business and the unions

Tony Blair told *The Guardian* in 1991, 'You can measure how well you're doing by the number of invitations you get to address businessmen'.[29] And in the 1997 election campaign Labour's first broadcast claimed it was a 'party business can do business with'. The signals suggested that if there was a clash between the interests of the business community and provision for ordinary people, every effort would be made to appease the former. As Andrew Rawnsley put it in *The Observer* in November 1997, the 'government will not do anything to be popular. Rather, it will do anything to avoid being unpopular with the well-connected, the well-organised and the well-heeled'.[30]

Anderson and Mann describe the launch of the Commission on Public Policy and British Business in 1997, an initiative set up 'to investigate the competitive position of the British economy and the role that public policy should play in it'. The commission's report 'backed a host of New Labour policies: a (low) minimum wage, tougher competition policy, improvements in education and training...tax incentives for long-term investment and strict adherence to a tight fiscal and monetary regime...it gave wholehearted endorsement to the Tory market liberalisations of the 1980s'.[31] At the launch, Blair's speech made his position clear:

Today I offer business a new deal for the future. The deal is this: we leave intact the main changes of the 1980s in industrial relations and enterprise... Our proposals for change, including the minimum wage, would amount to less labour market regulation than in the USA. Our aim is not to create inflexible labour markets... In the USA it would never occur to question the commitment of the Democrats to business. It should be the same here with New Labour.[32]

Hand in hand with Blair's wooing of business interests went his attempts to distance the Labour Party from its ties to the trade union bureaucracy. His speech to the Commission on Public Policy and British Business dovetailed with his statement during the election campaign that 'trade unions will have no special or privileged place within the Labour Party'.[33] The reduction of the voice of the union bureaucracy within the party as part of the battle to 'reform' Labour was crucial to the modernisers. In 1984 Neil Kinnock first proposed a change in the way parliamentary candidates were selected—to one member one vote, known as OMOV. Panitch and Leys argue that behind Kinnock's rhetoric about reducing the trade union block vote to 'increase activism in the party' lay the real desire for 'a new source of *in*activist (and hence "moderate") support for the leadership in the shape of a wider membership who could be directly consulted through postal votes'.[34] Eventually passed under John Smith in 1993, OMOV reduced the union block vote at conference and impaired the ability of the unions to get sympathetic candidates selected—which may partly account for today's lowest ever percentage of Labour MPs with a manual working class background, at 13 percent.[35]

As Panitch and Leys point out, 'As the unions' weight in party decision making was progressively reduced, the party's remaining policy commitments to them were also watered down'.[36] They cite the dilution of legislation on the minimum wage, union recognition and the right of public sector workers to take strike action as examples. The political victory for the modernisers does not at all mean that Labour cannot be influenced by the union leadership—almost all the Parliamentary Labour Party (PLP) are union members—but it removed the stigma of being in thrall to the unions. The campaign to replace Clause Four of Labour's constitution was similarly symbolic. In the desire to convince business that nationalisation was a thing of the past, despite the majority of the population supporting the return of the privatised utilities to public ownership, the new clause embraced the vision of a 'dynamic economy, rigour of competition and enterprise of the market'.

In addition, 'between 1986 and 1996 the union contributions to party funds declined from three-quarters to a half of the total. According to one insider, private business provided some £15 million for the party over a nine month period from June 1996'.[37] Figures from the election itself, however, indicate Labour's continuing reliance on union money. UNISON alone spent £1,112,000 on pro-Labour advertising, over an eighth of the total Labour advertising expenditure.[38] John Edmonds described the trade union contribution to the election campaign: 'We set up the general election fund which paid the bills. We funded the bright new Labour Party campaign centre. We paid agents in the key seats so that a sustained campaign was fought over three years and not just three weeks'.[39] A Labour victory mattered a great deal to the trade union leadership. According to Anderson and Mann, Labour's defeat in 1987 made the unions more ready to compromise with the Labour leadership. The Thatcher years, and its own complacency in the face of Tory attacks, led the trade union bureaucracy to a position of 'new realism'—an acceptance that Thatcherism had destroyed much of Britain's manufacturing base, emasculated the unions and wrought a sea change in working class attitudes.

The relationship between the acceptance of Tory anti-union laws and the electability of Labour after its third defeat is described by Lewis Minkin, who saw 'virtually complete agreement among TUC officials, and among a growing number of union leaders...that the Conservative government legislation on union industrial action had built upon and consolidated a more or less permanent body of opinion among union members and in the centre ground of the electorate. The Labour Party could no longer be saddled with a blanket commitment to repeal the entire legislation'.[40] However, such desperation to get Labour elected generates high expectations once it is in office. John Edmonds declared his belief in New Labour after the election when he said, 'Let us trust that, in the years ahead, every time a Labour MP walks through the House of Commons, they remember the help they received from the GMB and so many other trade unions'.[41] It may be difficult for Labour to continue to marginalise the bureaucracy. As Anderson and Mann rightly predicted, 'There are plenty of problems ahead for the unions' relations with the Blair government, most obviously public sector pay and the minimum wage, although there is also likely to be friction at some point over Labour's promised employment rights legislation'.[42]

Statutory union recognition is a manifesto commitment for Labour but the CBI is demanding that small firms are exempt, that at least 40 percent of the workforce must want recognition before a ballot can take place, and that recognition should only be granted if a majority of those eligible to vote is established, rather than a majority of those who actually vote. In addition, they want strikes to attain union recognition—like those on the Jubilee Line extension in 1997 and at Noon's in early 1998—outlawed. Several of the key business leaders advising the government are seasoned anti-union employers: Sir Peter Davis who derecognised unions at the publishing house Reed Elsevier; Sir Terence Conran, advising the government on business policy, who derecognised the union at his Design Museum; Lord Hollick who advises Margaret Beckett at the DTI and has not recognised the unions at United Newspapers and of course the notorious and seasoned union buster Rupert Murdoch.

While union leaders like John Edmonds dismiss the idea that Labour will betray the unions as rumour mongering,[43] all the signs point to Labour listening to its business allies above all others. Peter Mandelson has been quoted as saying, 'Trade union recognition of part of a company should not cut across or devalue other arrangements for employee communication which already exist'.[44] Five weeks before polling day Blair gave an interview to the *Daily Mail* stating, 'Even after the changes the Labour Party is proposing in this area [union rights], Britain will remain with the most restrictive trade union laws anywhere in the Western world'.[45] However, potential resistance from the unions could make the outcome of the union rights issue less restrictive than Blair wants.

Public sector pay is another potential source of conflict between Labour and the unions. The pay review bodies recommended in January 1998 an average pay rise of 3.8 percent—roughly equivalent to the rate of inflation in autumn 1997. However, Gordon Brown's pre-budget report in November 1997 indicated a target rate of inflation of 2.5 percent, and a matching pay policy. The report stated, 'The worst form of short-termism would be to pay ourselves more today at the cost of fewer jobs tomorrow and lower living standards in the very near future'.[46] The Treasury response to the review bodies was therefore to accept the awards but to phase them in, restricting the awards for the first eight months of the financial year to 2 percent. Brown is trying to avoid an increase in interest rates triggered by Bank of England fears of inflation rising if the pay bill rises too high:

> Average earnings...are rising at an annual rate of 4.75 percent. However, workers across the economy become more productive each year—their output increases by between 2 and 2.25 percent.
>
> As such, the real increase in the pay bill—after adjustment for the productivity growth factor—is around 2.5 percent—smack in line with the government's inflation target. But any further increase in earnings—to 5 percent or beyond—and the Bank would be concerned that inflation would rise above its target figures.[47]

However, it is doubtful that public sector pay can be held down indefinitely. As Larry Elliott and Seumas Milne observed in January 1998, 'Official figures show that in the year to November 1997, average earnings in the public sector rose by about 2.6 percent while in the private sector the figure was around 5 percent. Public sector employees have seen their average earnings fall behind the private sector by 16 percent since 1982, and pay deals have been achieved by shedding 250,000 jobs since the freeze was imposed in 1993'.[48] Rodney Bickerstaffe of UNISON protested, 'The rich are still getting richer and the poor poorer—and if the economy is in good shape, what better time is there for the government to tackle some of the most deserving cases?'[49]

Union leaders are likely to come under increasing pressure to defend their members as, in Elliott and Milne's words:

> This...crisis between public and private fields is now certain to become more difficult to live with as the labour market tightens and inflation is forecast to rise in the months to come. At the same time, the change of government has raised expectations among some four million workers still in the public sector. The speculation in both government and union circles is when, rather than if, the dam will break.[50]

Is there a left alternative to New Labour?

According to the modernisers, the blame for Labour's continued electoral defeat prior to 1997 lay in part with the attempts to shift the party to the left after Thatcher's election in 1979. The emergence of the 'new left' in the Labour Party was a response to the defeat of the Callaghan government, which had moved sharply to the right in office, introducing the Social Contract, implementing monetarist policies that entailed swingeing public sector cuts, and overseeing a rising unemployment rate.

The Labour left project was primarily concerned with democratising the party's structures to make the PLP accountable to the party as a whole. It also advanced an economic programme that returned the party to policies of government intervention, and called for withdrawal from the EEC and for unilateral nuclear disarmament. It reached its zenith with the deputy leadership election in 1981 in which Tony Benn narrowly lost to Denis Healey. A full discussion of Bennism is not possible here, but suffice to say that Benn's support was exaggerated by the left, to the extent that the split from Labour by the 'Gang of Four' to form the SDP was viewed by some—including Benn—as a move that would shift the whole Labour party leftwards. In fact, as Panitch and Leys point out, 'the split in the parliamentary party occasioned by the Social Democrats' Limehouse Declaration at the end of January 1981 actually had the effect of tilting the balance in the Labour Party further against the new left'.[51]

The 1983 election defeat, in which the SDP-Liberal Alliance polled

25.4 percent of the vote compared to Labour's 27.6 percent, galvanised the right in the party. Under the 'dream ticket' of Neil Kinnock and Roy Hattersley, Labour set about rolling back the public ownership promises of the 1983 manifesto and witch hunted the left in the party. *The Independent* columnist Ian Aitken, in a review of *The End of Parliamentary Socialism*, speaks the same language as the Labour right when he argues, 'Tony Benn and his allies...helped to keep [the Labour Party] out of office for so long that, in desperation, it swung all the way back in the opposite direction. If New Labour has now dumped even the remaining shreds of the Keynesian-style socialism it once espoused, and pretends to be enthusiastic about the global free market, that is the direct result of the Hard Left's disastrous crusade in the 80s'.[52] Anderson and Mann make concessions to the same argument, for example they write, 'In terms of party reform, expelling Militant...removed an anti-democratic virus from the party.' In fact, it led to the dominance of the right wing inside the party.

The parliamentary left, after the defeat of Bennism, either capitulated completely or became demoralised. As a result, many accept, as Anderson and Mann do, elements of the modernisers' project: 'One member one vote internal party elections were a long overdue democratisation as well as a useful symbolic victory for John Smith over the unions and the left'.[53] Panitch and Leys, however, differ. Their premise is that, while the defeat of the left led to New Labour, the attempt to pull Labour to the left was not in itself to blame. They argue it was the right who split the party and drove Labour further to the right. They suggest that the right were prepared to lose the 1983 election in order to destroy the left. Michael Meacher (then a left winger) is quoted as saying, 'There was never less than half a page of vitriol in the press per day and the source was the right wing of the Labour Party...even though it did cataclysmic damage to the Labour Party. It was like a bombing raid flattening everything in sight. It was more a cause of the defeat in 1983 than the Falklands'.[54]

Panitch and Leys are right about this, but their treatment of Bennism is inadequate. They rightly see that the new left project was obsessed with tinkering with Labour Party structures and failed to engage with forces in the wider working class, but they do not take account of the contradiction Benn was caught in. They identify with the political upturn that Benn was the main beneficiary of, without noticing that the working class was demoralised—by the previous Labour government's attacks. In such circumstances the strategy of starting from the Labour Party and hoping to generalise left ideas out into the class was mistaken. The strategy of electoralism led the left, and the workers who did follow them, *away* from collective struggle in the working class, which could have provided a real base for left wing policies inside Labour.

Panitch and Leys are ultimately naive about the capacity of a parliamentary left's ability to transform the party as a whole, and from there to create democratic structures in wider society. This is in part because they see Labour as having been potentially a genuine socialist organisation, and in part due to their relegation of the organised working class to simply one of a number of interest groups in society. This is a pity given that, within their own pages, they give examples of the limitations of fighting for fundamental change within the bounds of parliamentarianism. They do not draw the necessary conclusions that even an electorally successful left Labour Party would thus come into conflict with the unelected state.

Both *Safety First* and *The End of Parliamentary Socialism* are written by people disillusioned or ready to be disillusioned with New Labour's wholehearted embrace of untrammelled capitalism, yet they continue to cling to the possibility of a form of parliamentary socialism. Anderson and Mann were not quite ready to write Blair off in July 1997, with the government still in the first flush of victory: 'It seems rather churlish for anyone on the left to raise doubts about New Labour'.[55] But if Blair does not deliver, they are aware that the parliamentary left is very weak, disorganised and has no unifying ideological position. They reject revolutionary socialism, arguing that it is time for a new politics of the left. Unfortunately, it is a politics that yet again relies on parliamentary activity to change people's lives, albeit in a different guise than that offered by the Labour Party

The End of Parliamentary Socialism sets its sights somewhat higher, arguing for a socialism that can offer people a vision of the future: 'The essence of the socialist project—the idea of a social order capable of transcending the alienation and escalating risks of capitalist accumulation—is anything but finished; it seems more likely that it is just beginning to come into view again as a necessity...'[56] The authors conclude convincingly that operating purely within the Labour Party is a dead end for the left and that extra-parliamentary activity is crucial to the socialist project. But their proposals about what form of organisation such activity should take place with are vague. Ultimately, their prognosis is of a long, slow rebuilding of socialist organisation that can embrace organised labour without alienating the middle class—an organisation that widens its remit from class struggle and involves the entire 'community' collectively, combining parliamentary and extra-parliamentary activity. Such commitment to ending capitalism and fighting for socialism is to be welcomed, yet an acceptance of the notion that class struggle and the Leninist party are outmoded, and that parliament can be used in the interests of fundamental change, leaves them, as it leaves Anderson and Mann, unable to offer a clear direction forward.

This lack of a coherent strategy on the left does not mean revival is not possible. Yet there is no reason to believe that another attempt to shift Labour to the left would succeed where the last failed. Although such a move would be welcomed by socialists and by those workers already alienated from Blair, history is not reassuring about the possibility of a successful assault on the priorities of capitalism through parliamentary means. There are indications that New Labour will be under pressure to adopt more redistributive policies. Some mainstream commentators have already raised the spectre of Marxism. For example, Peter Kellner wrote:

> One hundred and fifty years after the publication of the **Communist Manifesto**, Marx's...underlying diagnosis holds up. Unbridled capitalism provokes inequality and insecurity; it shatters traditional social bonds; it denies people and even countries the power to control their own destiny...[Blair's] strategy towards the better-off should be not to reduce their benefits but to raise their taxes.[57]

Concretely, the Commons vote on proposals to cut single parent benefit in December was won easily—but 47 Labour MPs voted against. The revolt was muted but telling nonetheless. And the expulsion of Ken Coates and Hugh Kerr from the PLP for speaking out against Labour's plans for welfare highlighted the feelings of betrayal among many Labour activists. As *The Observer* editorial put it in December 1997, 'The row over disablement and the Kerr/Coates departures are not events to be shrugged off as the death pangs of Old Labour. They betray fundamental fractures in [Blair's] party that, unless mended, will threaten the success of his government'.[58]

In Hutton's words, 'Labour's refusal to analyse the facts, think straight, stop kow-towing to a defunct Conservatism and recognise its own distinct traditions and philosophy is leading it into a political crisis of the first magnitude'.[59] The difficulty in predicting the nature of such a crisis is obvious—New Labour is a moving target. What can be said with some confidence is that the class tensions and the ideological ferment will become greater as Labour tries to implement its policies. The prospects for independent socialist organisation under these circumstances are good—provided that its intervention in the working class involves both building protests against Labour's attacks and an ideological battle to win workers away from acceptance of Blair's ideas and from looking to parliamentary solutions as a whole.

Notes

1   *The Observer*, 5 October 1997.
2   *Tribune*, 2 January 1998.
3   D Draper, *Blair's Hundred Days* (Faber & Faber, 1997), p73.

4   Ibid, p69.
5   P Anderson and N Mann, *Safety First* (Granta, 1997), p22.
6   Ibid, p385.
7   The extent to which Thatcher had transformed the political landscape in Britain
     was greatly overstated, not least by the left. Even Ivor Crewe, the veteran pollster,
     admitted this in 1989: 'Quite simply, there has been no Thatcherite transformation
     of attitudes or behaviour among the British public. If anything, the British have
     edged further away from Thatcherite positions as the decade has progressed.' For
     a general discussion of this see D Kavanagh and C Seldon (eds), *The Thatcher
     Effect—A Decade of Change* (Macmillan, 1989).
8   L Panitch and C Leys, *The End of Parliamentary Socialism* (Verso, 1997), p241.
9   D Butler and D Kavanagh, *The British General Election of 1997* (Macmillian,
     1997), p250.
10   Ibid, p251.
11   Ibid, p52.
12   P Anderson and N Mann, op cit, p53.
13   D Butler and D Kavanagh, op cit, p184.
14   Ibid.
15   Ibid, p67.
16   Ibid, p232.
17   Quoted in P Anderson and N Mann, op cit, p25.
18   Ibid, p61.
19   D Draper, op cit, pp75-76.
20   Quoted in L Panitch and C Leys, op cit, p250.
21   Ibid.
22   Quoted in P Anderson and N Mann, op cit, p104.
23   Quoted in L Panitch and C Leys, op cit, p250.
24   *The Observer*, 9 November 1998.
25   *The Observer,* 18 January 1998.
26   *The Financial Times*, 25-26 April 1998.
27   *The Sunday Telegraph*, 5 April 1998.
28   Quoted in L Panitch and C Leys, op cit, p253.
29   P Anderson and N Mann, op cit, p26.
30   *The Observer*, ? November 1997.
31   P Anderson and N Mann, op cit, p40.
32   Quoted in P Anderson and N Mann, op cit, p40.
33   Ibid, p323.
34   L Panitch and C Leys, op cit, p224.
35   D Butler and D Kavanagh, op cit, p206.
36   L Panitch and C Leys, op cit, p254.
37   Ibid.
38   D Butler and D Kavanagh, op cit, p242.
39   Quoted in P Anderson and N Mann, op cit, p304.
40   P Anderson and N Mann, op cit, p317.
41   Ibid, p304.
42   Ibid, p326.
43   *Tribune*, 2 January 1998.
44   *The Observer*, 14 December 1997.
45   P Anderson and N Mann, op cit, p325.
46   *The Guardian*, 28 January 1998.
47   Ibid.
48   *The Guardian*, 28 January 1998.
49   *The Guardian*, 17 January 1998.
50   *The Guardian*, 28 January 1998.

51   L Panitch and C Leys, op cit, p193.
52   *London Review of Books*, 19 February 1998.
53   P Anderson and N Mann, op cit, p387.
54   L Panitch and C Leys, op cit, p197.
55   P Anderson and N Mann, op cit, p389.
56   L Panitch and C Leys, op cit, p262.
57   *The Observer*, 18 January 1998.
58   *The Observer*, 28 December 1997.
59   *The Observer*, 9 November 1997.

State of the art

A review of the 'Sensation' exhibition at the Royal Academy of Arts, September-December 1997

JOHN MOLYNEUX

The British art world is cock-a-hoop. It is convinced that in what has become known as Young British Art (YBA) it has found the answer to its dreams. Young, new, energetic, dynamic, cocky, cockney, rebellious (but not too rebellious, not Marxist or communist or anything old fashioned like that) sexy, successful, scandalous (in just the way that attracts the media and draws the crowds) and above all profitable and British—everything they ever wanted from an art movement and were afraid even to hope for. Already two books have been published specifically to cele-brate 'the world of YBA': *Blimey! From Bohemian to Britpop: The London Artworld from Francis Bacon to Damien Hirst* by Matthew Collings is ironic, hip, cool, a postmodern hagiography; *Moving Targets: A User's Guide to British Art Now* by Luisa Buck is just a hagiography. Its opening paragraph sums up the tone and message of the book and also the current mood of the art world:

> *More than at any other time in its history, British art is booming. For several years critics, curators and collectors from across the globe have been con-verging on the UK—especially London and Glasgow—to admire, to purchase and to select from Britain's artistic boldest and best. At home, a fully fledged mythology has grown up around the phenomenon of the Young British Artist as an uncouth entrepreneurial species that emerged fully formed from Goldsmiths' College in south London with Damien Hirst at its head to fly in the face of orthodoxy and the art establishment.*[1]

Everything about this passage and about the phenomenon as a whole seems designed to make socialist hackles rise. There is the crude nationalism reminiscent of the American chauvinism that accompanied the promotion of Abstract Expressionism in the 1950s (including its sponsorship by the CIA).[2] There is the unabashed commercialism of the language—note 'booming', 'to admire, to purchase' and 'uncouth entrepreneurial species'—straight out of the Thatcherite 1980s, which, of course, is where a lot of YBA comes from (the Goldsmiths' year of 1988).[3] There is the conscious emphasis on media hype, played to perfection round the Myra Hindley painting (of which more later). Above all there is the looming figure of Charles Saatchi, patron of Damien Hirst, owner of by far the largest collection of YBA (at the Saatchi Gallery in St John's Wood), supplier of all the works in the 'Sensation' exhibition at the Royal Academy in autumn 1997 and supposedly 'the Lorenzo de Medici of our times'. In many ways YBA fits exactly the scenario outlined by Trotsky in 'Art and Politics in our Epoch':

> *Bourgeois society showed its strength throughout long periods of history in the fact that combining repression and encouragement, boycott and flattery, it was able to control and assimilate every 'rebel' movement in art and raise it to the level of official 'recognition'. But each time this 'recognition' betokened, when all is said and done, the approach of trouble. It was then that from the left wing of the academic school or below it—ie from the ranks of a new generation of bohemian artists—a fresher revolt would surge up to attain in its turn, after a decent interval, the steps of the academy.*[4]

The only difference is that YBAs have omitted the decent interval. Nevertheless, socialists cannot just write a minus where the bourgeoisie writes a plus. In politics simply inverting the judgements of the bourgeoisie soon lets one down and in the sphere of art (as in science) it is completely hopeless. In its time the bourgeoisie has patronised Michelangelo and Rembrandt, Hogarth and David, Picasso and Pollock—all in their different ways great artists. The extremely backward Spanish monarchy managed to maintain Velázquez and Goya, and Diego Rivera was commissioned in turn by the San Francisco Pacific Stock Exchange, Edsel B Ford (son of Henry) and John D Rockefeller.[5] In general the bourgeoisie as a class is aware of the power of art and culture and, desirous of maintaining its hegemony in this sphere as in others, 'delegates' some of its number to specialise in this area. The latter—the likes of Sir Kenneth Clark and Lord Gowrie, Peggy Guggenheim and Charles Saatchi—seek, in their own way, to promote and embrace the best art, past and present. Which is not to say their taste can be trusted. In the second half of the 19th century the establishment and the bourgeoisie condemned or ignored, by turn, Courbet, Manet, the Impressionists, Seurat, Van Gogh and Cézanne. The bourgeoisie also at times endorses the bogus (Dali), inflates the mediocre (the Pre-Raphaelites) and rewards the downright awful (Landseer). We cannot, therefore, respond to the YBA phenomenon 'on principle'. There is no alternative to confronting the actual art and judging it on its merits. In this article I attempt to do this via consideration of the art and artists represented in the Royal Academy 'Sensation' exhibition.

The exhibition consisted of 110 works by 42 different artists and this in itself creates a problem for a review like this. It is impossible to respond to and comment meaningfully on all of them, either works or artists. At the same time there is a difficulty in responding to the show as a totality. 'Sensation' was not a collaborative effort, it was a *selection* from a *collection*, and therefore one cannot simply generalise or tar everything with the same brush. The Louvre contains paintings by Raphael, Rembrandt and Louis Le Nain. They are neither similar in style nor equal in merit. Max Ernst, Joan Miró and Salvador Dali are all known as Surrealists. This does not make a judgement of one hold true for the others. Nevertheless, some kind of holistic response to the experience of 'Sensation' seems both necessary and inevitable. I shall proceed by first discussing the work and artists I consider particularly significant (negatively and positively) and then by making some general comments.

Unfortunately it is necessary to begin by dealing with Marcus Harvey's *Myra*, the giant reproduction of the familiar newspaper image of Myra Hindley constructed out of children's handprints. This was the sign under which the exhibition was marketed, its logo, its shop window display, its loss leader. Whether or not this was the conscious intention from the outset, and whether there was actual conspiracy with the media, is hard to judge but this was how it worked out, and very successfully too. Everyone (artist, tabloids, curator, parents of Hindley's victims, outraged old Royal Academicians etc) played their required parts and the result was the record 300,000 plus attendance (which at seven quid a time is a lot of filthy lucre). I say unfortunately because as art, as a painting, *Myra* doesn't amount to much. Politically it is important to reject the media's hypocrisy about this image and the absurd inflation of its power. In so far as this particular image of Hindley possesses iconic power in our culture it is the media's constant use of it, not Harvey, that created it. When *The Mirror* denounced the painting as a 'disgrace' it plastered it all over its front page thus projecting it into 2 million homes. In other words, the fuss is not about the image itself but about making it into 'art', or calling it 'art'. Does this mean paintings of monstrous people cannot be art or morally speaking *ought not* to be art?[6] Where

does that leave Holbein's Henry VIII portraits or John Heartfield's pho-
tomontages of Hitler and Goering? However, defending the 'right' of the
Academy to show *Myra* is not the same as proclaiming its great artistic
merits. Technically there is nothing specially original, interesting or
excellent about its conception or execution. In so far as it makes a point,
it is that the image of Myra Hindley is made out of the bodies of murdered children—this is the function of constructing the image from
children's handprints. But we know this already and the painting does
not make the point with any particular power.

What really gives the game away as far as Marcus Harvey is concerned is his other work in the show: *Proud of his Wife* and *Dudley, Like
What You See? Then Call Me*, two crudely sexist nudes in which art imi-
tates pornography. Of course it is 'knowing' and 'ironic' so that's
supposed to make it alright. It doesn't. The catalogue tells us that these
paintings 'simultaneously contain and exceed their salacious imagery'.[7]
They don't. From John Berger's *Ways of Seeing* onwards Marxist and
feminist critics of the representation of the female nude by the likes of
Titian, Velázquez, and Ingres rejected the defence that these were 'great
artists' and 'wonderful handlers of paint'. Titian and Co *were* indeed
great artists and superb handlers of paint but this did not change the fact
that their representations of women were sexist or that because they were
sexist they were inferior *as art* to those exceptional works such as
Rembrandt's *Bathsheba* that managed to rise above the 'women as sex
object' tradition. The catalogue tries to justify Harvey in terms of his
'vibrant splashy brushstrokes' and 'expressionistic fervour'. But is
Harvey's handling of paint better than Titian's or Velázquez's? I think
not.

However, when it comes to being offensive, and I mean genuinely
offensive to human values, not shocking the bourgeois, Harvey's
'readers' wives' cannot hold a candle to Jake and Dinos Chapman. The
Chapman brothers' *Great Deeds Against the Dead* is a lifesize fibreglass
reconstruction of an etching of the same name by Goya from the series
known as *The Disasters of War*. These etchings depict scenes of
appalling brutality from the revolt of the Spanish peasantry against the
Napoleonic army of occupation. They show piles of dead bodies, people
being garrotted, mutilated and hacked to bits. *Great Deeds Against the
Dead* presents us with two figures tied to the front joint and back of a
tree trunk and castrated and a third figure hanging upside down over a
branch of the tree, castrated, arms cut off and decapitated—the ampu-
tated arms also hang from the branch and the severed head is impaled on
a smaller branch.

My objection to the Chapmans' piece, and I object to it vehemently, is
not based on the subject matter it depicts. That is identical to the subject

matter depicted by Goya and the Goya etchings are among the greatest works in the history of art: it is impossible to see them without being physically stunned by their utterly authentic presentation of the horror of war and, at the same time, moved by their profound humanity. Nearly 200 years on they retain—and thank god they do—all their power to shock but they contain (the word is appropriate) not an ounce of sensationalism. In contrast, the Chapman brothers have produced a piece of plastic kitsch in which the torture is drained of its terror and the art drained of its humanity. They have indeed committed 'great deeds against the dead'.

With *Zygotic Acceleration, Biogenetic, De-Sublimated Libidinal Model (Enlarged x 1000)* also by the Chapmans, it is not the dead but the living we have to worry about. Once again we have fibreglass mannequin type figures, this time children, about a dozen in all, melded together into an outward facing ring. Lacking sexual organs in the genital area, some of their noses are transformed into penises, some of their mouths into vaginas and anuses. The image as a whole is blatantly paedophiliac. This raises the question of whether the charge that a work of art is paedophiliac is in itself enough to condemn it? No doubt this would produce vigorous debate but let me put the question a slightly different way so as not to stray too far from this particular work. How might those wishing to defend *Zygotic Acceleration* respond to the charge that it is paedophiliac?

They might ask what's wrong with paedophilia. To my knowledge, no one has said this openly, but if they did, that would be a different debate. I intend to assume here that the sexual use of pre-pubertal children by adults is seriously damaging to children and that we condemn it. They might say that this is only an image, not the reality. This is true and we must remember it (I am not calling for the Chapman brothers to be prosecuted for child abuse) but the accusation is that this image appeals to and encourages paedophile tastes just as other images might appeal to and encourage racism or violence against women.

They might say that the charge is false, and that *Zygotic Acceleration* is not paedophiliac. This defence is not convincing. The mannequins are plainly children. The absence of breasts and normal genitalia, the 'innocent' expressions on their faces, their haircuts and the oversized trainers on their feet all reinforce this. Yet the transformation of their noses into penises and their mouths into anuses and vaginas immediately sexualises them; in particular, the rendering of the mouths as open orifices and the fact that one figure is bent over at the waist while another is upside down so that its anus/mouth and penis/nose are at genital level all suggests sexual access.

Then there would be what might be called the 'postmodern' defence, that the work is so *obviously* paedophiliac that it must be ironic. Along these lines it could be argued that the trainers signify commodification and therefore *Zygotic Acceleration* critiques the commodification of paedophiliac images. Clearly I am no expert on the conscious and unconscious motivations of the Chapmans but it seems probable that something like this was their intention. Unfortunately there is no necessary correspondence between intention and outcome in art. I am by no means convinced that it is even possible to play ironically with titillating paedophiliac visual material and in this particular case one is forced to conclude that, in a work which itself was and is bound to be commodified, the paedophiliac element of the mannequins overwhelms the commodity critique of the trainers.[8] Irony is always risky (Johnny Speight *intended* Alf Garnett's racism to be taken ironically but Alf became the racists' hero) and here, *if* irony was the intention, the work has been captured by that which it tries to ironise.

The curators and producers of the catalogue have been particularly dishonest on this question. On the one hand the catalogue makes no reference to this work's paedophiliac tendency—it fails even to acknowledge the existence of the accusation—covering up the issue in language that is simultaneously pretentious and disingenuous, speaking of 'genderless, self-reproducing manifestations of excess libidinal energy gone awry'.[9] On the other hand *Zygotic Acceleration* was placed in a room for over 18s only. Given this was an exhibition with *Great Deeds Against the Dead*, *Myra* and the readers' wives paintings on open view, there can only have been one reason for this restriction: an unacknowledged recognition that the work is paedophiliac or likely to be perceived as such.

Finally the paedophilia might be acknowledged and admitted as a problem but the work is still defended on the grounds of mitigating circumstances: either that it offered important insights into the nature of paedophilia or that paedophilia was only one element in an otherwise valuable work,[10] or that despite its content it was especially skilful or well made.[11] But none of these arguments work for *Zygotic Acceleration*. As for being well made, one has only to look at Ron Mueck's *Dead Dad* (also in 'Sensation') to see what can be done with these kind of materials and how shoddy the Chapmans' piece is. Nor does it offer any special insight into paedophilia (other than possibly the aforementioned point that paedophilia can be commodified) or into anything besides paedophilia. It simply *is* paedophiliac and that makes it into something quite rare—a thoroughly meretricious work of art.

But if the Chapman brothers plumb the depths there is also a substantial amount of serious, high quality, perhaps even major art in 'Sensation': notably the work of Damien Hirst and Rachel Whiteread. With eight pieces on show Damien Hirst is the best represented artist in

'Sensation' and as he is the central figure in the YBA movement this is fitting. Of the eight, two are paintings and six are the three dimensional 'sculptures' or 'installations' for which he has become famous. The paintings are, in my opinion, not of much consequence: *Argininosuccinic Acid* is a large multicoloured dot painting which is pretty but offers little beyond what has been achieved in much 20th century geometric abstraction; *beautiful, kiss my fucking ass painting* is a circular canvas on which bright primary colours have been spun but it doesn't even manage to be pretty. The 3D pieces are a different kettle of fish—at the very least they are an original and major provocation.

Much of the provocation and much of the 'scandal' attaching to Hirst derives from the materials he uses: the bodies of dead animals. In modern art there is a history to this question of materials. For about 500 years virtually all art was made from the same limited range of materials: tempera, oil paints, watercolours, bronze, marble, etc. Explicitly or implicitly these materials came to be regarded as inherently artistic and other materials as inherently non-artistic (just as certain subjects were regarded as fit for art and other subjects as unfit). The first breach in this convention was made by Picasso in his 'synthetic cubist' phase in 1912 when he introduced pieces of oilcloth, newsprint and wallpaper into his paintings. Picasso took the process further in his transformative sculptures like the bull's head made of handlebars and bicycle seat, and the monkey made of toy cars. So did Duchamp with his bottle rack and urinal 'ready mades' and his complex *Large Glass* 'sculpture'. Later came sculptors who used iron, steel, aluminium, plaster, bricks, fluorescent lights and so on, and Rauschenberg who combined painting with screen printing, photography, and objects found in the streets, including a motor tyre and stuffed goat. However, even against this 'anything goes' background Hirst's use of a large shark and cut up cows was a dramatic innovation.

In general in art, formal innovations occur not just for their own sake but because the artist has something new to say which requires the formal innovation for it to be said. Hirst's use of real dead animals is an example of this. Its purpose, I think, is to force a face to face confrontation with the brute fact of death on a blasé modern audience for whom *images* of death are superabundant while its *reality* becomes ever more removed and hidden. Short of exhibiting an actual human corpse this was about as far as Hirst could go.

In order to progress a little further in explaining how Hirst's art works I want to employ the concept of the 'objective correlative', developed by T S Eliot:

> The only way of expressing emotion in the form of art is by finding an 'objective correlative'; in other words, a set of objects, a situation, a chain of events

*which shall be the formula of that **particular** emotion; such that when the
external facts, which must terminate in sensory experience, are given, the
emotion is immediately evoked.*[12]

This seems to me exactly what Hirst is doing: constructing an object
(using, as we have noted, unusual and original materials) which will be
the objective correlative of certain thoughts and emotions, of certain 'felt
ideas'. Thus the huge shark piece works as the 'objective correlative' of
death in at least four ways: (1) it is an actual dead shark; (2) the shark is
a powerful cultural signifier of the fear and threat of death; (3) the curvature in the glass of the tank containing the shark reinforces point 2 by
making the shark appear to move threateningly in the direction of the
viewer; and (4) the title of the work, *The Physical Impossibility of Death
in the Mind of Someone Living*, works in tension with the piece itself and
with the taboo on 'death' in our culture. Thus the one object serves as an
objective correlative for the fact, fear, threat and taboo of death.

In *A Thousand Years* with its cow's head, breeding maggots, flies and
insect-o-cutor we have a work that is even more transgressive in its
materials—not only dead flesh but living creatures that are killed before
one's eyes—and which incorporates a new element, smell (or rather
stench). Here we have represented not just death but a whole life-death
cycle, a mini-ecosystem complete with breeding, feeding and human
intervention. If it is a spectacle which evokes disgust and nausea, then that
too is part of its statement. It asks us to examine our responses. *Away from
the Flock*—a white lamb with black face and feet suspended in a white
steel and glass tank—serves as objective correlative for rather different
ideas and emotions. The work itself interacts with its title (titles usually
play an important role with Hirst) to represent and evoke separation, isolation, loneliness and abandonment, especially as these might pertain to a
child. As such it generates an acute pathos. *Isolated Elements Swimming
in the Same Direction for the Purpose of Understanding* works with a
related theme but to different emotional effect. It consists of a large glass
cabinet containing six shelves and on each shelf is placed a row of six or
seven perspex cases each containing a suspended fish, all 'swimming'
head to tail. We are presented here with an embodiment of individuals as
part of a conformist collective yet all isolated and hermetically sealed
from one another (a 'series' not a 'fixed group' in the old language of
Sartre). Of course it might be objected, à la Lukács, that this is a profoundly false view of life. In the final analysis I would agree, but it is also
the case that this is an important element of human experience in this
alienated society and that here Hirst has succeeded in giving powerful
visual expression to this experience. The construction, it should be said, is
very beautifully composed in terms of its ordering of forms and colours,
possessing some of the visual qualities of a Mondrian or Klee.

Emotionally it induces not pathos or sympathy but an almost terrifying chill.

Mother and Child Divided was not in this show but I want to comment on it here (in preference to the cut up cow and pig works in 'Sensation') because I think it is Hirst's most important work to date and because it brings together a number of the themes from the other works. It consists of a bisected cow and a bisected calf. Each half of the cow is placed in its own glass tank and the tanks are adjacent to one another but with enough space to walk between the tanks and observe close up the insides of the cow. The same is done with the halves of the calf but the two calf halves are placed several yards away from the cow. Of all Hirst's pieces this is the one that seems to have made the biggest impact on the public consciousness and this in itself testifies to the power of its conception.[13] However, what is most impressive about it is the way in which it functions as objective correlative for a range of different almost conflicting ideas and emotions. First there is the confrontation with death and dead flesh. Then there is the 'shock' of the violence of the bisection (shock like the shock of Goya, not the Chapmans) and disgust and distaste at the exposure of the innards. But this works in tension with the knowledge that this is how we treat animals and this is what we eat as food. One does not need to be an animal rights supporter or vegetarian to feel the force of this, just as one does not need to be a pacifist to respond to Wilfred Owen: Hirst is merely insisting we face facts. Finally the title (again) and the placing of the cow/mother and calf/child evokes the pathos, despair and separation anxiety of *Away from the Flock* and *Isolated Elements Swimming*. *Mother and Child Divided* has the integration of thought and feeling and the combination of complexity with visual and emotional power that is characteristic of major art.

Two final comments on Hirst. First significant art, no matter how 'new' or 'original', always turns out to be the next step in an ongoing tradition. Nevertheless Hirst, on examination, is seen to be the point of confluence of a remarkable number of artistic streams. Most immediately there is the influence of Francis Bacon in the themes of framed and caged flesh (and also a distant echo of Rembrandt's great painting of a beef carcass, *The Slaughter House*). In the use of ready made materials, in the making of art out of apparent anti-art moves, in the mix of playfulness and high seriousness, he is clearly the heir of Marcel Duchamp. The use of the glass case also looks back to Duchamp (*The Bride Stripped Bare by her Bachelors, Even*, aka *The Large Glass*) and the vitrines of Joseph Beuys. The white steel boxes expand the form pioneered by Sol LeWitt and the minimalists in the 1960s.[14] And in the self conscious deployment of hype there is the unmistakable legacy of Warhol.

Second, it is an art cliché that reproductions cannot compare with the original works. Often there is an element of myth involved here for the extent to which this is true varies greatly from artist to artist and work to work. In fact you can get a better idea of the ceiling of the Sistine Chapel from good reproductions than you can from the floor of the chapel. Gauguin, Miró and Mondrian reproduce excellently: Van Gogh (because of the texture of the paint) and Pollock (because of the texture and the importance of the size) much less well. Indeed with most paintings and some sculpture you get 'a pretty good idea' from quality modern reproductions. This is not the case with much of Hirst's work. The curvature in the glass in the shark piece and its visual effects do not appear in photographs. The same is true of the flying and dying flies in *A Thousand Years*, not to speak of the smell, and you have actually to walk through the bisected cow and calf in *Mother and Child Divided* to experience its full effect. In short, Hirst demands to be seen first hand. Whether this is a good or bad thing is a debate for another occasion but it is a fact which must be taken into account in discussing his merits.

The same applies to Rachel Whiteread who makes casts in plaster and other materials of the insides and underneaths of things. Indeed it applies to her with particular poignancy for of her two most important works, *House* and the Judenplatz Holocaust Memorial in Vienna, to be called *The Nameless Library*—the former was destroyed and the latter never built. Whiteread had five works in 'Sensation', casts of: the underspaces of 100 chairs and stools, a kitchen sink, two baths and the inside of a Victorian room.

Before discussing these let us reflect a moment on Whiteread's distinctive method—the casting of the negative space of an object—and consider its slightly uncanny nature. It is tempting to say that to make a cast of the inside or underneath of something is to make the invisible visible—before you couldn't see it, now you can. Except that isn't quite right. You might as well say that before you could see the space and now you cannot because it has been filled up, obliterated—the visible has been made invisible. The 'things' whose negative spaces Whiteread casts are (so far at least) domestic, familiar. So perhaps she makes the familiar unfamiliar, but perhaps one can become familiar with a tangible object in a way one cannot become familiar with a space. So the intangible is rendered tangible? Yes, except that in the gallery they won't let you touch it. Christo, the Bulgarian artist famous for wrapping the Reichstag and the Pont Neuf, has argued that wrapping a building blots out the decorative details and brings out its underlying structure. Does making a cast do the same thing? Nearly, but not quite, since it is the structure in reverse. Can we compare the cast to a fossil? Yes, and it bears those associations, and yet an internal cast is an inverted fossil. So what is Whiteread's art—just a play on words, a clever but soluble conundrum or a real enigma? The answer depends, I think, on how her technique is realised in specific works.

Untitled (One Hundred Spaces) consists of 100 resin castings in various colours of the spaces beneath different sized chairs and stools. It is visually attractive, arguably beautiful (in fact it is rather more beautiful in the catalogue photograph, where it is placed in a pure ice blue gallery space, than it was in the cluttered Academy) but in the end rather inconsequential. The 'underneaths of chairs' simply do not carry enough associations or meanings with sufficient emotional charge to give the work any real point or power. *Untitled (Square Sink)* works better in this respect—it is an object of genuine curiosity, at once highly modern and suggestive of the past, both recent and distant. Nevertheless it is still a relatively minor piece. The two bath pieces are on a higher level. *Untitled (Bath)* in white plaster with a glass top manages, almost effortlessly, to condense a multitude of 'bath associations': the enamel bath in the cold bathroom that once marked the English petty bourgeoisie (in contrast to the tin bath of the working class), signifier of narrow respectability, genteel impoverishment and austere aspiration; but also the sinister bath, the bath as site of murder, the bath in the Chamber of Horrors; and finally the white plaster suggests stone and the stone suggests sarcophagus. *Untitled (Orange Bath)* is remarkable in a different way. Made of rubber and polystyrene it is the nature of the material itself that comes to the fore. To the viewer it resembles a giant rubber eraser which might be bent or broken in two, or scratched with the fingernails or have its corners worn down through use. It is enormously intriguing and the attendants have to be constantly on the alert to inhibit the probing fingers of visitors.

However, it is in the large *Ghost*, the cast of the inside of a room, that Whiteread's method really bears fruit. *Ghost* is not like the Hirst pieces where one can attribute fairly precise feelings and ideas to particular aspects of the works: it is an altogether more mysterious object. Nevertheless it has extraordinary presence. In the Academy its looming bulk made me feel pressed up against the gallery walls or perhaps it was pressed against the walls of the room that are no longer there—a kind of claustrophobia in reverse. In a way the title—*Ghost*—sums up the work. It is the trace of what has departed, the presence of an absence, the materialisation of memory. Indeed it is haunting, despite the all too obvious pun. But what is remarkable—the measure of Whiteread's achievement—is that one can talk in these terms, the terms of ghostliness, about 1,000 cubic foot, apparently solid, white cube which also manages to look as if it were made of concrete.

The success of *Ghost* is what makes me so regret not having seen the original *House* in Grove Road, Bow, before it was demolished in 1994.[15] More or less everything I have said about the casting technique in general and about *Ghost* would probably have applied to *House* but my guess is that the poignancy of the work would have been greatly increased by its positioning alone in an otherwise bulldozed street in a traditional working class area. Even more regrettable is the non-construction of the proposed Holocaust Memorial in Judenplatz, Vienna. Tremendous aesthetic/political problems attend any attempt to memorialise the Holocaust. How can the work be adequate to that which it is meant to commemorate and if it is not how does it avoid being an insult? Clearly the Holocaust cannot be visually depicted or described as a totality—in naturalistic mode all that could be achieved would be the illustration of an instance, and is that good enough? If it is shocking it runs the risk of being insufficiently solemn, if it is solemn of being too undemanding. It is just possible, I think, that Whiteread would have overcome these problems. Her proposal was for a huge concrete cast of the inside of a library. In one way, therefore, it would have been a place of quiet dignity, redolent of study and reflection, of the preservation of civilized values in the time of barbarism and of the recording of history. Yet, following *Ghost*, it might also have had the same effect of filling that Viennese square to bursting, of pressing itself insistently on every visitor and every passer-by so that they could not have avoided the reminder and the challenge that it constituted. Which was just what was needed in Judenplatz in Vienna.*

I have now discussed the worst and the best of 'Sensation' and should make it clear that I think Hirst and Whiteread are not just the best of this show but probably the major artists of this generation. Nevertheless the exhibition contains a number of other works I want to mention. There are two outstanding individual pieces: Mat Collishaw's *Bullet Hole*—a huge close up of a head wound mounted on 15 light boxes which is genuinely painful to look at, as it should be—and Marc Quinn's *Self*—a frozen perspex cast of his head filled with his own blood which achieves an intense lyrical beauty. But I suspect that both of them may be one-offs. There are three women artists[16]—Jenny Saville, Sarah Lucas and Tracey Emin—all of whom make an immediate 'sensational' impact. It is easy to see the appeal of Saville's huge nudes but they are painted in the style of Lucian Freud only not as well and the fat-is-a-feminist-issue type points they make are by now rather obvious and well worn. With mass media that preach puritanism and practise prurience Lucas's up-front sexual pieces are bound to cause a minor stir. Some of her sexual symbolism (the cucumber, oranges, bucket and melons of *Au Natural*) is too unimaginative to take very seriously, but *Two Fried Eggs and a Kebab*

*Since this article was written it has been reported in the press that the Judenplatz memorial now will be constructed. However, whether or not it actually happens remains to be seen.

(which neatly combines references to street slang and Magritte) is a witty and pointed challenge to sexist putdowns. Also there is *Sod You Gits*, made of large, blown up photocopies from the *Sunday Sport* which both exposes and somehow copes with the assault of alienated tabloid culture.[17] Tracey Emin's *Everyone I Have Ever Slept With, 1963-95*, in which the names of her bedmates are stitched to the inside of a tent, is based on a powerful idea, both sad and grimly funny, but it lacks visual impact. Emin's vulnerability is so evident that where her future is concerned one hopes for the best but fears the worst. In a different league is Palestinian exile Mona Hatoum who may well prove to be the third major figure alongside Hirst and Whiteread. Unfortunately Hatoum has only one piece here, *Deep Throat*, showing film of her throat in the middle of a plate at a place set on a table, and this is one of her weakest, least evocative works.[18]

Finally there are the photographs of Richard Billingham. These depict members of Billingham's family—principally his parents—with apparently alarming candour in their daily life of drunkenness, squalor and TV dinners. The point about this work and the reason for leaving it until last is the way it forces one to choose: for or against. I don't mean decide whether it is good, bad or indifferent or whether one likes it or even whether it is socially progressive. I mean one has to make a fundamental decision as to whether or not it is in good faith. In this case that means trying to decide on the nature of the relationship between the work and the subjects it depicts. Is it, fundamentally, a work of solidarity and sympathy or a work of exposure and exploitation? I repeat, this is a decision about the *work,* not the artist. The artist's motives are doubtless relevant but not decisive; in the end the choice must be made on the evidence of one's eyes, not the evidence of history or gossip. Personally, in this instance, I have decided against. I think Billingham has humiliated his parents by holding up working class life as an exhibit for the bourgeois gaze much as the inmates of Bedlam were exhibited to bourgeois visitors in the 18th century.[19] Could I be wrong and doing Billingham an injustice? Certainly I could—the dividing line is a fine one—but what I want to stress is that the work *forces* me to make the decision, at least implicitly, and in this it is representative of the 'Sensation' exhibition as a whole. One has to make very much the same decision about the Chapman brothers' work, about Harvey's readers' wives, about Hirst's bisected animals and putrefying cow's head, about Collishaw's bullet wound and Mueck's dead dad.

It could be objected that all serious art confronts one with choices and judgements. This is probably true but it is not usually this particular *kind* of choice. Faced with Seurat's *Bathers* in 1884 the choice was, is it great art or is it irredeemably vulgar and commonplace? With Salvador Dali it is, are these really profound images from the human subconscious or are they artificial and fabricated? With Carl André's *Equivalent VIII* (the infamous 'bricks') it is, can something so minimal be art, can it be meaningful and can it be beautiful? With *Guernica* in 1937 a number of questions arose. Does it work as a painting? Is it moving? In what way is it moving? Which side am I on in Spain? Does it help the anti-fascist cause? But *not,* is the painting in solidarity with those on the receiving end of the bombing or is it relishing and exploiting their suffering? Yet that is precisely the question posed by Billingham's work and the dominant question posed by the exhibition as a whole.

Why? Why does this question arise in relation to this body of art more insistently than is generally the case in the history of art? Because the underlying theme of all the more striking work here, its common denominator, is alienation—the alienated individual in an alienated society.[20] This is the other side of the coin of the Thatcherite entrepreneurialism of the 1980s. It is smack and crack on estates in Hackney (where many of the YBAs live[d] and have/had their studios). It is poverty, the dole and a sense of collective powerlessness in the face of 'a power which has become more and more enormous and, in the last instance, turns out to be the world market'.[21] It is personal rebellion in the absence of any felt connection to a wider force for social change.

In this situation art can go different ways. Hypothetically it could retreat into formalism and decoration (what Clement Greenberg in *Avant Garde and Kitsch* called 'Alexandrianism') but the history of art in the 20th century has more or less closed off that option.[22] It can embrace the alienation, wallow in it, internalise it and as a result produce art that is itself alienated in the extreme, alienated to the point of cruelty and collusion in cruelty—with a repudiation of all ties of human solidarity. Or, even in its alienation and isolation, it can battle through by exploring the depths of its condition 'in the place of excrement',[23] with intelligence and without surrender to produce work that in its own way is positive and life enhancing. Hence the polarisation in 'Sensation'. The first option produces work that is the stuff of Lukács' worst nightmares. The second produces work that can stand in the tradition of Kafka and Ginsberg, Goya and Picasso, Duchamp and Brancusi.

This then is the moment of 'Sensation'. Soon it will pass (life has already moved on) but not before it has left its mark on our culture and on the history of art for both better and worse.

Notes

Thanks are due to Steve Edwards and John Roberts who both endured lengthy arguments with me about the contents of this article. They will not agree with it, unless I have persuaded them, but hopefully they will see in it how much I learned from the dialogue.

1   L Buck, *Moving Targets: A User's Guide to British Art Now* (London, 1997), p7.
2   See E Cockcroft, 'Abstract Expressionism, Weapon of the Cold War', in F Frascina (ed), *Pollock and After* (London, 1985).
3   In 1988 Damien Hirst, in his second year at Goldsmith's College, curated the *Freeze* exhibition which marks the origin of Young British Art.
4   L Trotsky, *On Literature and Art* (London, 1977), p105.
5   Until he insisted on including a portrait of Lenin in his proposed mural for the Rockefeller Centre!
6   People get into the most absurd confusions about subject matter and 'art'. Can you make great art out of a man being slowly tortured to death? Yes! In fact it is probably the most common theme in the history of European art—the Crucifixion. Titian painted someone being hung upside down and flayed alive (*The Flaying of Marsalis*). Can you make art out of a pair of old boots? Both Van Gogh and Chaplin managed it. The question is not what the subject matter is but how it is painted or represented or used.
7   Royal Academy of Arts, *Sensation—Young British Artists from the Saatchi Collection* (London, 1997), p198.
8   I am reminded of Vivienne Westwood and others associated with punk in 1976/77 attempting to 'play' with the swastika for shock value, attempts which socialists had to firmly oppose.
9   Royal Academy of Arts, op cit, p194.
10 For example, such a defence might be offered in relation to the anti-Semitism in T S Eliot's poem *Gerontion*.
11 All three of these arguments might be used to defend Nabokov's *Lolita*.
12 T S Eliot, *Selected Prose* (Harmondsworth, 1965), p102.
13 It is worth noting that those works of art which became exceptionally well known—like the *Mona Lisa*, *The Hay Wain*, Monet's *Water Lilies*, Munch's *The Scream* etc—are often despised for this reason, but usually are powerful and important works in their own right.
14 For this point see D Batchelor, *Minimalism* (London, 1997), p95.
15 Bitter controversy surrounded the decision by the local authority to destroy *House* which had been erected on a temporary basis. Doubtless the decision was motivated by philistinism and it can easily be seen as an artistic tragedy (as well as a financial blunder). However, it seems to me that there is also a sense in which, just as Duchamp decided to regard the cracks received in transit by *The Large Glass* as part of the work, so the demolition of *House* is its fitting dialectical completion.
16 It is worth noting that, of the 42 artists represented, 11 are women—still a small minority but probably a higher proportion than would have been found in a supposedly representative survey of British art at any time in the past.
17 I have revised upwards my opinion of Lucas's work as a result of a number of discussions with students, colleagues and comrades, epecially Sarah Dryden, Paul Clarke, Jenny Walden and Alison Jones.
18 Far more powerful are *Light Sentence* and *Corps Etranger* by which Hatoum was represented in the Turner Prize show of 1995.
19 As depicted by Hogarth in the last of *The Rake's Progress* series (but Hogarth shows and implicitly condemns the voyeurs).
20 It is possible, thanks to the shift to the right in academia in the 1980s that many of these artists do not know either the name or the analysis of the condition in which they are immersed.
21 K Marx and F Engels, *The German Ideology* (London, 1985), p55.
22 Traces of this are to be seen in some of the work, such as that by Chris Ofili, Glen Brown and Jason Martin.

23   'But love has pitched his mansion in /The place of excrement/For nothing can be
     sole or whole/That has not been rent.' W B Yeats, 'Crazy Jane Talks with the
     Bishop', *Collected Poems* (London, 1982), p285.

In perspective: Sergei Eisenstein

A review of the special centenary edition of **The Eisenstein Collection**
(Tartan Video, Faber & Faber), £39.99

ANNA CHEN

The movies directed by Sergei Eisenstein during the 1920s provided much of the defining imagery of the Russian Revolution. Described as the father of film montage, he was certainly the first major theorist of cinema. The year 1998 marks the centenary of his birth. It is also 50 years since he died, leaving behind an invaluable legacy of writings but with very few of his scripts actually produced. A boxed set of videos of his 'Revolution' trilogy—*Strike*, *The Battleship Potemkin* and *October*,[1] which includes his first collection of essays and articles, *The Film Sense*, published in 1943—has been released to commemorate Eisenstein's centenary.

A prolific writer yet an underproduced film maker with only eight mostly monochrome epics completed, why is this director considered so important even today? What power was unleashed in *The Battleship Potemkin* which led UK authorities to ban it until 1954? Why do mainstream Hollywood directors pay him homage through direct reference, pastiche and even parody? In Spielberg's black and white feature film *Schindler's List* a small girl is picked out in red as she tries to escape her Nazi persecutors, the same device also finding its way into a TV ad for Peugeot. It was first seen, however, in *The Battleship Potemkin*, wherein the the director himself painstakingly hand tinted the flag, frame by frame, a flaming revolutionary red. Coppola's powerful use in *Apocalypse Now*, of the bull's slaughter from the end of *Strike* signifies, not the victim's pain—as with the 1,800 strikers killed at the end of the Russian film—but the horror that has fed the megalomania of Brando's

Kurtz, extinguished only when he is hacked to death by Martin Sheen's Marlow.

Ken Russell filches *Alexander Nevsky*'s knights on ice battle spectacular for *Billion Dollar Brain*, whilst De Palma shamelessly and thoroughly pastiches the Odessa Steps sequence from *The Battleship Potemkin* in *The Untouchables*. *Naked Gun* is by no means the silliest of many other screen references: the cliché of the baby carriage careering down the Odessa Steps (of which there were only 120, not the hundreds of the cinematic illusion Eisenstein created through rapid repetitive intercutting) is now instantly recognisable even to people who have never watched an Eisenstein movie.

When reading Eisenstein's own words, what strikes you is how driven he was as an artist. Possessed of a dazzling intellect that drew from sources as diverse as da Vinci, Dickens, Disney, Shakespeare, Goethe and Haiku poetry, Eisenstein's eclectic interests fuelled his search for a definitive theory of cinema. Pursuing his obsession in the early years of the Russian Revolution, when cinema was barely crawling from the womb and the creative possibilities of the first generation of Russian artists were seemingly without limit, Eisenstein turned pioneer and hunted down evidence for his theories, trawling western and eastern culture for clues. He called on Marx for support, quoting his 'definition of the course of genuine investigation'[2] in *The Film Sense*: 'Not only the result, but the road to it also, is a part of truth. The investigation of truth must itself be true, true investigation is unfolded truth, the disjuncted members of which unite in the result'.[3]

Eisenstein was born in Riga in 1898 to 'a tyrannical Papa', the architect and civil engineer Mikhail Osipovich, who fought for the White Russians during the civil war and died in Berlin in 1920. In the latest attempt to reclaim Eisenstein for liberals everywhere, his biographer, Ronald Bergan, attempts to rescue him from his claim 'to be a Marxist all his life'[4] by seizing on the oedipal nature of Sergei's relationship with this small minded philistine. Bergan's psychologism denies Eisenstein's capacity to transcend his own personal interests. His case seems to be sustained by Eisenstein's own account of his conflict with his father: 'The reason why I came to support social protest had little to do with the real miseries of social injustice, or material privations, or the zigzags of the struggle for life, but directly and completely from what is surely the prototype of every social tyranny—the father's despotism in a family, which is also a survival of the basic despotism of the head of the "tribe" in every primitive society'.[5]

But, as for many people from a similar background who joined the international revolutionary movement, claustrophobia and rebellion against the middle class family were only the beginning of a profound transformation. Eisenstein had, after all, witnessed government troops brutally clearing demonstrators from Nevsky Prospect in 1917. Even Bergan himself produces evidence which contradicts his case, quoting Eisenstein's foreword to his 1946 memoirs, *Beyond the Stars*:

> *The revolution gave me the most precious thing in life—it made an artist out of me. If it had not been for the revolution I would never have broken the tradition, handed down from father to son, of becoming an engineer... The revolution introduced me to art, and art, in its own turn, brought me to the revolution...*[6]

It was Yulia Ivanovna, his mother, who grounded Sergei in bourgeois culture. She surrounded him with books, bought him a camera, took him to the theatre and, in 1907, treated him to a memorable trip to Paris. But, according to Peter Wollen, it was the extraordinary upheavals of the 1917 revolution, when Sergei was 19, that brought his interest in art to fruition. At a time when 'authentic intelligentsia' was ousting 'academic hierarchy':

> *He was not prepared for the overthrow of the existing order of society, the collapse of his ideology and the dissolution of his family... The revolution destroyed him, smashed the co-ordinates of his life, but it also gave him the opportunity to produce himself anew...he was compelled to become an intellectual, to construct for himself a new world-view, a new ideological conception both of society and art...we cannot separate the ideas which he developed from the matrix in which they were formed, the matrix of the Bolshevik Revolution.*[7]

Eisenstein was steeped in accounts of the 1905 Revolution, and in particular 'Bloody Sunday', when troops opened fire upon a peaceful demonstration at the Tsar's Winter Palace in St Petersburg. Because of 'the wild outburst of reaction and repression...the brutality in my pictures is indissolubly tied up with the theme of social injustice, and revolt against it...'[8] His early working years included stints with the Petrograd militia, as a cartoonist for the *Petersburgskaya Gazeta*, decorating the agitprop trains leaving for the front, and as an engineer in the Red Army during the civil war, serving on the Eastern Front. 'The melting pot of the civil war and military engineering work at the front...' gave him '...a fascinating sense of history in the making, which had made a deep impression with the broad canvas of the fates of nations and epic ambitions, and was then realised in the thematics of future films of monumental scale'.[9]

Eisenstein's studies at the Institute of Civil Engineering in Petrograd were disrupted by the 1917 revolution. Any thoughts of renewing them were rapidly eclipsed by his fascination with theatre, especially that of his future mentor, the actor and theatre director Vsevolod Meyerhold, who ran the Proletkult Theatre in Moscow. Along with the poet Mayakovsky, and the artists Malevich and Tatlin, Meyerhold reassessed the Futurist and Symbolist movements in the pre-revolution years and came up with Constructivism, which would 'be a branch of production, in the service of the revolution' rather than 'pure' art.[10] Meyerhold had rejected the naturalism of Stanislavsky's acting methods at the 'monolithic' Moscow Arts Theatre, which would later be 'enshrined as the apogee of Stalinist art'.[11] He sought instead to prove the 'primacy of physiological gesture over psychological emotion'[12] (as Pavlov was attempting to establish through his experiments concerning reflex conditioning at the time). Subscribing to William James's dictum that 'we weep not because we are sad; we are sad because we weep,' Meyerhold used circus spectacular and body mechanics and drew from *commedia dell'arte* in order to produce a 'non-verbal, stylised, conventional theatre'. Even F W Taylor, whose time and motion studies in American factories led directly to the deepening of workers' exploitation, exerted an influence. Theoretical faultlines cracked wide open as Stanislavsky sank deeper into mysticism, exploring the Hindu concept of 'prana' and trying to get people to feel radiation rays emitted from his actors' fingertips, provoking an attack by Meyerhold for being 'out of key with the epoch of the machine, the mass, urbanism and Americanism'.[13]

However, the Proletkult movement was hardly beyond criticism itself. Tony Cliff points out that one of the chief aims of the revolution according to Trotsky was the 'awakening of human personality in the masses—who were supposed to possess no personality'.[14] The passionate cultural debates in post-war revolutionary Russia centred around raising the masses out of the quagmire of illiteracy, giving them the confidence that would prevent the growth of a cultured bureaucracy. Otherwise 'this would push the masses back into passivity and and lead to the degeneration of the revolution'.[15] The adherents of Proletkult wanted to cut free from the existing culture, rather than bring it to the masses, because they thought it 'was the last refuge of the bourgeoisie in retreat'.[16] (The Italian Formalists had similarly cast off their cultural roots, but were absorbed into the ideology of fascism.) In 1919 Lenin was scathing:

> *Proletarian culture is something that suddenly springs from nobody knows where, and is not invented by people who set up as specialists in proletarian culture. Proletarian culture is the regular development of those stores of knowledge which mankind has worked out for itself under the yoke of capitalist society, of feudal society, of bureaucratic society.*[17]

Trotsky acknowledged that because the bourgeoisie 'owned both physical and mental means of production...they possessed the comfort and abundance necessary for art to grow and become subtle'.[18] But Proletkult's ideology demanded both the rejection of this wellspring and the fetishisation of an imagined proletarian culture that would replace it. Trotsky also asserted that 'the proletarian regime is temporary and transient,' and not a permanent edifice, its purpose being to lay 'the foundations of a culture which is above classes and which will be the first culture that is truly human'.[19] Besides, there was little point in cutting the umbilical cord to a bourgeois culture to which the tiny Russian proletariat was not even attached in the first place.

Against the background of this controversy and attracted by the freeing up of artistic experimentation, the young Eisenstein set out to join Meyerhold's avant-garde group. Starting work as a set designer for the Proletkult Theatre in 1920, he rapidly progressed to directing stage productions, which gave him the preparation he needed for his first foray into film.

Early development of film art

Although Eisenstein is widely credited as the 'father of montage'—a form of editing technique—he wasn't strictly the first director to cut film in order to construct scenes. Early film makers such as George Méliès and the Lumière brothers had lifted existing theatrical methods for the screen wholesale, with little or no adaptation to the new medium. A stationary camera, the equivalent of a static audience, was placed at a fixed distance from the actors, where it passively recorded the basic *mise-en-scène* (literally, 'putting into the scene',[20] the composition of all the elements within the individual frame). Scenes were shot in their entirety with no zooming or tracking of camera and no close ups of the actors, rendering them completely self contained in time and space.

One of Thomas Edison's cameramen, Edwin S Porter, then revolutionised film narrative by constructing a story film, *The Life of an American Fireman*, from previously shot material in 1902. By cutting from one scene of incomplete action to another—from the firemen arriving at an actual burning building to the studio scene of the mother and child trapped inside—Porter was able to create the illusion of continuous story development. 'It implied that the meaning of a shot was not necessarily self-contained but could be modified by joining the shot to others'.[21] Eisenstein insisted that the shot was the basic *unit* of montage and not, as director Lev Kuleshov had insisted, merely an element of it. Because these units were small and manageable, directors were freed from the tyranny of theatricality.

However, Porter still filmed everything in long shot, maintaining a constant distance from the object. The American director D W Griffith, considered by Eisenstein to be (despite his politics) the first great storyteller in film, took Porter's parallel montage technique and introduced different camera lengths, giving us the *close up* and the *extreme long shot*. Instead of Porter's objective distancing from the action, Griffith pulled the spectator into the scene through the subjective close up and different viewpoints, controlling what the spectator saw and manipulating their emotional and intellectual response. In his seminal films, *Intolerance* and *The Birth of a Nation*, Griffith not only utilised close ups for emotional emphasis, he also used flashbacks and dissolves, maximising tension and excitement by increasing the pace of cutting towards the climax. Eisenstein traced the origins of montage back to literature. Parallel montage—cutting away to simultaneous action—can be summed up simply by the literary device, 'Meanwhile, back at the ranch...' As for the close up, Eisenstein cites Dickens, who opened *The Cricket on the Hearth* with a Griffith-esque close up: 'The kettle began it...'[22]

However, Eisenstein's appreciation of Griffith was not uncritical. Eisenstein took him to task for political and ideological reasons. The notorious racist depiction of the blacks and the heroic portrayal of the Ku Klux Klan in *The Birth of a Nation* made Griffith 'an open apologist for racism'.[23] Neither did Griffith's support for the Dry Law (alcohol prohibition) in *The Struggle* or 'the metaphysical philosophy of the eternal origins of Good and Evil'[24] in *Intolerance* go down well. Eisenstein detected:

> ...the inseparable link between the cinema and the industrial development of America. We know how production, art and literature reflect the capitalist breadth and construction of the United States of America. And we also know that American capitalism finds its sharpest and most expressive reflection in the American cinema.[25]

Meanwhile, back in Russia, the young revolutionary directors—including V I Pudovkin, Lev Kuleshov and Eisenstein—studied the old masters and then resolved to step up the director's degree of control over his material:

> They planned, by means of new editing methods, not only to tell stories but to interpret and draw intellectual conclusions from them...[they] saw themselves as propagandists and teachers rather than as conventional entertainers. As such, their task was twofold: to use the film medium as a means of instructing the masses in the history and theory of their political movement; and to train a young generation of film-makers to fulfil this task.[26]

Pudovkin rationalised Griffith's practical work and then developed his theoretical explanation further. The close ups of significant details that Griffith used to heighten the drama were, to Pudovkin, the very stuff of the film story. His contention, that each new shot must make a new and specific point rather than merely punctuating long shots of actors acting, was supported by Kuleshov whose experiments found that juxtaposition gave meaning to hitherto neutral shots. Depending on whether the same neutral close up of the actor Mosjukhin was joined with shots of a plate of soup, a shot of a dead woman in a coffin, or a child playing, the audience:

> *...raved about the acting of the artist. They pointed out the heavy pensiveness of his mood over the forgotten soup, were touched and moved by the deep sorrow with which he looked on the dead woman, and admired the light, happy smile with which he surveyed the girl at play. But we knew that in all three cases the face was exactly the same.*[27]

The Russians had discovered that emotions and ideas could be stimulated simply through the juxtaposition of pieces of film. Pudovkin wrote that 'Kuleshov maintained that the material in filmwork consists of pieces of film, and that the composition method is their joining together in a particular, creatively discovered order'.[28]

Eisenstein took the process a crucial stage further so that conventional narrative was all but abandoned, and individual characters and their motivation left undeveloped. He wanted to lead 'towards a purely intellectual film, freed from traditional limitations, achieving direct forms for ideas, systems and concepts, without any need for transitions and paraphrases'.[29] But whereas Pudovkin argued that the most effective scene is made through *linkage*—smoothly linking a series of selected details from the scene's action—Eisenstein insisted that film continuity should progress through *collision*—a series of shocks arising out of conflict between spliced shots: '...the juxtaposition of two shots by splicing them together resembles not so much the simple sum of one shot plus another—as it does a creation'.[30]

In his essay, 'A Dialectic Approach to Film Form', Eisenstein sets out his stall with a quote from Goethe: 'In nature we never see anything isolated, but everything in connection with something else which is before it, beside it, under it and over it'.[31] Eisenstein cites Marx and Engels, for whom the dialectical method was only the conscious reproduction of the dialectic of the external events of the world. He then explains that existence is in a state of constant evolution resulting from the interaction of two contradictory opposites. For Eisenstein, the basis of every art is this sort of dialectical conflict, 'an "imagist" transformation of the dialectical principle',[32] dynamically yielding new concepts in the form of a constantly developing argument of opposites. 'In the realm of art this dialectic principle of dynamics is embodied in CONFLICT as the fundamental principle for the existence of every work and art form'.[33]

Eisenstein developed his cinematographic theory which he would put into practice in making his films. Not only should there be conflict *between* shots, there should also be conflict *within* the frame at every level: conflict of graphic directions (lines—either static or dynamic: eg calming horizons broken by energised verticals of trees or walls; the dead boy lying 90 degrees against the strong diagonals of the steps in *The Battleship Potemkin* Odessa Steps sequence), scales (large and small), volumes (eg the full sails of the Odessa flotilla greeting the *Potemkin*), masses (volumes filled with various intensities of light) and depths. Also necessary was conflict of close and long shots; conflict of tempo (activity within the frame); light conflict (pieces of darkness and pieces of lightness). And 'conflicts between an object and its dimension—and conflicts between an event and its duration',[34] and so on. Eisenstein was building a cinematic art with a painter's eye and the method of an engineer. In him, music, literature, painting and science all converged.

The Revolution trilogy

Eisenstein's three great films about the Russian Revolution—*Strike, The Battleship Potemkin* and *October*—were all made between 1924 and 1928, before Stalin had consolidated his power and gained an iron grip on the arts. During this period the Communist Party initially favoured Proletkult artists. *Strike*, made in 1924, Eisenstein's second film and the first of the trilogy, was originally planned as the first of a series of films documenting the pre-revolutionary working class. It turned out to be an artistic success as well as an educational aid and it won an award at the 1925 'Exposition des Arts Décoratifs' in Paris, as well as being commercially exhibited in Germany.

In this fictionalised account of a factory strike, a highly stylised collection of capitalist exploiters do battle with the striking workers of a factory in a surreal series of set pieces. Midget bourgeoisie tango on table tops amid the detritus of excessive consumption; three identical top-hatted bosses make up a single composite capitalist; spies metamorphose into animals; a panorama of barrels sunk into the ground spews out troglodyte lumpenproletarians. Against this backdrop, the film presents the workers as a single group protagonist instead of as individual heroes. Eisenstein maintained that this was the first time collective and mass action had been seen on the screen in contrast to individualism and the 'triangle' drama of bourgeois cinema (which distils down to boy meets girl and then has to overcome obstacles—invariably in the form of a rival—in order to keep girl and resolve drama). Years later he criticised his 'beginner's piece' for its tricksiness and overuse of effects such as the cross-dissolve which proved 'the "infant malady of leftism" existing in these first steps of cinema',[35] and also because the development of the individual within the collective, 'a conception irreconcilably opposed to bourgeois individualism', had been neglected.[36]

On its release in 1925, *Strike* was poorly received by the Russian public, whose imagination had already been gripped by American films and the comfy folkloric familiarity of their conventional questing heroes and tightly developed narratives. *The Battleship Potemkin*, however, proved more successful. David O Selznick, then an MGM associate producer, wrote to one of his executives in 1926:

> *It was my privilege a few months ago to be present at two private screenings of what is unquestionably one of the greatest of motion pictures ever made, **The Armoured Cruiser Potemkin**... the film is a superb piece of craftsmanship. It possesses a technique entirely new to the screen... The film has no characters in an individual sense; it has not one studio set; yet it is gripping beyond words—its vivid and realistic reproduction of a bit of history being far more interesting than any film of fiction... Notable, incidentally, are its types and their lack of make-up, and the exquisite pieces of photography.*[37]

Running one of the major Hollywood studios, Selznick might also have been impressed that *The Battleship Potemkin* was made for a fraction of the hit German movie *Metropolis*'s budget of five million marks. A domestic flop in the Soviet Union, *Potemkin* was loved by German audiences, although the armed forces were forbidden to see it for fear of mutiny, as were Pennsylvanian audiences on the grounds that it gave American sailors 'a blueprint as to how to conduct a mutiny'.[38] When it was eventually screened in the US in 1926, Chaplin declared it to be 'the best film in the world'. In France the authorities burnt all copies they could find—it received only a limited art house screening at Paris film clubs. Despite being banned in the UK until 1954, *The Battleship Potemkin* has rarely been out of the annual BFI critics' top ten list, and only then when another Eisenstein film has been voted in.

It is easy to see why. The Odessa Steps sequence has even now the power to move and excite: '...Eisenstein, in forcing the spectator to create the image by putting together all the relationships between attractions (relationships existing because of the interpenetrating theme), gives to the spectator not a completed image, but the "experience of completing an image".'[39] All Eisenstein's elements come together in this perfect piece of cinema and the audience participates in the process of producing meaning.

The film documents an event that helped precipitate the 1905 Revolution which shook the Tsarist regime. The battleship *Potemkin* is a microcosm of Russian society. The ship's officers, doctor and priest—all representing the ruling power structure—pile abuse on top of abuse until maggot infested meat and a threatened mass execution push the sailors to mutiny. The mutineers eventually find sanctuary at the Black Sea port of Odessa, the setting for the film's penultimate sequence, showing Odessa's population supporting the *Potemkin* mutineers anchored in the bay. The sudden appearance of Tsarist soldiers abruptly reverses the joyous mood as the troops mercilessly advance, shooting everything that moves. Rhythm (cutting) builds with tempo (the pace of action within the frame) as the soldiers descend the steps in relentless solid formation behind the chaotically scattering crowd. This descending action travels left to right across the screen for rapidity (because we read left to right, top to bottom in English, our brains process screen information better in this direction, enabling us to read the images faster).[40]

Furthermore, Eisenstein plays with the planes of the shot so that we are not simply looking through a window at staged action, but also at a flat surface where the picture is composed, like a painting on a canvas. The film is not so much a substitute for the real world as 'an image existing for significant perception'.[41] Every visual and musical element is an aspect of a composition specifically designed to elicit the audience's participation in the construction of the scene in their minds. When the mother carries her murdered son towards the troops, she travels right to left against graphic lines formed by the edges of the steps and the fleeing crowd. Trudging up the steps and against the descending mass, she occupies her own distinct emotional space. At the point where she stands in front of the rank of anonymous soldiers, her figure is caged in by the diagonal lines of the steps; the prison bar like shadows of the soldiers and their rifles below her; and, foregrounded nearest the camera, the actual figures of the soldiers pointing their rifles straight at her.

Eisenstein increases the illusion of depth in this shot by clothing the many small far off dead bodies in dark shadings which recede into the distance; and foregrounding three soldiers and their officer in brightly lit white uniform, utilising conflict of mass and volume to locate the power in this scene. This is where this sequence's central idea reaches its peak, expressed in the graphic representation. With the corpses of the towns-folk behind her, the agents of death in front of her and their shadows falling across her, the mother is now the sole point of humanity within the frame. In the shot, she occupies the point of maximum tension—about two thirds towards the right and a little above centre, conforming to the proportions of the classical composition: compelling evidence of the virtuosity with which Eisenstein applied lessons learned from the study of centuries of classical painting to the new medium.

The full exploitation of suspense and tension highlights Hitchcock's artistic debt to Eisenstein. Will the nanny be shot? For how long can the baby carriage teeter on the top step before it begins its fall? The tracking camera shot which introduces the runaway pram increases the scene's tempo so that the pram runs at double time against the march of the soldiers, also raising the dramatic stakes. The final climactic destruction of innocence—the death of the baby and the attack on the conciliatory, bespectacled old woman by the sabre wielding cossack to whose better nature she vainly appeals—puts paid to any notion that verbal persuasion in powerless isolation can ever be an effective part of any revolutionary's armoury against monstrous reactionary forces.

Eisenstein's next film, *October*, was based on *Ten Days that Shook the World*, journalist John Reed's eyewitness account of the period leading up to the 1917 revolution. Released in 1928, the film takes the director's experiments in juxtaposition to new heights. *October* reconstructs the critical period between the revolutions of February and October 1917, when prime minister Kerensky's Provisional Government clung to power. (Incidentally, Bergan quotes Grigori Alexandrov, the assistant director on *October,* as saying, '...it has long been a joke in the Soviet film industry that more casualties were caused by Eisenstein's storming of the Winter Palace in June 1927 than by the attack of the original Bolsheviks in October 1917.' He attributed this to enthusiastic extras who had served at the front bringing along their ancient live cartridges. The original storming had ended in a peaceful surrender.)[42] Influenced by the climate of the rising bureaucracy and its conflict with Trotsky, the film shows Trotsky arguing for postponement of an armed uprising, finally voting reluctantly with Lenin on 10 October for immediate action. Once the counter-revolutionary forces are repelled, Kerensky escapes. At the election of the Second Congress presidium, the Bolsheviks win an overwhelming vote against the Mensheviks on the eve of the storming of the Winter Palace. As a result of their victory, the new revolutionary government under Lenin wins peace and grants bread and land to the masses.

Some critics have observed that in making *October* Eisenstein displayed a 'lack of interest in the simple mechanics of storytelling and... ruthless suppression of any footage not directly relevant to his thesis'.[43] The lack of a conventional bourgeois hero means that there is no emotional door into the story; the group protagonist—the revolutionaries and working class—is fragmented across the film. However, the mostly episodic narrative still contains a few vestigial plot points such as the entrance of the Tsarist general Kornilov, which presents a major moment of crisis: a short lived turning point maximising both jeopardy and opportunity for the revolutionaries before the resolution.

Trotsky's role in these events—head of the Military Revolutionary Committee based in Petrograd—is reduced to a single appearance as a craven weakling pitted against Lenin, warning against immediate action and nearly wrecking the revolution. Yet, according to John Reed's absorbing account, Trotsky was operating at full revolutionary throttle, urging the Bolsheviks to yield no ground to their detractors: 'All these so-called Socialist compromisers, these frightened Mensheviki, Social Revolutionaries, Bund—let them go! They are just so much refuse which will be swept away into the garbage heap of history!'[44] Foreshadowing Stalin's infamous predilection for rewriting history, all other scenes featuring Trotsky were cut from the film. At the time there was a major power struggle surrounding Trotsky's opposition to, among other matters, Stalin's directive that the Chinese communists should unite with the Kuomintang nationalists against Japanese imperialist invaders. Although this led the communists to their slaughter, the Stalinist bureaucracy was still able to grab total power in the Soviet Union. Bergan notes that after Stalin's interference with *October*, 'Eisenstein did confide to his diary his disgust at "the barbarism of Stalin".'[45]

Technically, *October* was Eisenstein's most ambitious project. It places excessive reliance on cross-cutting between the story and shots of details commenting on and shaping the main action. However, Eisenstein uses these details chiefly within the realm of *symbol*—where an image is juxtaposed with another, unconnected, image which has no subtext and therefore can sustain only a single interpretation. For example, relatively lengthy screen time is given up to crosscut shots of Kornilov and Kerensky with plaster busts of Napoleon, '...a juxtaposition of purely symbolic significance',[46] which draws obvious parallels and underlines their ambition. Elsewhere shots of Kerensky enjoying the opulence of the Tsar's Winter Palace are matched with shots of a gilded mechanical peacock, suggesting his vanity. Such heavy handed symbolism would not work for a modern cinema literate audience, who would get the point way ahead of the film. Even Eisenstein was aware of potential pitfalls: 'As soon as the film-maker loses sight of this essence [emotional dynamism of the subject] the means ossifies into lifeless literary symbolism and stylistic mannerism'.[47] He is critical of his own work:

> ...the sugary chants of the Mensheviki at the Second Congress of Soviets—during the storming of the Winter Palace—are intercut with hands playing harps. This was a purely literary parallelism that by no means dynamised the subject matter.[48]

Eisenstein has been taken to task for frequent obscurity. In the scene that introduces Kornilov:

In illustrating the monarchist **putsch** *attempted by General Kornilov, it occurred to me that his militarist* **tendency** *could be shown in a montage that would employ religious details for its material... So we intercut shots of a Baroque Christ (apparently exploding in the radiant beams of his halo) with shots of an egg-shaped mask of Uzume, Goddess of Mirth, completely self-contained. The temporal conflict between the closed egg-form and the graphic star-form produced the effect of an instananeous* **burst**—*of a bomb or shrapnel.*[49]

It is unlikely that many viewers would follow Eisenstein's exact line of logic, making the connection between Kornilov's militarism and what the film maker reads as an explosion.

When Eisenstein went to Hollywood in 1928 he was feted by movie moguls and powerbrokers like Douglas Fairbanks, Chaplin and Paramount's Jesse Lasky, all hailing him as the genius who would teach the philistines who populated this commercial hell how to make film. Eistenstein churned out scripts by the cartload, but Paramount failed to green light any of them for actual production. Eventually Eisenstein accepted the financial backing of novelist Upton Sinclair and commenced filming *Que Viva Mexico!* but Sinclair pulled the plug following one too many interventions by Stalin. Eisenstein's near complete work was sold to studios for use as stock footage.

He returned to the Soviet Union in 1932, finding a vastly different climate to the one he had left. Proletkult had petered out. Few of his friends remained active. Many of them had been purged. The 1932 edition of the *Soviet Encyclopaedia* accused him, regarding *October* and *The General Line*, of giving 'no deep analysis of the decisive stages of the Socialist Revolution' and stated that he 'made a diversion to formal experiments. Eisenstein is a representative of the ideology of the revolutionary section of the petty bourgeois intelligentsia which is following in the path of the proletariat.'

So, years after making *October*, Eisenstein was denounced as a Formalist. The Formalism movement used the method of *defamiliarisation* —making objects strange in order to make them seem more real. Eisenstein's technique expressed their idea that mere reproduction is never valid unless it is a deviation from the norm, a risky thing to do under Stalin. Subsequently he directed *Old And New*, which advanced the arguments of Stalin's collectivisation policy. Toeing Stalin's nationalistic line with *Alexander Nevsky* (1938) at a time when the Soviet state was gearing up for war with Germany, Eisenstein portrayed medieval Russian knights as heroic defenders of the motherland. *Ivan TheTerrible I* (1944) depicts a tough but misunderstood tyrant battling single handed against the evil Boyar conspiracy, the enemy within. Eisenstein's brilliant earlier technique has congealed: the storytelling is stolid and turgid; the performances verge on self parody. The 1,376 editing cuts of *The Battleship Potemkin*, double that of the average film, give way to long, repetitive shots of actors mugging to camera. In 1946, with Eisenstein recovering from a near fatal heart attack, his work print of *Ivan the Terrible II* was screened and critically mauled. Finally released in 1958, during Khrushchev's 'thaw' and ten years after Eisenstein's death, its antiquated style rendered it an ill received dinosaur.

Eisenstein threw in the towel shortly before he died in 1948, weakened by poor health and the stultifying political climate in which he was trying to work. Bergan quotes a magazine article published in 1947 in which he wrote:

> *In the light of the resolutions of the Central Committee, all workers in art must...fully subordinate our creative work to the interests of the education of the Soviet people. From this aim we must not take one step aside nor deviate a single iota. We must master the Lenin-Stalin method of perceiving reality and history... This is a guarantee that our cinematography will be able to surmount all the ideological and artistic failures...and will again begin to create pictures of high quality, worthy of the Stalinist epoch.*[50]

What, then, remains of Eisenstein's legacy? Without the Russian Revolution we might never have heard of him at all. He was at his most inventive and innovative during the initial throes of the revolution, in unprecedented conditions of mass creative liberation. In the early days state finance allowed him to pursue his ideas to their limits, whereas even Griffith encountered great difficulty in securing backing for his films in the US. Griffith and his successors eventually defined the art of film for the mass market, if not for the masses; but whilst little of Eisenstein's work transcended brilliant experimentation, it was nevertheless Eisenstein who embodied the promise of the fulfilment of human potential under socialism.

Notes

1   As there is no definite article in the Russian language, *Strike* and *Battleship Potemkin* are sometimes translated with definite articles attached. I have used the Tartan Video titles as stated on the box throughout this piece.

2   S Eisenstein, 'Word and Image', *The Film Sense* (Faber, 1943), p35.

3   K Marx, *Werke und Schriften* (quoted in *The Film Sense*, op cit, p35). *Bis Anfang 1844, nebst Briefen und Dokumenten* (Berlin, Marx-Engels Gesamtausgabe, section

1, vol 1, semi-volume 1). *Bemerkungen über die neueste preussische Zensurinstruktion*, von ein Rheinlander.

4   Eisenstein quoted in R Bergan, *Eisenstein: A Life In Conflict*, (Little, Brown & Company, 1997), p28.
5   Ibid, p28.
6   S Eisenstein, *Beyond the Stars: The Memoirs of Sergei Eisenstein* (BFI Publishing, 1995), p45.
7   P Wollen, *Signs and Meaning in the Cinema* (Secker & Warburg, 1969), p19.
8   Eisenstein Archives at TsGALI (State Archives of Literature and Arts), Moscow. Quoted in R Bergan, op cit, p27.
9   P Wollen, op cit, p21.
10 Ibid, p21.
11 Ibid, p21.
12 Ibid, p28.
13 Ibid, p27.
14 T Cliff, *Trotsky 1923-1927: Fighting the Rising Stalinist Bureaucracy* (Bookmarks, 1991), p98.
15 Ibid, p99.
16 Ibid, p113.
17 Quoted ibid, p115.
18 Ibid, p115.
19 Quoted ibid, p115.
20 I Konigsberg, *The Complete Film Dictionary* (Bloomsbury, 1988), p213.
21 K Reisz and G Millar, *The Technique of Film Editing* (Focal Press, 1953), p19.
22 S Eisenstein, 'Dickens, Griffith, and the Film Today', *Film Form* (Dennis Dobson, 1951), p195.
23 Ibid, p234.
24 Ibid, p234.
25 Ibid, p196.
26 K Reisz and G Millar, op cit, pp27-28.
27 V I Pudovkin, *Film Technique* (Newnes, 1929), p140.
28 Ibid, pp138-139.
29 S Eisenstein, *Film Form* (Dobson, 1951), p63
30 S Eisenstein, *The Film Sense* (Faber & Faber, 1943), p17.
31 Goethe in *Conversations with Eckermann* (5 June 1825) translated by John Oxenford, quoted in S Eisenstein, *Film Form*, op cit, p45.
32 S Eisenstein, *Film Form*, op cit, p38.
33 Ibid, p46.
34 Ibid, p39.
35 Ibid, p15.
36 Ibid, p16.
37 *Memo from David O Selznick* (Viking Press, 1972) quoted in R Bergan, op cit, p118.
38 Ibid, p117.
39 J D Andrew, *The Major Film Theories* (Oxford, 1976), p73.
40 More on the subject of the physiology of perception can be read in 'The Language of Film: Signs and Syntax' in James Monaco's *How To Read A Film: The Art, Technology, Language, History, and Theory of Film and Media* (Oxford University Press, 1981).
41 J D Andrew, op cit, p81.
42 R Bergan, op cit, p131.
43 K Reisz and G Millar, op cit, p36

44   J Reed, *Ten Days That Shook The World: The Illustrated Edition* (Sutton
     Publishing, 1997), p78.
45   R Bergan, op cit, p21.
46   S Eisenstein, 'A Dialectic Approach to Film Form', *Film Form*, op cit, p59.
47   Ibid, p58.
48   Ibid, p58.
49   Ibid, p56.
50   R Bergan, op cit, p347.

Vietnam veterans

A review of C Appy, **Working Class War: American Combat Soldiers and Vietnam** *(University of North Carolina Press, 1993), £12.50, and A Young,* **The Harmony of Illusions: Inventing Post-Traumatic Stress Disorder** *(Princeton University Press, 1995), £14.99*

JONATHAN NEALE

Christian Appy's *Working Class War* is an almost perfect socialist history of United States combat soldiers in Vietnam. Here is the story he tells. About 80 percent of soldiers came from blue collar families. About 20 percent had fathers in white collar jobs, but mostly routine ones. It was a working class war. These men were forced to go to Vietnam. The majority were drafted (conscripted). Many more joined the military because they were about to be drafted. And some joined to get steady work or because they were in trouble at home.

The government and the draft boards protected the sons of the rich. College students were not drafted until they finished their studies. And as the demand for men increased, the army began taking the young men who failed the army's intelligence tests. At the time everybody knew the draft was discriminatory. Appy quotes a 1970 interview with a firefighter who lost his son Ralph in Vietnam:

> *I'm bitter. You bet your goddam dollar I'm bitter. It's people like us who gave up our sons for the country. The business people, they run the country and make money from it. The college types, the professors, they go to Washington and tell the government what to do... But their sons, they don't end up in the swamps over there, in Vietnam. No sir. They're deferred, because they're in school. Or they get sent to safe places. Or they get out with all those letters they have from their doctors. Ralph told me. He told me what went on at his physical. He said most of the kids were from average homes; and the few rich*

kids there were, they all had big-deal letters saying they weren't eligible…
Let's face it: if you have a lot of money, or if you have the right connections,
you don't end up on a firing line in the jungle over there, not unless you want
to. Ralph had no choice. He didn't want to die. He wanted to live. They just
took him.[1]

Some 58,000 Americans died in Vietnam. So did between 1.5 and 2
million Vietnamese—civilians and soldiers on both sides. As Appy says,
to insist on the scale of Vietnamese dead does not belittle the suffering of
US soldiers:

Without some awareness of the war's full destructiveness we cannot begin to
understand [the US veterans'] *experience. As one veteran put it: 'That's what*
I can't get out of my head—the bodies…all those bodies. Back then we didn't
give a shit about the dead Vietnamese. It was like: "Hey, they're just gooks,
don't mean nothin'." You got so cold you didn't even blink. You could even
joke about it, mess around with the bodies like they were rag dolls. And after
a while we could even stack up our own KIAs [killed in action] *without*
feeling much of anything. It's not like that now. You can't just put it out of your
mind. Now I carry those bodies around every fucking day. It's a heavy load,
man, a heavy fucking load'.[2]

Why were there so many bodies? From 1945 to 1954 the Vietnamese
fought the French colonialists. In 1954 the French gave in. The northern
half of the country became a Stalinist dictatorship: North Vietnam. The
southern half became a military dictatorship backed and funded by the
US. Everybody knew that if there was an election in the South the
Communists would win. There was no election.

From the late 1950s on the Communists in the South began a guerrilla
war, against the orders of the Communist government in the North. In
the end the North was morally obliged to support the movement in the
South. But the great bulk of the fighting was always done by Southern
guerrillas. Not everybody in the South supported the guerrillas, but the
majority preferred them to the corrupt generals who ran the South. Then
the US troops came: 11,300 in 1961, 185,300 in 1965, 536,000 in 1968.
The more Americans came, the more it became a nationalist war and the
less support the Southern government had.

So the US army and marines faced a population who mostly supported the guerrillas. They outnumbered the US forces. They had
200,000 to 300,000 full time combat troops. The US, with at least five
support troops to every combat soldier, had 90,000 men at most in the
field.[3] The US government, the CIA and the senior generals understood
all this. But once they had thrown their support behind the South
Vietnamese government they felt compelled not to lose.

Why? Appy does not say. I think the answer is this. Between 1945 and 1975 the US or the local armies it supported smashed mass movements in Greece, Malaya, Indonesia, the Philippines, Iran, Iraq, Guatemala, the Dominican Republic, Kenya, Brazil, Argentina and Chile. The ability to do this rested, in the end, on the threat of US intervention. The US did not, and does not, rule the world. But the US government does serve as the organising centre for local ruling classes in many places. After the defeat in Vietnam the US government could not send troops to fight anywhere for almost 20 years.[4]

To return to Appy's argument: there was much at stake and the US government had few strategic alternatives. It decided to use its massive firepower in what General Westmoreland, the US commander in Vietnam, called 'a war of attrition'. This meant killing so many of the enemy—civilians or soldiers—that they just gave up. The pressure for this was relentless. The Pentagon demanded statistics. In rear units the officers chalked the cumulative kills on a board. Officers knew their careers would depend on their numbers. And while the officers seldom said, 'Kill all the civilians you can,' they seldom criticised anybody for it and often praised them. This put the soldiers in a horrific position.

They arrived in Vietnam as individuals and were assigned to companies. They had no training for what they faced, because the army and marines could not admit what kind of a war they were fighting. So the slightly more experienced soldiers had to train the new men, and fast. One marine remembered his training at Khe Sanh:

That first patrol, we went to where some marines had ambushed a bunch of Vietcong. They had me moving dead bodies, VC and NVA (North Vietnamese Army). Push this body here out of the way. Flip a body over. See people's guts and heads half blown off. I was throwing up all over the place.

'Keep doing. Drag this body over there.'

'For what?'

'You're going to get used to death before you get in a firefight and get us all killed. You're a [machine] *gunner and gunners can't panic on us.'*

I moved some more bodies and after a while I stopped throwing up...

[Then] *they gave me about a ten-minute rest. They're laughing and joking.*

Next, I had to kick one dead body in the side of the head until part of his brain started coming out the other side. I said, 'I just moved a dead body. What are y'all telling me?' The logic, I didn't see it then. I understood it later. At the time I thought, 'These fuckers been up here too long. They are all insane.' I'm going through my changes and the rest of these guys are laughing.

'Kick it,' they said. 'You are starting to feel what it is like to kill. That man is dead, but in your mind you're killing him again. Man, it ain't no big thing.

Look-a-here.' And they threw some bodies off the cliff...
*   'So... Kick.' They meant it. The chant started, 'Kick... Kick... Kick...'*
*   I'm kicking now. I'm kicking and I'm kicking and all of a sudden, the*
brains start coming out the other side...

Later he understood:

They were serious men, dedicated to what they were doing. [They were]
teaching me...not to fall apart. I saw it happen. I saw guys get themselves
killed and almost get an entire platoon wiped out, because they panicked or
because they gave up or because they got wounded and they couldn't deal
with their own blood. They had this thing about teaching a boot [a new man]
exactly what he's got to deal with and how to accept the fact of where he
really is.[5]

Where he really was at Khe Sanh was: he was bait. The population
either supported the guerrillas or were too scared to tell on them. So the
US generals could only find the guerrillas by sending the US soldiers
and marines out on patrol. If and when the guerrillas chose to attack, the
Americans on the ground would then call in artillery and bombers to
blast them. This terrified the GIs: they were always waiting to get hit.
Their enemy almost always chose the time and place of battle. And
between 15 and 20 percent of Americans killed in Vietnam died from
'friendly fire': the artillery and bombs they called in.
   Another 20 to 25 percent died when they stepped on mines. They
could not see the enemy. But they had seen villagers a few minutes or
hours before they stepped on the mines. The villagers knew where the
mines were—the guerrillas told them or left warning marks. And the US
soldiers learned: the villagers were their enemy.
   They were fighting an enemy they could not see. They were constantly afraid. They felt helpless. They were losing. The officers were
pushing them relentlessly to report dead Vietnamese. And they were on
the wrong side. They knew it. Again and again returning veterans in the
1960s said that the other side were the only people in the country who
knew what they were fighting for. But the GIs felt the choice was to fight
or to die. They knew they were oppressing poor people, but that only
made them angrier and more desperate.
   With care and sympathy Appy lets the reader feel what those soldiers
felt, so that by the time he gets to the atrocities you understand why they
did them. This is a short article, so it will be harder for the reader to
follow the process. But let us take one example.
   The US soldiers were particularly angry with the Vietnamese children. The soldiers expected the children to like them. From their first
moments in Vietnam they met children begging for food. The soldiers

were appalled by the poverty, and their fathers had told them of giving food and candy to grateful children in Europe. But if they did not feed the Vietnamese children, the kids screamed abuse at them. If they did, the children fell on them, tearing at their clothes, going through their pockets, making clear their need and their hatred.

The old soldiers told the new soldiers the truth: those children hate us. They know where the mines are. They want us to die. The hardest thing was: the US soldiers saw themselves in those children. They had grown up poor. Many of them knew what it was to go to bed hungry. Most of them had been laughed at in high school because they didn't have the right clothes. And now, suddenly, they were unimaginably rich compared to those children. But they would still be poor when they went home. So they hated it when the children begged. Soldiers who served in different parts of Vietnam remember throwing full cans of combat rations at children from trucks: throwing them as hard as they could. Appy quotes an army combat engineer:

> *We threw full C-ration cans at the kids on the side of the road. They'd be yelling out, 'Chop, chop; chop, chop,' and they wanted food. They knew we carried C-rations. Well, just for a joke, these guys would take a full can... and throw it as hard as they could at a kid's head. I saw several kids' heads split wide open, knocked off the road, knocked into the tires of the vehicle behind.*[6]

Appy then quotes a marine who 'served at the opposite end of South Vietnam':

> *When they originally get in country* [Americans] *feel very friendly toward the Vietnamese and they like to toss candy at the kids. But as they become hardened to it and kind of embittered against the war, as you drive through the ville you take the cans of C-rats and the cases and you peg 'em at the kids; you try to belt them over the head. And one of the fun games that always went was you dropped the C-rats cans or the candy off the back of your truck so that the kid will have time to dash out, grab the candy and get run over by the next truck.*[7]

Appy comments:

> *This is not easy to understand, and veterans who are plagued with guilt for incidents like this do not themselves fully understand what led them to behave so cruelly or how they might have found in it a 'joke' or a 'fun game'. Somehow those roadside children became the emblems and the targets of the war's contradictions.*[8]

The soldiers saw the children's hatred and need, and could not bear it. And then the soldiers went home.

> *Away from the war, veterans found it difficult to numb themselves to the suffering they endured, witnessed and inflicted... [One] soldier, just a long plane flight away from the war, was met by his parents at the airport:*
>
> *'They drove home in silence and then sat together in the kitchen, and his mother, in passing, apologised for there being 'nothing in the house to eat'. That did it; he broke. Raging, he went from cupboard to cupboard, shelf to shelf, flinging doors open, pulling down cans and boxes and bags, piling them higher and higher on the table until they spilled over onto the floor and everything edible in the house was spread out in front of them.*
>
> *'I couldn't believe it,' he said, shaking his head as he told me. 'I'd been over there...killing those poor bastards who were living in their tunnels like rats and had nothing to eat but mud and a few goddamn mouldy grains of rice, and who watched their kids starve to death or go up in smoke, and she said **nothing to eat**, and I ended up in the kitchen crying and shouting: **nothing to eat, nothing to eat!**'* [9]

As Appy comments, 'Beyond this veteran's rage one can imagine the hurt and confusion of his parents.' But how could a man in this situation make sense of his experience? The GIs came home to a mass anti-war movement. But they saw it as movement against them. Over and over, they told each other stories of being spat on by anti-war hippies upon their return. They saw the protesters as college students. They had learned in Vietnam that the officers and the professionals were their enemies. Learned it the hardest way possible, and learned it forever. Earlier I quoted a firefighter who lost his son Ralph in Vietnam. His wife said:

> *I told (my husband) I thought (the anti-war demonstrators) want the war to end, so no more Ralphs will die, but he says no, they never stop and think about Ralph and his kind of people, and I'm inclined to agree. They **say** they do, but I listen to them, I watch them; since Ralph died I listen and I watch as carefully as I can. Their hearts are with other people, not their own American people, the ordinary kind of person in this country... Those people, a lot of them are rich women from the suburbs, the rich suburbs. Those kids, they are in college... I'm against this war, too—the way a mother is, whose sons are in the army, who has lost a son fighting in it. The world hears those demonstrators making their noise. The world doesn't hear me, and it doesn't hear a single person I know.* [10]

This woman does not support the protesters, but she opposes the war. All the public opinion surveys at the time showed that blue collar workers opposed the war as much as or more than professionals. A larger proportion of blue collar workers than professionals voted for George McGovern, the anti-war candidate in 1972.[11] And the great majority of veterans were clear: the US should not be in Vietnam.

Only a minority of veterans supported the organised Vietnam Veterans Against the War. But more important, under the pressure of their own experience and the anti-war movement at home, the soldiers and marines in Vietnam began to act against the war. During the war roughly 500,000 people deserted from the US forces, many to avoid going to Vietnam.[12] Think about that: half a million deserters.

In Vietnam many units began refusing patrols they thought were too dangerous. Some of these mutinies were televised back home. Throughout the war small units of enlisted men had 'sandbagged' night patrols—they went and hid somewhere and simply called in false reports on the radio. Now more and more junior officers joined in sandbagging.

Officers who forced men into patrols were killed by their men. I remember a friend in 1967, just returned from combat in Vietnam, telling me that killing officers was common but never reported. By 1969 there was a name for it—'fragging', from the fragmentation grenades commonly used. And the army was collecting statistics: 126 fraggings in 1969, 271 in 1970 and 333 in 1971. About 80 percent of these were killings of officers and NCOs, but these figures do not include officers and sergeants simply shot in the back on patrol.

By 1971, under pressure from the anti-war movement, US forces were down to 200,000.[13] Killing 300 or more gung-ho officers and NCOs from among that number was enough for the rest to get the message. The US forces were withdrawn from Vietnam because they had ceased to fight. The courage and endurance of the Vietnamese peasants won the war. The anti-war movement in the US mattered, and so did the fragging of officers by US enlisted men.

Post-traumatic stress

But that was forgotten. The men who killed their officers didn't talk about it much when they came back. There was nobody who celebrated their resistance. The half a million deserters kept quiet. In one way, almost everybody who fought in Vietnam knew that their lives had been damaged, and sometimes ruined, by the US class system. They returned with a hatred of that system. But at the same time they heard no voice that explained their suffering in class terms. They were alone. And they returned to a generation of recession, and employers who discriminated against them. Most of them coped, as people do, and got on with building lives.

But the more they thought about the war, the more desperate some of them felt. 'No one knows how many veterans have committed suicide…but most specialists who have worked closely with veterans believe the number of suicides far exceeds the number of men who died in the war itself.'[14] Many more drugged themselves, or drank hard, or woke up screaming or exploded in rage or went mad.

The Vietnam Veterans Against the War, however, left a legacy of political organisation. The veterans were able to insist that something must be done. The Veterans Administration (VA), part of the federal government, was already responsible for medical care of all veterans. In the 1980s they began to offer psychiatric help to people suffering from what the psychiatrists now called 'post-traumatic stress disorder'.

Allen Young's *The Harmony of Illusions: Inventing Post-Traumatic Stress Disorder* includes a study of staff and resident patients in one such VA psychiatric centre in 1986-1987. Young is an anthropologist, and he spent a year in the centre watching and listening.

One man was both manager of the centre staff and director of the treatment offered. He had a model of post-traumatic stress the staff had to use. It went as follows: Men with post-traumatic stress disorder are split between their aggressive and sexual sides. At a moment in the past they did one wrong thing, and they did it because they enjoyed it. After they enjoyed that thing, they were overwhelmed with guilt. So they split their desire from their aggression. The cure is for them to recall that moment in detail in group therapy. When they have returned to that moment, and accepted that they wanted to do evil, they then can leave the guilt behind and become whole people.

Note carefully: they *did one wrong* thing. Terrible things that were done to them don't really count. Terrible things they saw don't really count. It has to be an atrocity they wanted to commit. And only one atrocity. A lot of time in therapy is spent trying to find that one time.

It's all nonsense, as Young shows clearly. But it serves a function. This centre treats men wounded by the war. But it's a government centre. It cannot say, 'The officers and the government are to blame.' It cannot say, 'What was done to you in Vietnam is of a piece with what has been done to you since.' And it cannot allow the patients to say these things. So the psychiatric theory blames the men: they wanted to kill. The men keep trying to say what was done to them. In group therapy 'Henry' explains some of why he is upset:

Henry: Well, the word gutting has a special meaning for me. It makes me think of a time when a guy in my outfit threw some ears on the lieutenant's table. The ears were still wet with blood, and the lieutenant got pissed off, because he had to begin his report over again: his paper was bloody. In our outfit, it was policy to bring in ears as proof of confirmed kills, for body counts. And when we'd do this, it reminded me of hunting. You know, you go out, track your deer, shoot it, and then you gut the carcass.

Lewis [a psychologist, co-leader of the group]: *But yesterday you used this word toward the group.*

Henry: *Yes, I know. I don't like feeling that way. I don't feel that I'm too tightly wrapped. Maybe I am crazy. I was raised a Baptist. I went to church every Wednesday and Sunday, and I went to Bible camp. By the time I was 18, I was in Vietnam. After I was in country for only three days, I killed a 16 year old boy. I began questioning my religion. I was asking myself what kind of god would put me in a position like this and let me do this. At first, I felt sad. But then people started telling me, 'Way to go,' and the captain and the sergeant congratulated me for having a kill after such a short time. After a while, I fell into the programme. I'd see guys lose legs and other shit happen, and it didn't bother me any more. I began to enjoy it and went back for a second tour* [a second year]. *I wanted to get revenge, and I wanted to do as much destruction as possible.*[15]

Here is part of group therapy a week earlier. Lewis the psychologist explains the theory. Henry listens for a while. Then he speaks, and Lewis immediately shuts him up:

Lewis: *Forgetting traumatic events originates in a conflict. You don't want to remember. Your conflict is always driving you back to the original event, but you don't want to go back to it. Stress responses do two things for you. First, you don't have to face your conflict, and second, you punish yourself... One of the jobs of combat training is to remove some of the conflict over aggression, so that you can be aggressive...*

Martin [another patient]: *Well, I can tell you we had no problem being aggressive in Vietnam.*

Lewis: *Okay, Martin. Give us an example, but use the word 'I' instead of 'we'.*

Martin: *Well, you get orders to burn a village, and a gook tries to put the fire out while you're trying to burn his hootch* [house]. *He fucks with you, and you show him that you can fuck with him. You can push him away, or you can kick his ass, or you can do what we usually did: you can shoot him.*

Lewis: *The word 'gook' is a good example of how we depersonalise people, turn them into objects. It's how we make it easier to—*

Martin: *I wasn't even conscious that I was using this word.*

Henry: *My aggression is against Americans: against the smug, sanctimonious, hypocritical, silent majority of Americans. My fantasy is to release the black plague on them. If I could do that, then maybe I'd have some satisfaction.*

Lewis: *OK, Henry, what you need to do now is examine what you've said and ask yourself why you said it when you did. It was what we call a 'displacement'. The real target of your aggression is somewhere else. You may have a* *legitimate complaint about these people, the silent majority. But you're using them as a target for your anger. The real source of the conflict is hidden in these feelings against the silent majority. If you take the time to think about it, you'll discover two things at the bottom of it. First, there's the intent to do harm, and second, there's the intent to punish yourself. You need to stop trying to see what makes sense 'logically'—whether or not the majority of Americans earned the negative feelings you have for them. You need to see what makes sense emotionally and psychologically.*[16]

Lewis, the psychologist, was a conscientious objector during the Vietnam War. So he has to acknowledge there was something wrong with the war. It is not clear if he really believes the 'American people' are at fault. But if he regularly told the group, 'Look, why don't you just blame the rich,' he would lose his job. Two weeks later Carol, a counsellor, shuts Henry up again in group therapy:

Carol: Yesterday you were wearing all black, Henry, a black shirt, black jeans. And what was Paul's response? He said the clients are like troops being shot at by people [Vietnamese] *in black pyjamas.*
*Henry: Listen, the people who were shooting **at me** in Vietnam weren't wearing black uniforms. Black clothes don't mean anything to me. There was **no** aggressive intent. After the session, when I realised that my clothes produced a stress response, I went to my room and changed, and I came to lunch in different clothes.*
*Carol: Even if it's not your conscious experience right now, its meaning will come to realisation. Same thing about the meaning of your remark yesterday, about the Vietcong not being **your** enemy.*
Henry: Well, that's right. The Vietcong were acting the same way we would have acted in their place. I had no anger against them. My anger's against the people who sponsored the war.
Carol: Which is equivalent to saying, 'My anger is against all Americans'.[17]

Which shuts him up and forces him to blame himself. Again and again in Young's book you can hear the class struggle in therapy. It goes on all day every, every day in this clinic. The therapists, controlled by the managing psychiatrist, try to make the veterans responsible for the war. The veterans fight back.

*Carol: Say to yourself, I've been punishing myself and people around me for 20 years. Say, Jack, you **can** choose to stop!*
Jack: Listen, Carol. On some nights, I feel anxiety going through my body like it's electricity. It started in Vietnam. It wasn't just a feeling. It was anxiety together with terrible chest pains and difficulty breathing. Just like having a heart attack. They sent me over to the field hospital to get an ECG. The

doctors told me there was nothing wrong. They said I was just hyperventi-lating. They told me to breathe into a paper bag when I got those feelings, and they gave me a supply of Valium to take back. But I got those attacks anyway. And I'm still getting them.

Carol: *What would you call it?*

Jack: *Well, I know that it's called a 'panic attack'. But I didn't know it then.*

Carol: *No, I mean what would you call it using the terms of the model—the model that you learned about during orientation phase?*

Jack: *I don't really know, Carol. My mind is confused right now.*

Carol: *The model says that we're dominated by two drives, aggression and sex, and that—*

Jack: *Listen, Carol. When I got those attacks, I sure didn't want to get fucked, and I can't believe it was my aggression.*[18]

Or:

Gary: *What's your success rate?*

Carol: *It's normal to doubt, but—*

Gary: *I'm not doubting. I just want to know the name of one graduate: someone who has no flashbacks, bad dreams, etcetera.*

Carl: *You can go to the alcohol ward, and they'll give you the name of a reformed alcoholic they've treated. Will this program allow us to get back on the street? I came here all the way from North Carolina, and I spent 41 days on the alcohol ward—that was the condition you people set for me to get into this programme. I put a lot into getting here; now I want to get some answers.*

Flip: *The programme won't change anything. We have to change ourselves. But I'm in a state of confusion now. My mood changes from minute to minute. You can get something from this programme, Carl, and you can just reject the rest.*

Carl: *There's a difference between you and me, Flip. I've been going to the VA [Veterans Administration] for years—long before PSTD. They browbeat you at the VA, and then they send you out on the street. [To the therapists] When I ask if you have answers, don't fuck with me. Everywhere in the VA, it's the same. Patients against staff. We don't need their rules. They've got to treat us like men. We don't need to take their bullshit any more. All over the country you get the same bullshit.*[19]

The staff have a way of explaining away the patients' anger. They say: anger is a defence. The patient gets angry so he doesn't have to get in touch with his feelings of guilt about what he did. He seems to be angry with me. Actually, he's angry with me because I'm pushing him to reveal his guilt.

Sometimes patients test the 'limits' set by the staff. Maybe they become violent. Maybe they leave the room during group therapy to have a piss. Maybe they wear dark glasses in group. Maybe they disagree with the therapists too effectively. If they break these limits, they face a 'panel'. This panel is made of all the staff the patient has told his intimate secrets to. They discuss everything about him behind his back. Sometimes they throw him out of the hospital. The other patients regard this as a punishment—just like the army. The staff disagree. They feel they are only setting limits.

The centre Young studied is one of the best in the Veterans Administration. It is Freudian, progressive. The patients are encouraged to talk. Many of these men have been to other hospitals, where they were drugged to the eyeballs, shot full of thorazine, strapped to tables for weeks, given electric shocks over and over, given electric shocks while they were awake.

Money

These are men whose median income—except for Veterans Administration disability benefits—is less than $1,000 a year. If they don't get a good report from the staff, they could lose those benefits. If the staff decide they have 'post-traumatic stress disorder', they could get $40,000 to $60,000 in back benefits. So there's a lot of pressure to be good. But not too good—if you're cured, you might lost your benefits, and still not have a job.

In this situation it's hard to be honest and open in therapy. Yet these men often are. They try desperately. They have suffered for years. This is the only help available. And so they wait, days or weeks, for each man to gather the courage to say what he did, what was done to him. As each man tells his worst 'event', they sit silent, leaning forward, willing him on to tell the truth. They want to tell and hear the truth. They have seen enough lies. But they also hope the therapists are right—this will cleanse him.

The man tells the truth. It does not cure him. The therapists say once a man has returned to that moment and owned his responsibility, he will be whole. He is not. He is ashamed. And in the eyes of the men who were there too, he is right to be ashamed. The therapists say he can put the guilt behind him. He can't. Somebody has to bear the guilt. It should be the guilty—not the working class boys sent to hell, but the rich and powerful men who sent them there.

It would help these veterans in pain if they could be angry with the men who sent them there—titanically angry, encouraged in their anger, supported in their anger, honoured for their rage. Instead they are silenced, so those who ruled the US then can still rule the US today.

Academic writing

That's all I have to say about the war. Now I want to use these two books to talk about writing socialist books. Socialists need books about class struggle because we want to fight. So we need to know what our rulers are doing, how and why they rule us, both in the corridors of power and day by day in the clinic and the workplace. We need to understand how the class struggle structures our lives. We need to understand how we can win and why we might lose. And we need books ordinary socialists and workers can understand.

Appy has written such a book. It's a book working class veterans can read. Their children, many of them students in US colleges, can read it too. It does justice to the veterans' experience. It also shows what the ruling class and the officers did to them. It does not tell us fairy stories about people making their own lives. It shows us how the soldiers were brutalised and brutalised others. But it also shows us how the same men fought back: the half a million deserters, the sandbaggers, the men who refused patrols, the mutineers and the fraggers.

There are two things missing. Appy's book is clearly based on Marxist ideas of class. But he does not mention Marxism. And he does not explain why the US ruling class felt they had to stay in Vietnam. I think in both cases Appy is worried about losing the veterans for whom he is writing. He might lose the readers who do not agree with his analysis of US foreign policy. And the veterans fought people who were called Marxists.

The way round this problem is to say that the Vietnamese Communists were no more Marxist than the US government is freedom loving. The Vietnamese government now is a state capitalist regime, not a socialist one. But I suspect Appy is confused about this, so he avoids the subject.

Young's book is also about the class struggle. He shows us in detail, in conversation after conversation, how the manager makes the junior therapists oppress the patients. He shows us how the patients argue back and how they support each other. In that way, it's a brilliant book. It made me shout out loud and made me cry. But it's written so veterans won't read it. Before we get to life in the veterans' clinic there are 144 pages of a history of psychiatric ideas about trauma and stress. Much of it is very insightful, but I had a lot of difficulty following it. And I have 13 years experience as a counsellor and a PhD in social history. Those first 144 pages make quite sure veterans won't read the book.

The next 120 pages describe the clinic. The transcripts of therapy are electrifying and the analysis is spot on. But here again the reader needs more explanation and more signposts. Why did Young write in this way? I don't know his individual circumstances, but I can guess.

Academics move in a world suffused with the ideas of the rich and powerful. It's in the air they breathe, the seminar papers they listen to and the reading lists they assign. They depend upon senior professors for job security, promotion and even personal and intellectual approval. When academics write in opposition to the prevailing ideas, they feel vulnerable. They often try to protect themselves. One way to do that is to begin the book with a chapter which reviews other academic books in the field. Unfortunately, this chapter acts as a barrier to ordinary people reading the book.[20]

Another way is to write in a language which only other academics can read. (Some write in a language even other academics have great difficulty understanding.) I am not saying that academics should simplify their ideas for a working class audience. The more complex the ideas, the simpler the language needs to be. In Appy's book, for instance, the ideas are complex. The writing is not. In fact, clear language helps a writer think through complex ideas.

Appy's strength comes partly from his topic and circumstances. He is writing about an old and discredited war. He is writing about the military for liberal academics. His book comes from a thesis at Harvard supervised and defended by Robert Coles, a left winger of great moral and intellectual stature. Young is more exposed. He is writing about now. He is writing about how a liberal, professional institution attacks workers. He is writing about a psychiatrist he knows who allowed him to do the fieldwork. And, like Appy, he is writing about class struggle.

Most academics don't write *about* the oppressed. Those who do, usually write about the oppressed *for* the professors, not *about* the class struggle *for* the oppressed. In other words, they write about the feelings, families, gender, rituals, networks, work and culture of the oppressed. They do not focus on the class struggle: strikes, demonstrations, unions, parties, the state and the daily battle at work.

So Young was vulnerable. I suspect he decided to write a book which would be professionally bombproof, because he could show he knew more about psychiatric history and ideas than the psychiatrists themselves. He didn't have to. He could have put the hospital stuff first and the history afterwards. Then veterans could have read the first half and left the rest. And when he wrote the first half he could have said to himself: I must write this so veterans will understand it.

Does this matter? Yes. Here's more group therapy. 'Henry' is the man we met before, remembering the severed ears and being silenced by the therapists:

Peter: In Vietnam we didn't have an objective. We weren't allowed to accomplish anything. They just sent people there to fart around and to die.

Carol: *And the centre—is it like this too?*
Peter: *Well, I wonder if there is a cure for PATS* [post-traumatic stress disorder]. *Lewis* [another therapist] *says that what we're into here is 'a recovery on the way to a cure'.*
Henry: *Everything I've read before coming here says that PATS can't be cured.*[21]

'Everything I've read...' Here is a man who reads everything he can to understand his life. He's still out there somewhere. There are many like him. They need a book by Young. He knows what they know, but are constantly forced to doubt. Reading it in a book will confirm them, strengthen them. And in some ways Young understands more clearly than they do what happened to them. They keep feeling they should blame the American people. Young can show them it was the officers who did it to them there, and the manager who did it to them in the hospital.

For Young shows clearly how the frontline therapists struggle, caught between the managing psychiatrist and the patients. These therapists, counsellors and nurses are at the bottom of the profession, without graduate degrees. They know that what the patients say is true. You can hear them bending to the patients in group therapy. You can see them arguing among themselves, angry with the 'model' they are forced to use. And you can read how the psychiatrist fired one therapist who disagreed with him and reduced another to tears.

These frontline therapists are confused. In one way, they know what's happening. In another way, they are afraid of losing their jobs. And they have no alternative politics for understanding and helping the patients. They could use a book which explained what happened in clinics like theirs. They would read it. As it is, this book is presented in such a way that mental nurses and junior counsellors won't read it. Young can and should write the book the therapists, mental nurses *and* veterans need. I hope it's his next book.

Notes

1   R Coles, *The Middle Americans* (Boston, 1971), quoted in C Appy, *Working Class War: American Combat Soldiers and Vietnam* (University of North Carolina Press, 1993), p42.
2   C Appy, op cit, pp16-17.
3   Ibid, pp166-167
4   See J Neale, 'Imperialism' in *Socialist Review*, 1990, 137, pp20-21 and A Callinicos et al, *Marxism and the New Imperialism* (Bookmarks, 1994).
5   M Baker, *Nam: The Vietnam War in the Words of the Men and Women Who Fought There* (New York, 1981), quoted in C Appy, op cit, pp143-144.
6   Vietnam Veterans Against the War, *The Winter Soldier Investigation: An Inquiry into American War Crimes* (Boston, 1972), quoted in C Appy, op cit, p294.
7   Ibid, pp294-295.

8   C Appy, op cit, p295.
9   P Marin, 'Coming to terms with Vietnam', *Harpers*, 1980, quoted in C Appy, op cit, p296.
10 R Coles, op cit, quoted in C Appy, op cit, pp42-43.
11 C Appy, op cit, pp38-43.
12 Ibid, p95.
13 Ibid, p246.
14 Ibid, p9.
15 Ibid, p247.
16 Ibid, pp244-245.
17 Ibid, p251.
18 Ibid, p245.
19 Ibid, p235.
20 If you find yourself pressed by an editor or publisher to write such a chapter, write a bibliographic essay for the end instead. It looks classier and it's more use to the reader.
21 A Young, op cit, p254.

Bookwatch: Marxism and science

PHIL GASPER

Marxists have more than one reason to take an interest in science. From a straightforwardly practical point of view, it is hard to be a political activist in the 1990s without dealing with some of the many ways in which science and technology have an impact on modern society—from the development of computers, to global warming, to the use of biological determinist arguments to defend the status quo. So from this perspective alone, there are obviously good reasons to have at least some understanding of science and the ways in which it is used and misused. But science is not just important for Marxists—Marxism is important for science. Marxism attempts to offer a comprehensive framework for understanding human society, and whatever else it is, science is obviously a product of human society. Marxists thus reject the view that science can be adequately understood in abstraction from the social and historical circumstances in which it develops. At the same time, however, Marxists (at least those who are genuinely attempting to continue the tradition initiated by Karl Marx and Friedrich Engels) reject the currently fashionable view that science is *merely* a social construct, simply one point of view among many, lacking any special objective validity.

This means that Marxists have to be both critics and defenders of science. We are critical of the way in which capitalist priorities distort the development of science. It is not simply that many scientific discoveries are misused in capitalist society, although it is certainly true that, for example, technology which could make work easier for everyone often means instead speed-up for some and unemployment for others. More fundamentally, however, scientific theories themselves often reflect, either implicitly or explicitly, assumptions which are rooted in capitalist ideology. One central example of this phenomenon is the reductionist assumption that complex systems can always be adequately explained in terms of the interaction of their parts, an assumption which reflects the individualism of capitalist society itself, and which has proved totally inadequate as the basis for a satisfactory scientific understanding of the world.

Yet Marxists are also defenders of science and its accomplishments—indeed, sometimes even enthusiasts for scientific research and discoveries. It is a basic assumption of Marxist theory that human beings have the capacity to expand their understanding of, and control over, the world in which we live. The development of the natural sciences thus represents, albeit in a distorted form, a triumph of human reason. Marx and Engels' admiration for science is clear from the fact that they describe their own materialist conception of history as providing a scientific understanding of the social world, and not simply the view of a single social class or historical period. Despite the distortions of science that often result from the influence of ruling class ideology, the natural sciences under capitalism have achieved a high degree of objectivity. Indeed, the relentless competition of capitalist society and the system's constant need to expand, promote theoretical and technical innovations which are then rigorously tested in terms of their practical consequences. Thus shortcomings in our understanding of the natural world are often ruthlessly exposed, and we are forced to come up with ideas that describe the world around us more accurately. As the philosopher of science Peter Railton has put it:

> In contrast to the contemplative or speculative ideal of precapitalist intellectual elites and the heavily restricted possibilities for competition and innovation under feudal modes of production or within such feudal institutions as the early universities, the rise of capitalism gives enormous impetus and scope to the pursuit of inquiry in ways that increase the possibility of receiving and responding to causal feedback from natural phenomena.[1]

The Marxist understanding of science thus offers a third way between the increasingly sterile opposition between 'internalist' rationalists (who attempt to explain the development of science internally, without reference to its social context) and 'externalist' relativists (who argue implicitly or explicitly that science develops as the result of external, and non-rational, social forces) that dominates mainstream history, sociology and philosophy of science.[2] Unlike the internalists who believe that science can be understood as a self contained body of ideas, with a fixed method that guarantees its rationality and objectivity, Marxists argue that science is a socially embedded practice and that its basic concepts and methods have changed significantly over time. Unlike the externalists who conclude that, because science is a social practice with no fixed canon of methodological principles, its findings have no objective validity, Marxists claim that, at its best, science is a way of discovering the world's hidden causal structure, and that the development of science may even help to undermine assumptions which reflect the dominant ideology.

This article will briefly review what some of the major figures in the Marxist tradition have had to say about science (for those who want to examine this tradition in greater detail, Helena Sheehan's *Marxism and the Philosophy of Science* can be recommended as a generally reliable one volume guide[3]) and then go on to make some suggestions about where to start reading about both the history of science and the current state of the natural sciences. I begin with Marx himself, partly for the obvious reason that he is the founder of our tradition, and partly because it is often falsely claimed that admiration for science, and the belief that Marxism throws light on the natural sciences, represent a distortion of Marx's views begun after his death by Engels. This view, as we shall see, is mistaken.

The Marxist tradition

Marx himself wrote no systematic treatise on science, but throughout his writings there are numerous scattered passages in which he comments on the nature of science and on general questions of methodology. There are also several places in which Marx compares his own historical, economic and political studies with the kind of research carried out by natural scientists. In *Capital*, for instance, he likens his 'scientific analysis of competition', based on an account of the 'inner nature of capital', to the way in which astronomers explained the 'apparent motions of the heavenly bodies' by developing a theory of 'their real motions...which are not directly perceptible by the senses'.[4]

There are few discussions of Marx's views on science, and those which do exist (such as David-Hillel Ruben's *Marxism and Materialism*[5] or Patrick Murray's *Marx's Theory of Scientific Knowledge*[6]) tend to be highly academic, so there is little alternative to plunging into Marx's writings themselves. Most of Marx's explicit comments on methodology and science are scattered in such works as *The Holy Family*, *The Economic and Philosophical Manuscripts*, the *Theses on Feuerbach*, *The German Ideology*, the *Grundrisse*, *Capital*, and in his correspondence.[7] But two of the most extensive discussions—the Introduction to the *Grundrisse* and notes Marx made on a book by Adolph Wagner—are conveniently available in a single volume, *Texts on Method*, edited by Terrell Carver.[8]

From Marx's direct remarks and his own practice, a relatively systematic account of science emerges. To begin with, while recognising that 'sense-experience must be the basis of all science',[9] Marx is well aware that sense experience cannot always be taken at face value (to take a simple example, it does not appear that the earth is moving) and he emphatically rejects the empiricist view that science is largely concerned with systematising what is directly observable rather than with discovering underlying causes. Empiricism is a restricted method of thought which views the world as a collection of dead facts. As the philosopher Allen Wood notes, Marx 'criticises empiricists for emphasising observation too much at the expense of theory, and for treating scientific concepts and theories only as convenient mechanisms for relating isolated facts rather than as attempts to capture the structure of reality'.[10]

In the contemporary philosophical jargon, Marx is a scientific realist who holds that science aims to give us knowledge of the underlying structure of an independently existing material world.[11] He notes that 'all science would be superfluous if the outward appearance and the essence of things directly coincided'.[12] He takes it to be obvious that there are 'sensuous objects, really distinct from the thought objects'[13] so that 'the priority of external nature remains unassailed',[14] and he mocks the views of the Young Hegelian philosophers in the 1840s by likening them to what he obviously regards as the absurd view that the world is constructed by consciousness:

> *Once upon a time a valiant fellow had the idea that men were drowned in water only because they were possessed with the idea of gravity. If they were to knock this notion out of their heads, say by stating it to be a superstition, a religious concept, they would be sublimely proof against any danger from water. His whole life long he fought against the illusion of gravity, of whose harmful results all statistics brought him new and manifold evidence. This honest fellow was the type of the new revolutionary philosophers in Germany...*[15]

This much ought to be elementary. Yet surprisingly enough, many influential commentators have argued that Marx was not a realist, and that he did not believe that the natural world exists independently of our knowledge of it. Perhaps the first to come to this conclusion was the 20th century Hungarian Marxist Georg Lukács, who claimed in the 1920s that to distinguish between 'thought and existence' is to accept 'a rigid duality'.[16] Lukács abandoned this view in the 1930s after reading Marx's

Economic and Philosophical Manuscripts, which convinced him of the importance of recognising the 'ontological objectivity of nature',[17] but many others (including the Polish philosopher Leszek Kolakowski[18]) have advocated similar views since then. Often, Marx's 'Second Thesis on Feuerbach' is taken to support this interpretation:

> The question whether objective truth belongs to human thinking is not a question of theory but a practical question. It is in practice than man must prove the truth, ie, the actuality and might, the this-sidedness of his thinking. The dispute over the actuality or non-actuality of thinking isolated from practice is a purely scholastic question.[19]

Commentators who deny that Marx was a realist claim that this passage shows that he defined truth in terms of practical success, not in terms of some kind of correspondence with independent reality, and that he rejected arguments about whether thought actually does correspond with reality as 'scholastic'. But this is to misread Marx's (admittedly somewhat obscure) formulation. His claim is that practical success is a *guide* to truth, not that truth is literally no more than practical success, and what he rejects as scholastic is not the question about whether thought corresponds to reality, but the attempt to answer that question purely theoretically, without reference to practice. In fact there are numerous passages where Marx explicitly accepts a correspondence view of truth. In the Afterword to the second German edition of *Capital*, for instance, Marx says that an adequate description is one in which 'the life of the subject-matter is ideally reflected as in a mirror', and he adds that 'the ideal is nothing else than the material world reflected by the human mind, and translated into forms of thought'.[20]

What this all amounts to is that our beliefs and theories are correct only in so far as they copy, correspond to, or reflect some aspects of a distinct reality, just as an accurate map represents some aspects of an (obviously distinct) geographical area. However, Marx is quite clear that it does not follow from this that truth can be obtained simply by, so to speak, holding a mirror up to nature. That, he thinks, was the mistake of the empiricists who thought that the world would simply imprint knowledge on our passive minds. But knowledge can only be obtained by a combination of actively constructing theories which attempt to understand what is going on beneath surface appearances, and by actively intervening in the world to see if these ideas can survive the test of practice. A theory of what it is for a claim to be true is one thing. A theory of knowledge (which will tell us how to obtain truth) is quite another. Our ideas are correct when they correspond with independent reality, but it is generally no simple matter to establish that such a correspondence actually holds.

Most importantly, Marx is aware that there is no timeless, ahistorical set of concepts out of which scientific theories are to be constructed, and no timeless, ahistorical scientific method by which such theories can be tested. As our knowledge of the material world develops, our understanding of the appropriate methods to use to find out more about the world, and our understanding of the concepts appropriate to describe it, develop as well. Moreover, methods and concepts may well be subject matter specific—what is appropriate in one area will probably not be appropriate in another. As one commentator notes, Marx insists that there is 'a dialectic of *concept* and *fact*', because the categories which we use to describe experience must be carefully scrutinised and grounded in the particular subject matter under examination.[21] The various concepts in physics—such as mass, velocity and energy, for example—did not arise automatically from experience, but were developed by a long and complex process of abstraction, and the same holds true for the very different concepts employed in cell biology or in meteorology or in any of the other areas of science.

Marx thus sees science as a dialectical process in the sense that its methods and concepts, as well as its theories, develop over time in dynamic interaction with one another and with the material world, allowing progressively more accurate descriptions of reality to emerge. But science for Marx is also dialectical in two other senses. First, empirical scientific inquiry reveals a world of dynamic, interconnected processes—processes which frequently involve elements which not only interact but are in conflict with one another, and which thus give the system to which they belong an inherent tendency to develop. Over time these developments can lead to sudden radical changes in the system as a whole. The dialectic, according to Marx, 'includes in its comprehension and affirmative recognition of the existing state of things, at the same time also, the recognition of the negation of that state, of its inevitable breaking up; because it regards every historical developed social form as in fluid movement, and therefore takes into account its transient nature not less than its momentary existence'.[22] Marx is here speaking specifically of society, but it is clear from other comments he made—for example, his observations on Darwin's theory of evolution discussed below, and his remark that 'Hegel's discovery regarding the *law that merely quantitative changes turn into qualitative changes*…holds good alike in history and natural science'[23]—that he thought the same general description applied to the natural world too. Nature, in other words, is itself dialectical, so adequate theories in the natural sciences will have a dialectical structure.

Second, because the natural world has a complex, dialectical structure, the best way to present a scientific account of some aspect of that world may be to begin with a relatively abstract model that attempts to isolate the system's underlying tendencies, and then to show how more complex models, which capture more and more of the concrete phenomena, can be developed dialectically from the original abstraction. Marx's own presentation of economic theory exhibits this dialectical structure. In *Capital* he presents 'a hierarchy of theoretical models, ascending by successive approximation from very abstract models representing the basic social forms present in modern bourgeois society up to fuller, more detailed models of this society'.[24] If Marx is right, then essentially the same process is likely to be followed in other successful areas of science as well, as indeed it is.[25]

In addition to advocating a realist and dialectical conception of science, Marx emphasises that science can only be fully understood in its broader social context. Where, he asks in *The German Ideology*, 'would natural science be without industry and commerce? Even this "pure" natural science is provided with an aim, as with its material, only through trade and industry'.[26] Or as he puts it in *Capital*, 'modern industry ... makes science a productive force distinct from labour and presses it into the service of capital'.[27] Thus, for example, the scientific revolution and the rise of modern physics in the 17th century can only be properly understood in the context of the development of capitalism. Bluntly put, the new science emerged because it met the material interests of the bourgeoisie.

It does not follow from this, however, that science is no more than bourgeois ideology. It is true that capitalism may set the agenda for scientific research, and that capitalist ideology may have a significant influence on the development of scientific theories. Thus for example, Marx notes that 'Descartes, in defining animals as mere machines, saw with the eyes of the manufacturing period'.[28] But at the same time, economic competition, the expansion of production and the need to find more efficient ways of generating profits gives the bourgeoisie an interest in acquiring objective knowledge of the natural world, since without such knowledge they will fail to accomplish their goals. So while capitalist ideology may often limit scientific development, the need to construct practically successful theories allows natural science under capitalism to achieve a considerable degree of objectivity. To put the point slightly differently, Marx recognises that the objectivity of scientific results does not require impartial or value-free motivations for engaging in scientific research, but only requires that the values which drive science are ones which are likely more often than not to lead to more accurate theories of the world.[29]

Moreover, once the process of scientific inquiry is under way, it can produce results that are at odds with its initial assumptions—results which contradict bourgeois ideology and which fit more satisfactorily into a Marxist world view. Thus, for example, by the mid-19th century it was already becoming evident that purely mechanical models—which attempt to explain all natural phenomena in terms of simple forces acting on the unchanging elements of a system[30]—were inadequate in physics (let alone in biology), and much 20th century work in physics and biology has led to the questioning of reductionist assumptions, which claim that complex wholes can always be fully understood by decomposing them into their constituent parts.

All these themes in Marx's writings are developed at much greater length in the works of Engels, particularly in his *Anti-Dühring* (1878), *Ludwig Feuerbach and the Outcome of Classical German Philosophy* (1888) and *Dialectics of Nature* (not published during Engels' lifetime). These books present Engels' attempts to formulate a sophisticated, non-reductionist and dialectical version of materialism, to develop a comprehensive, scientific world view which sees a fundamental unity between the natural and social worlds, and to articulate a dialectical account of scientific method. Unfortunately, for much of the 20th century Engels' discussions of these questions suffered a dual fate. In the Soviet bloc, at least from the 1930s, a caricatured version of Engels' views was treated as holy writ, and serious critical discussion was virtually non-existent. By contrast, in the West Engels' work was either completely ignored or rejected as worthless, even by authors who are otherwise relatively sympathetic commentators on the Marxist tradition. David McLellan, for example, asserts that 'it is difficult to believe that Engels' views contain much of lasting value either to science or to philosophy'.[31] Such dismissive judgments are typically coupled with the claim that Engels' views on such issues marked a sharp break with Marx's own ideas.

I have already indicated how seriously mistaken the latter view is, and recent scholarship has confirmed that there is no evidence of any fundamental disagreement between Marx's and Engels' ideas about science.[32] What is true is that Engels had a much more detailed grasp of contemporary scientific developments than Marx. In fact, the 20th century biologist J B S Haldane regarded Engels as 'probably the most widely educated man of his day',[33] and the contemporary philosopher of science Hilary Putnam describes him as 'one of the most scientifically learned men of his century'.[34] Particularly in the *Dialectics of Nature* (which, it should be noted, was still a work in progress at the time of his death), Engels uses his wide ranging scientific knowledge to illustrate the claim that science reveals a world of complex, interacting processes that can only be adequately understood from a dialectical perspective. Some of Engels' examples are not very convincing, and others depend on scientific views which have since been superseded, but in general the ideas that Engels develops—and in particular his rejection of the mechanistic view that attempts to understand wholes as no more than the sum of their passive, unchanging parts—have stood the test of time remarkably well. There is much more to be said about Engels' views, but I shall not explore them further here, since they have already been extensively discussed in two excellent essays in this journal—John Rees's article 'Engels' Marxism' and Paul McGarr's article 'Engels and Natural Science' (both in *International Socialism* 65).

Following Engels' death in 1895, the major intellectual figures of the Second International produced little of interest on the nature of science. This may be a reflection of the general fact that thinkers such as Karl Kautsky had a profoundly undialectical grasp of Marxist theory, as well as the specific fact that none of the Marxist theorists of the next generation came close to matching the breadth of Engels' scientific knowledge. In addition, Engels' most detailed discussion of science, in the *Dialectics of Nature*, remained unpublished until the 1920s. If this work had been available at the time of Engels' death, it might have stimulated more thought on these questions.

It was mainly among Russian Marxists that science became a central topic of discussion, following the defeat of the 1905 Revolution.[35] In this period a number of Marxist intellectuals became highly influenced by philosophical ideas about science that had emerged in western Europe in the previous two decades. From the late 19th century onwards a general mood of pessimism came to characterise influential segments of the bourgeois intelligentsia in western Europe as they became increasingly aware of the disruptive and dehumanising effects of capitalist development, and this pessimism provided the intellectual soil in which religious, idealist, irrationalist and even mystical ideas could flourish. This mood coincided with a major crisis in the natural sciences, where it was becoming increasingly evident that the basic ideas of classical physics did not provide an adequate basis to understand new phenomena such as electromagnetism and radioactivity. Against this background, various European scientists and philosophers, such as the Austrian physicist Ernst Mach, and Henri Poincaré and Pierre Duhem in France, in effect offered a compromise. They attempted to reinterpret science in such a way that its rationality was preserved and the crisis in physics resolved, while at the same time denying that science had any broader metaphysical (and in particular materialist) implications. This left the door open for those (like the Catholic Duhem) who wanted to embrace science together with the anti-materialist metaphysics of their choice.

It was in fact the extreme empiricism of Mach,[36] which he called 'empirio-criticism', that had the biggest impact on a group of Russian

Marxists that included prominent Bolshevik activists and intellectuals such as Alexander Bogdanov, Anatoly Lunacharsky and Maxim Gorky. Mach himself had no time for religion or irrationalism, but he came to view science as simply a way of systematising patterns in the sensory experience of observers. According to Mach, all we are directly aware of are our own sensations, and all that scientific laws tell us is that in some particular set of circumstances one set of sensations will be followed by another. The problems in physics are sidestepped by resolutely refusing to interpret a theory's conceptual and mathematical machinery as referring to anything that cannot be directly observed—all that matters, on this view, is that the theory is capable of predicting observable phenomena. Since, however, Mach holds that the only directly observable phenomena are our own sense experiences, his ideas amount to little more than a sophisticated revival of the subjective idealism of Bishop Berkeley (the 18th century Irish philosopher who argued that only minds and their ideas exist). Nevertheless, Mach's philosophy proved highly influential. Einstein, for example, claimed to be influenced by Mach when he rejected the idea of absolute simultaneity in his special theory of relativity, on the grounds that such a relation cannot be measured (see below).[37] Of course, the fact that Mach's views helped Einstein to reach some creative conclusions does not mean that the former are correct. Whatever Einstein may have believed at the time, the theory of relativity is logically quite independent of Mach's epistemology.[38]

Among the Russian Marxists, it was Bogdanov who most enthusiastically welcomed Mach's ideas, and who attempted to integrate them with Marxism in his multi-volume study *Empirio-Monism* (1904-1906). Bogdanov attempted to bridge the chasm between idealism and materialism by arguing that neither mind nor matter is fundamental, but that both are constructs from experience, and that his version of monism which emphasised the active intervention of the subject, captured the spirit, if not the letter, of what Marx had meant by 'materialism'.[39] Bogdanov's views came under attack from the founder of Russian Marxism, Georgi Plekhanov (by this time a Menshevik), and Plekhanov's protégé Lyubov Axelrod, but the definitive refutation was produced by Lenin in his *Materialism and Empirio-Criticism* (1909), which (despite being repetitious at times) is both a powerful argument against all versions of empiricism, and an analysis of the social circumstances which give rise to such views. Like Berkeley before them, Mach and his fellow thinkers claimed that their views are quite compatible with the commonsense belief that there is a physical world, since the commonsense belief can supposedly be translated into a claim about sensations. Lenin points out the absurdity of this proposal:

> *The 'naive realism' of any healthy person who has not been an inmate of a*

*lunatic asylum or a pupil of the idealist philosophers consists in the view that things, the environment, the world, exist **independently** of our sensation, of our consciousness, of our **self** and of man in general. The same **experience**... that has produced in us the firm conviction that **independently** of us there exist other people, and not mere complexes of my sensations of high, short, yellow, hard, etc—this same **experience** produces in us the conviction that things, the world, the environment exist independently of us. Our sensation, our consciousness is only **an image** of the external world... Materialism **deliberately** makes the 'naïve' belief of mankind the foundation of its theory of knowledge.*

A little later Lenin raises another uncomfortable question for the defenders of empirio-criticism: 'Did nature exist prior to man?'—and he then proceeds to dissect the contortions in which they engage in an effort to avoid the apparent contradictions of their view:

*No man in the least educated or in the least healthy doubts that the earth existed at a time when there **could not** have been any life on it, any sensation...and consequently the whole theory of Mach and Avenarius, from which it follows that the earth is a complex of sensations...or 'complexes of elements in which the psychical and physical are identical'...is **philosophical obscurantism**, the reduction of subjective idealism to absurdity.*[40]

However, Lenin does not confine himself to the entertaining task of picking philosophical holes in his opponents' views. In an important chapter on 'The Recent Revolution of Natural Science and Philosophical Idealism' he takes up the crisis in physics (though not Einstein's proposed resolution of the problems) and in particular the claim that 'matter has disappeared', arguing that while the new developments in areas such as electrodynamics refute mechanistic materialism, they actually support a dialectical materialism that conceives of the elements of the physical world as dynamic and interactive, rather than as passive and unchanging.

The one serious weakness of Lenin's discussion is that, in his eagerness to refute idealism, he sometimes bends the stick too far and ends up apparently advocating a crude copy theory of knowledge, according to which knowledge of our surroundings is not the result of our active intervention in the world, but is simply imprinted directly on our passive minds in a way that immediately enables us to grasp that our ideas are correct. The claim that Lenin is committed to this untenable view was first made by Axelrod and later repeated by the Dutch council communist Anton Pannekoek, the German philosopher Karl Korsch and others. If Lenin did hold this view in 1909, he abandoned it later—certainly by the time he composed his *Philosophical Notebooks* (1916), which discuss Hegel's logic. But it is also true that in some passages in *Materialism and Empirio-Criticism* he seems to make the mistake of confusing an account of what it means for a claim to be true (a theory of truth) with an account of how the truth of a claim can be established (a theory of knowledge), and is thus led from a perfectly sensible correspondence theory of truth to an unacceptable copy theory of knowledge.[41]

However, there are other passages in *Materialism and Empirio-Criticism* which make it clear that it is not Lenin's considered view that establishing the truth of a scientific claim is a straightforward matter. Indeed he is aware that our scientific views are generally only partially, relatively or approximately true, and that scientific progress does not result in absolute knowledge, but only in closer and closer approximations to the truth:

> *In the theory of knowledge, as in every other branch of science, we must think dialectically, that is, we must not regard our knowledge as ready-made and unalterable, but must determine how **knowledge** emerges from **ignorance**, how incomplete, inexact knowledge becomes more complete and more exact.*

Moreover, 'for dialectical materialism there is no impassable boundary between relative and absolute truth', even though all knowledge is historically conditioned:

> *From the standpoint of modern materialism, ie Marxism, the **limits** of approximation of our knowledge to the objective, absolute truth are historically conditional, but the existence of such truth is **unconditional**, and the fact that we are approaching nearer to it is also unconditional.*[42]

Lenin treats these ideas with greater subtlety and sophistication in the *Philosophical Notebooks*, but if we read *Materialism and Empirio-Criticism* charitably, there is no fundamental incompatibility between these works. *Materialism and Empirio-Criticism* defends the existence of an independently existing material world. The *Notebooks* explore the complex ways in which knowledge of such a world can be obtained. For further reflections on Lenin's views, see Sebastiano Timpanaro's *On Materialism*,[43] which also contains interesting discussions of several other issues surveyed in this article.

Despite Lenin's polemics, Bogdanov, Lunarcharsky and others did not renounce Mach's philosophy and continued to play a prominent role in the Bolshevik Party. Indeed, after the 1917 revolution, as intellectual life flourished, many of them were given prominent political and academic positions. Lunarcharsky became Commissar of Education. Bogdanov was appointed to the Communist Academy where he quickly became an advocate of 'proletarian culture' and helped launch the 'Proletkult' movement, which sought to replace bourgeois science, art and culture with new proletarian ideas. This movement soon came under attack from both Lenin and Trotsky, who criticised both its philosophical presuppositions and its political programme. In an essay on 'Proletarian Culture and Art' in *Literature and Revolution* (1923), Trotsky argues that despite its one sidedness science under capitalism has produced genuine knowledge which it would be folly to reject:

All science, in greater or lesser degree, unquestionably reflects the tendencies of the ruling class. The more closely science attaches itself to the practical tasks of conquering nature (physics, chemistry, natural science in general), the greater is its non-class and human contribution. The more deeply science is connected with the social mechanism of exploitation (political economy), or the more abstractly it generalises the entire experience of mankind (psychology, not in its experimental, physiological sense but in its so-called 'philosophic sense'), the more does it obey the class egotism of the bourgeoisie and the less significant is its contribution to the general sum of human knowledge. In the domain of the experimental sciences, there exist different degrees of scientific integrity and objectivity, depending upon the scope of the generalisations made. As a general rule, the bourgeois tendencies have found a much freer place for themselves in the higher spheres of methodological philosophy... But it would be naive to think that the proletariat must revamp critically all science inherited from the bourgeoisie, before applying it to socialist reconstruction. This is just the same as saying with the Utopian moralists: before building a new society, the proletariat must rise to the heights of communist ethics. As a matter of fact, the proletariat will reconstruct ethics as well as science radically, but he will do so after he will have reconstructed a new society, even though in the rough.

The supporters of Proletkult believed that the new society could not be built by using the tools inherited from the old. Trotsky argues in response that what such critics ignore is the dialectical nature of the envisaged social transformation:

The proletariat rejects what is clearly unnecessary, false and reactionary, and in the various fields of this reconstruction makes use of the methods and conclusions of present-day science, taking them necessarily with the percentage of reactionary class-alloy which is contained in them. The practical result will justify itself generally and on the whole, because such a use when controlled by a socialist goal will gradually manage and select the methods and conclusions of the theory. And by that time there will have grown up scientists who are educated under the new conditions. At any rate the proletariat will have to carry its socialist reconstruction to quite a high degree, that is, provide for real material security and for the satisfaction of society culturally before it will be able to carry out a general purification of science from top to bottom.[44]

In the mid-1920s Trotsky gave a number of speeches and wrote several short articles elaborating these themes, emphasising both the overall unity of the sciences and the specificity of methods and theories within particular domains. Scientific problems cannot be solved simply by mastering the general principles of Marxist theory. On the other hand, mastering a particular field of science is not a substitute for Marxist theory. 'Communism', he wrote, 'is not a substitute for chemistry. But the converse theorem is also true'.[45] Some of Trotsky's articles on science can be found in *Problems of Everyday Life*.[46] Despite his other preoccupations, Trotsky found time to write more on these and related scientific issues while in exile in the 1930s. The later writings are available as *Trotsky's Notebooks 1933-35: Writings on Lenin, Dialectics and Evolutionism*.[47] There is a helpful review of these notebooks in Chapter 5 of *The Algebra of Revolution* by John Rees.[48]

For much of the 1920s there was lively debate in the Soviet Union between various schools of thought on scientific questions, but this slowly came to an end as Stalin rose to power and consolidated his counter-revolution. Nevertheless, some of the path-breaking work done during this period was given a wider audience in 1931 when Stalin decided at the last minute to send a Soviet delegation headed by Bukharin to the Second International Congress of the History of Science and Technology in London. The various members of the delegation disagreed with one another about many issues, but the group as a whole had an electrifying—and polarising—effect on the conference. An extra session was added so that all of their papers could be discussed, and they were published as soon as the congress was over, in a volume entitled *Science at the Crossroads*,[49] which contains some of the most important Marxist discussions of science since Engels' *Dialectics of Nature*.

The most famous of the contributions to *Science at the Crossroads* is Boris Hessen's paper 'The Social and Economic Roots of Newton's *Principia*', which provides a detailed and brilliant analysis of the way in which classical physics was rooted in the economic and technological developments of the 17th century, decisively refuting the 'individual genius' view of the history of science. Hessen focuses on the period of the English Revolution of the 1640s, and examines the impact on theoretical physics of factors such as communications, water transport, mining, armaments and ballistics:

We have compared the main technical and physical problems of the period with the scheme of investigations governing physics during the period we are investigating, and we come to the conclusion that the scheme of physics was mainly determined by the economic and technical tasks which the rising bourgeoisie raised to the forefront.

But Hessen does not offer a crudely reductionist view. While economic and technical factors play a crucial role in shaping the development of science, they are not the whole story, and Hessen also discusses the influence of philosophical and political ideas, arguing that it is necessary to 'analyse more fully Newton's epoch, the class struggles during the English Revolution, and the political, philosophic and religious theories...reflected in the minds of the contemporaries of these struggles.'

Hessen's outstanding essay remains to this day the high watermark of 20th century Marxist analyses of science, expertly tracing the way in which a major scientific theory emerged from the interplay of material and ideological factors. Tragically, however, the period of intellectual vitality and debate which had begun with the 1917 revolution, and which eventually produced *Science at the Crossroads*, was almost at an end. Two years later, on the 50th anniversary of Marx's death, Bukharin was still able to edit another important collection, *Marxism and Modern Thought*,[50] which contains important discussions of 'Marxism and Natural Science' (Y M Uranovsky), 'The Old and the New Physics' (SI Vavilov) and 'Marx and Engels on Biology' (V L Komarov). But soon many of the contributors to the two volumes (including Bukharin and Hessen) were to become victims of Stalin's purges. The Stalinist destruction of critical scientific thought (indeed critical thought of all kinds) laid the groundwork for the great debacle of 'Lysenkoism', the movement named after the agronomist Trofim Lysenko who rose to a position of ascendancy in Soviet biology by denouncing modern genetics as inconsistent with dialectical materialism. Lysenko's views were not only a travesty of Marxist thought (since Marx and Engels utterly rejected the idea that one could refute or establish any scientific view on the basis of abstract philosophical categories), they were also eventually to result in major damage to Soviet agriculture.

While in the Soviet Union serious Marxist analysis of science came to an end in the 1930s, the work of Bukharin, Hessen and others had a major impact elsewhere, particularly in Britain, where a generation of radical scientists—including the physicist J D Bernal and the geneticist J B S Haldane became members or fellow travellers of the Communist Party and often brilliant popularisers of modern science.[51] Haldane wrote a regular column for the *Daily Worker* in the 1930s, some of which can be found in *On Being the Right Size*,[52] a contemporary collection of his essays edited by the evolutionary biologist John Maynard Smith. The prolific Bernal wrote numerous books offering a Marxist perspective on science. Before the war the most important was *The Social Function of Science*,[53] a long work which contains many interesting discussions, but which is also, unfortunately, thoroughly imbued with the spirit of 'socialism from above'.

History of science

After the Second World War a number of British Marxists continued the kind of detailed materialist analyses of the history of science pioneered by Hessen. Joseph Needham laboured for many years on his multi-volume *Science and Civilisation in Ancient China*.[54] Bernal wrote a comprehensive four volume study called *Science in History*[55] (originally published in 1954 and still in print). Stephen Mason covered the same territory more briefly in *Main Currents of Scientific Thought*[56] (also published under the title *A History of the Sciences*). However, the Cold War climate made it difficult to pursue such work. For example, according to the historian of science Robert M Young, Mason 'had to return to chemistry because he could not find work as a historian of science'.[57] As a result, there is disappointingly little history of science available from a Marxist point of view, apart from what are now the 'classics' of the 1940s and 1950s.

The books by Bernal and Mason mentioned above are still the best overall surveys. Bernal also wrote a history of physics before the 20th century called *The Extension of Man*.[58] The origins of science are briefly discussed in V Gordon Childe's *What Happened in History*.[59] On science in the ancient world see *Greek Science*[60] by Benjamin Farrington and *The Origins of Materialism*[61] by the American Trotskyist George Novack. Much of Greek science was lost after the collapse of the Roman Empire, but important ideas were preserved and developed in the Arab world and eventually passed on to western Europe. A brief survey of developments from the 12th century on can be found in Edward Grant, *Physical Science in the Middle Ages*.[62]

Standard works on the scientific revolution of the 16th and 17th centuries include Thomas Kuhn's book on *The Copernican Revolution*[63] and *The Birth of A New Physics*[64] by I Bernard Cohen, but the latter in particular should be supplemented by Hessen's classic essay. Another short, readable account, which covers chemistry and biology as well as physics, is Richard Westfall, *The Construction of Modern Science*.[65] Moving on to the 1800s there is *Science and Industry in the Nineteenth Century* by (once again) Bernal.[66] Most of the books mentioned here deal mainly with physics. For a history of chemistry see Mason's *Chemical Evolution*[67], and for a short history of geology read Stephen Jay Gould's excellent *Time's Arrow, Time's Cycle*.[68] Some books on the history of biology are mentioned below.

The physical sciences

Physics in the 20th century has undergone two major intellectual revolutions which Marx and Engels could obviously not have anticipated, but which nevertheless accord well with their general views about the dynamic of scientific development. The first revolution was the overthrow of Newton's classical mechanics by Einstein's special, and later general, theories of relativity. Contrary to popular misunderstanding, relativity theory does not say that 'everything is relative'. What Einstein did argue is that various physical properties and relations that Newtonian mechanics supposes to be independent of any particular frame of reference, and hence 'absolute', are in fact relative to particular frames of reference (just as whether one object is to the left or to the right of another, to use a rough analogy, depends on the frame of reference). These properties and relations include, contrary to 'common sense', spatial distances, time intervals and mass. Thus, for example, according to Einstein, whether or not two events take place simultaneously varies from one frame of reference (or, more precisely, inertial system) to another. From my frame of reference, two events may be measured as occurring at the same time, but if you are moving with respect to me, you may measure them as occurring at different times. If Einstein is right, neither measurement is incorrect. The events are simultaneous relative to the first frame of reference, but non-simultaneous relative to the second.

Einstein was led to this remarkable conclusion from his commitment to the principle of relativity, which holds that the fundamental laws of physics hold in every frame of reference and that no possible measurement can be performed that would distinguish one uniformly moving reference system from another. Thus a passenger in a sealed train moving at uniform velocity with respect to its surroundings would experience the same laws of physics as if the train were stationary. The principle of relativity had been accepted by many physicists since the 17th century, but Einstein recognised that, if it is true, then it is impossible to reconcile Newtonian mechanics with the theory of electromagnetism developed by Faraday, Maxwell and others in the 19th century.

According to Newton, a body accelerated long enough can reach any velocity, including the speed of light. But if this were possible, then Maxwell's equations would not correctly describe the behaviour of electromagnetic phenomena (which, of course, includes light waves) in every frame of reference. To take one of Einstein's own examples, imagine an observer illuminated by a light source and holding a mirror in front of himself. If the observer and the mirror moved at the speed of light, the observer would not see his own reflection, since light from the source would never reach the mirror. Einstein concluded that the speed of light must be constant in every frame of reference (so that the speed of light is independent of the speed of its source), and that nothing can move faster than the speed of light. If time is simply a system of relations between physical events and objects, then the relativity of simultaneity follows from this. More generally, Einstein preserved the principle of relativity by saying that the measurements of space, time and mass are dependent on the relative motion of the measurer, thus modifying our notions of all three.

Various amazing consequences follow from Einstein's theory. One is the claim that the rate of moving clocks is slower than that of clocks at rest. Another is the claim that as a body accelerates its mass increases, making it impossible for it to exceed the speed of light. Yet another is Einstein's most famous equation, $E = mc^2$, which asserts the equivalence of energy and matter and is the theoretical basis for nuclear fission. The mass of an object is, as it were, concentrated energy, so that what were once two separate concepts turn out to be inextricably linked. The theory of relativity also leads to the unification of space and time into the single notion of space-time, an idea first proposed by Hermann Minkowski in 1908. 'Henceforth', wrote Minkowski, 'space by itself and time by itself, are doomed to fade away into mere shadows, and only a kind of union of the two will preserve independent reality'.[69] The special theory of relativity, initially put forward by Einstein in a series of papers published in 1905, develops these ideas in the context of frames of reference moving uniformly relative to one another. The general theory, which took a further decade to develop, considers accelerating frames of reference and brings in gravitational phenomena.

Einstein's initial conviction that his theories were correct was based as much on 'intuition' (in other words, a hunch) as empirical data, but experimental and observational evidence soon demonstrated that his ideas were right. Several things concerning his success are interesting from a Marxist perspective, including how Newtonian physics, a set of ideas that had dominated science for over two centuries, and which appeared to be invincible—eventually ran into insuperable contradictions, and came crashing down. At the same time, however, the new Einsteinian synthesis preserves the elements of truth in classical mechanics, showing how Newton's laws are approximations to the truth for systems in which velocities are low compared to the speed of light. Moreover, Einstein's theory showed that the basic concepts of classical physics—not just the laws it had formulated using them—needed to be modified, and that apparently distinct features of the world are in fact deeply interrelated.

My exposition of these ideas has been of necessity highly compressed, but hopefully it will whet your appetite to read more about them. Einstein wrote a number of popular introductions to his own views, including one simply titled *Relativity*.[70] My favourite, however, is *The Evolution of Physics*,[71] which he co-authored with his student Leopold Infeld in the 1930s, and which also gives a historical account of physics from Galileo to the mid-20th century. *Einstein's Legacy*,[72] by the Nobel laureate Julian Schwinger, is a clear and up to date presentation. On the general theory in particular, see Clifford Will, *Was Einstein Right?*,[73] a systematic account of the evidence for Einstein's theory and the way in which subsequent thinkers have built on his ideas. For discussion of the evolution of Einstein's views, the essays in Gerald Holton's *Thematic Origins of Scientific Thought*[74] are helpful. The most comprehensive biography is *Einstein: The Life and Times*[75] by Ronald Clark, which, in addition to Einstein's early scientific work, also discusses his pacifist-socialist politics, his soft Zionism and his role in the development of the atomic bomb.

The second major revolution in 20th century physics came with the rise of quantum mechanics in the 1920s. Relativity theory proposes radically new conceptions of space and time. Quantum physics breaks with the idea of a deterministic universe in which every event has some prior cause, and proposes instead that at the subatomic level some events are matters of pure chance or, more precisely, take place in accordance with probabilistic rather than deterministic laws. Ironically, although quantum mechanics developed out of work done by Einstein and another German physicist, Max Planck, in the early 20th century, Einstein himself refused to reconcile himself to this idea, arguing to his death that 'God does not play dice with the universe' and thus that there must be something wrong with the theory. Yet quantum theory is enormously successful. It allows physicists to describe with great accuracy the behaviour of subatomic phenomena, the properties of the atomic nucleus and the structure and properties of molecules and solids. Quantum mechanics also provides the basis for technological innovations ranging from lasers to silicon chips.

At the same time, however, there is no clear understanding of why the theory works so well, or any agreed solutions to the conceptual and philosophical problems which it raises. For example, quantum physics does not simply tell us that there is radical indeterminacy in the world, it also seems to require that subatomic phenomena behave both as particles and as waves, which common sense tells us is impossible, and that in some circumstances physical particles can influence each other even though physical interaction between them is impossible. The physicists David Bohm and B J Hiley interpret 'the quantum interconnectedness of distant systems' in terms that Marx and Engels would have relished:

*A quantum many-body system cannot properly be analysed into indepen-
dently existent parts, with fixed and determinate dynamical relationships
between each of the 'parts'. Rather, the parts are seen to be in an immediate
connection, in which their dynamical relationships depend, in an irreducible
way, on the state of the whole system (and indeed on that of broader systems
in which they are contained, extending ultimately and in principle to the
entire universe). Thus one is led to a new notion of **unbroken wholeness**
which denies the classical idea of analysability of the world into separately
and independently existing parts.*[76]

The views of Bohm and Hiley, however, are accepted only by a minority.
On the standard view of quantum theory (known as the Copenhagen
interpretation), subatomic particles do not have determinate properties
prior to an act of measurement. Instead the various possible states the
system can be in are defined by a probability wave which only 'collapses' when an observation is made. This gives rise to the by now
well-known paradox of Schrödinger's cat. We are asked to imagine the
animal locked in a box with a vial of poison gas that will only be
released if a radioactive atom decays within a certain time. But if the
atom has no determinate state until a measurement is taken, does this
mean that the cat is also poised in an indeterminate state, neither dead
nor alive, until the apparatus is observed? Puzzles like this have led some
physicists to embrace bizarre idealist views, in which human consciousness determines the nature of the physical world (despite the fact that
human consciousness only evolved comparatively recently). Others have
suggested that each time an indeterministic quantum event takes place
the universe 'splits' so that for each possible outcome there is a separate
reality in which it takes place.

The genuine problems associated with quantum physics give plenty
of opportunities for mystics and cranks to claim that the theory supports
their own views, so care is needed in navigating between the large
numbers of popularisations that have been published. One of the better
guides is Nick Herbert's *Quantum Reality*,[77] which gives a clear exposition of the basic theory, and carefully explains the various interpretations
of the theory that have been proposed and why none of them is fully satisfactory. *In Search of Schrödinger's Cat*[78] by the prolific science writer
John Gribbin is also a good introduction. Gribbin has recently published
a sequel called *Schrödinger's Kittens and the Search For Quantum
Reality*.[79] A more advanced discussion is provided by David Albert in
Quantum Mechanics and Experience.[80] In the early 1980s the BBC
broadcast a series of radio interviews with leading quantum physicists
which are now available as *The Ghost In the Atom*[81] edited by P C W
Davies and J R Brown. The first chapter of this book is another good
brief introduction to quantum mechanics.

A slightly more advanced introduction, but still reasonably accessible, is Alastair Rae's short book *Quantum Physics: Illusion or Reality?*[82] Rae concludes with a sympathetic discussion of how the anti-reductionist ideas of the Nobel Prize winning physicist Ilya Prigogine may offer a solution to the problems of quantum theory. Prigogine, whose main work has been in the field of thermodynamics, rejects the idea that we can understand the changes that take place in, say, a gas, in terms of its micro-constituents, and argues that we must instead explain the micro-world in terms of changes at the macro level. In terms that Engels would have approved, Prigogine describes this as a shift from 'being' to 'becoming'. Exactly how this relates to the problems of quantum mechanics is too complicated to explain here, but if you are intrigued read Rae's book or Prigogine's own popular introduction to these ideas, *Order Out of Chaos*[83] (co-authored with Isabelle Stengers).

The development of relativity theory and quantum physics, together with technological developments, have enabled cosmologists to develop detailed models of the history and structure of the universe. The most well known introduction to this field is Stephen Hawking's bestselling *A Brief History of Time*.[84] Duncan Blackie's review article 'Revolution in Science' (in *International Socialism* 42) discusses Hawking's book from a Marxist perspective and points out some of its weaknesses. *Perfect Symmetry*[85] by Heinz Pagels covers the same territory as Hawking's book but in greater detail. Steven Weinberg's discussion of the 'big bang' theory, *The First Three Minutes*,[86] is now a little dated but still worth reading. Gribbin's *In Search of the Big Bang*[87] is a slightly more recent discussion.

Today Weinberg is one of a number of physicists who believe that a 'theory of everything', which unifies relativity theory and quantum mechanics, may soon be within our grasp. He makes his case in *Dreams of a Final Theory*.[88] Another introduction to these controversial ideas can be found in Davies and Brown (eds), *Superstrings: A Theory of Everything?*[89] which, like their book on quantum physics, is a collection of interviews originally broadcast on the BBC. It is worth remembering, however, that in the late 19th century physicists had similar hopes that their discipline was nearly complete. Given the serious difficulties that continue to exist with quantum theory, and the fact that current models of the structure of the universe all face problems, the 20th century scientists who dream of the end of physics are likely to prove as far off the mark as their forerunners 100 years ago.

One other area of physics (or more accurately, applied mathematics)—chaos theory—deserves at least brief mention here, if only because it has been so frequently misrepresented by postmodernists and others who want to claim that the world is essentially beyond rational understanding. In fact, chaos theory does not claim that the world is essentially unintelligible, but rather attempts to use sophisticated mathematical techniques to show that even apparently random behaviour in dynamic systems can be analysed and understood. The best book length introduction to the field is still James Gleick's *Chaos*.[90] A more advanced account is *Does God Play Dice?*[91] by Ian Stewart. Stewart also has a very short introduction to chaos theory (called 'Do Dice Play God?') in his more recent book *Nature's Numbers*,[92] which is a good non-mathematical introduction to some basic ideas in mathematics. There is also an excellent brief overview in Paul McGarr's article 'Order Out of Chaos' in *International Socialism* 48.

The biological sciences

The Russian biologist Theodosius Dobzhansky (one of the founders of the modern 'synthesis' of evolutionary biology and genetics in the 1930s) once remarked, 'Nothing in biology makes sense except in the light of evolution'.[93] The development of the theory of evolution marks the beginning of modern biology, and for anyone who has the time, the best starting point is the work of Charles Darwin himself. *The Origin of Species*,[94] originally published in 1859, is perhaps the last great work of science written for, and still accessible to, a general audience. The main difficulty that faces the contemporary reader is not so much Darwin's prose, but grasping the overall structure of his most famous book. Darwin tells us in the final chapter that 'this whole volume is one long argument', but the *Origin* is so densely packed with discussions of specific cases that it can be difficult to see the wood for the trees. Nevertheless, as the book proceeds, Darwin painstakingly builds an overwhelming case for evolution by natural selection, carefully presenting the detailed evidence which he had spent over 20 years accumulating.

Darwin begins the *Origin* by drawing our attention to the ability of plant and animal breeders to drastically alter the characteristics of a group of organisms over a series of generations by permitting only individuals with desired traits to reproduce. He then argues (in chapters 2 and 3) that an analogous process takes place in nature without conscious human intervention.[95] The organisms in a given population typically differ in various ways from one another, and some of these differences can be passed on to their progeny. If there are too many organisms for a given environment to sustain, then those that by chance are slightly better suited to survive and reproduce will tend to have more offspring, so that the favourable traits will tend to proliferate from one generation to the next. Evolutionary change is thus the result of a 'struggle for existence' which:

...inevitably follows from the high rate at which all organic beings tend to increase. Every being, which during its natural lifetime produces several eggs or seeds, must suffer destruction during some period of its life, and during some season or occasional year, otherwise, on the principle of the geometrical increase, its numbers would quickly become so inordinately great that no country could support the product. Hence, as more individuals are produced than can possibly survive, there must in every case be a struggle for existence, either one individual with another of the same species, or with the individuals of distinct species, or with the physical conditions of life.[96]

Over time a population of organisms can become better and better adapted to its environment, and the characteristics of its members at the end of the process may be very different from those of their ancestors. Darwin later claimed that the basic idea of natural selection was suggested to him by Thomas Malthus's reactionary *Essay On Population*, which argues (on the basis of no evidence) that human populations will always outgrow the available food supply. Recent scholarship has shown that Darwin's claim is something of an oversimplification,[97] but Malthus was an influence, as was the economic thought of Adam Smith. As the contemporary evolutionary biologist Stephen Jay Gould notes, however, 'the source of an idea is one thing, its truth or fruitfulness is another.' He goes on:

In this case, it is ironic that Adam Smith's system of laissez faire does not work in his own domain of economics, for it leads to oligopoly and revolution, rather than to order and harmony. Struggle among individuals does, however, seem to be the law of nature.[98]

Having established the reality of natural selection, Darwin goes on to argue (in chapters 4 and 5) that this process is capable of giving rise not simply to new varieties but, if it continues long enough, to new species. In the next few chapters (6 to 8), he deals with objections to the idea that natural selection—or 'descent with modification'—can account for the characteristics of all existing species (even 'organs of extreme perfection' like the human eye, and the sterility of certain kinds of insect).

The first two thirds of the *Origin* have thus shown that natural selection is a genuine phenomenon and that it is *capable* of explaining where existing species came from and why they are typically so well adapted to their environments. Now at last Darwin presents the evidence that natural selection is not only a *possible* explanation of the origin of species, but that it is the only reasonable one available (chapters 9 to 13). The evidence ranges from the pattern of development revealed in the fossil record, to facts about the geographical distribution of organisms, to structural and developmental similarities between otherwise very different living things. Darwin demonstrates that his view can provide satisfying explanations of such matters, while from the point of view of those who believe in divine creation (far and away the majority view among naturalists before the publication of the *Origin*) they remain inexplicable conundrums. In his final chapter Darwin recapitulates his central argument and looks forward to the 'revolution in natural history' that he rightly believed his theories would bring about.

But Darwin's views did not, of course, only have revolutionary implications for the study of biology. The theory of evolution by natural selection suggests a thoroughly materialist picture of the world which banishes vital forces and pre-ordained purposes from nature, and which implies that mental phenomena emerge when matter is arranged in complex ways.[99] Such views undermine not only traditional religious views of divine creation but also more 'sophisticated' versions of theism which claim that God works through evolution, and they were a direct challenge to the dominant ideology of Victorian England. One early reviewer of Darwin's book, the great geologist Adam Sedgwick, spoke for many: 'I cannot conclude without expressing my detestation of the theory, because of its unflinching materialism'.[100] Darwin was well aware of the materialistic consequences of his views, and as a respectable bourgeois gentleman, he was made extremely nervous by them (and was never prepared to embrace atheism). This probably explains why he took so long to publish his ideas, finally doing so only when he became aware that the young Welsh naturalist Alfred Wallace had reached similar conclusions which he was about to make public.[101]

It also explains why Marx and Engels were so enthusiastic about Darwin's theory. Less than a month after the *Origin* was published, Engels remarked in a letter to Marx that 'Darwin, whom I am just now reading, is splendid.' Marx himself read the *Origin* the following year and commented to Engels that, 'although it is developed in the crude English style, this is the book which contains the basis in natural history for our own view'.[102] Marx's point was not that evolution by natural selection automatically implies the truth of historical materialism—there is no contradiction in accepting Darwin and rejecting Marx. But Darwin's views, by supporting a general materialist perspective and by demonstrating the centrality of historical change in the biological world, certainly enhance the general plausibility of a materialist approach to human society as well.

If you want to read more of Darwin's work, I would recommend first his short *Autobiography*, second *The Voyage of the Beagle*, his account of his five year voyage around the world during which he gathered much of the evidence which he later presented in the *Origin* and first came to doubt the biblical account of creation, and third *The Descent of Man*, his most important work after the *Origin*, which discusses human evolution.[103] All that Darwin had to say about this topic in the *Origin* itself was that, when the theory of natural selection gained general acceptance, 'light will be thrown on the origin of man and his history', but it took him more than a decade before he was prepared to put his views on these matters into print. Darwin's *Descent* also contains one important theoretical advance over the *Origin*—the recognition of sexual selection as a special category of natural selection. In cases of sexual selection, certain characteristics (such as the peacock's flamboyant tail) develop in one sex, not because they make the individuals who possess them better adapted to their environment, but because they enable them to attract mates more effectively. Finally, Darwin's early notebooks on evolution have been republished under the title *Metaphysics, Materialism, and the Evolution of Mind*, and make fascinating reading.[104]

Mark Ridley's *The Problems of Evolution*[105] is a short contemporary introduction to evolutionary theory. The best biography of Darwin, which firmly places his ideas in the social and political context in which they arose, is Adrian Desmond and James Moore's *Darwin*.[106] Also well worth reading are Desmond's earlier study *The Politics of Evolution*,[107] which examines the development of evolutionary ideas in the generation before Darwin, and his two volume biography of Thomas Huxley (*Huxley: The Devil's Disciple* and *Huxley: Evolution's High Priest*[108]), who quickly became the most vocal public defender of evolutionary theory after the *Origin*'s publication and earned himself the nickname 'Darwin's bulldog'. Ronald Clark's biography *The Survival of Charles Darwin*[109] is also worth a look, primarily because the second half of the book is a useful survey of the development of biology from Darwin's death in 1882 to the present day. A more sweeping and detailed history of biology can be found in *The Growth of Biological Thought*[110] by Ernst Mayr, perhaps the most distinguished living evolutionary biologist. Although Mayr takes some potshots at vulgar Marxist approaches to history in his introduction, he also admits 'that I share some of Engels' anti-reductionist views, as stated in his *Anti-Dühring*, and that I am greatly attracted by Hegel's scheme of thesis-antithesis-synthesis...This view has dominated my presentation.'

As I mentioned above, Darwin's argument in the *Origin* provides a detailed and devastating critique of creationism. As a result, particularly in the United States, evolutionary theory has come under concerted attack over the past 20 years by the religious right, who demand equal time for 'scientific creationism' in the schools. While they have been unsuccessful in this demand, they have effectively been able to exclude evolutionary biology from the curriculum in many high schools. Today opinion polls in the US show that only about 10 percent of the population accepts the truth of Darwinian evolution, while nearly 50 percent believe that humans were created by God in the last 10,000 years.[111] There are several good books which both demolish the arguments of the 'scientific' creationists and provide useful summaries of the evidence in favour of evolution. *Abusing Science: The Case Against Creationism*[112] by the philosopher of science Philip Kitcher is one of the best, except for its final chapter which attempts to reconcile evolution with liberal theology. A good discussion by a biologist is contained in Tim Berra's *Evolution and the Myth of Creationism*.[113] The sociologist of science Dorothy Nelkin gives a social history of the dispute in *The Creation Controversy*.[114]

Here is probably a good place to mention the writings of Stephen Jay Gould (quoted above), whose books are no doubt already familiar to many readers of this journal. Gould, who is an evolutionary biologist and paleontologist at Harvard, is perhaps the best contemporary populariser of scientific ideas. I particularly recommend his first two collections of essays, *Ever Since Darwin*[115] and *The Panda's Thumb,*[116] both of which contain chapters setting Darwin's ideas in their historical context, discussions of contemporary issues in evolutionary theory, critiques of biological determinism, and much else. More recently, in books like *Wonderful Life*[117] and *Life's Grandeur*[118] (published in the US as *Full House*), Gould has argued against the common misconception that life must evolve along a single path and that human beings have somehow emerged as the inevitable outcome of this process. But while this is right, Gould sometimes seems to throw the baby out with the bathwater, apparently denying that there are any discernible evolutionary patterns, and implying that evolutionary history is nothing more than a series of accidents. This is an important mistake because—just as in human history—determinism and randomness do not exhaust the possibilities. There can be recognisable trends in a historical process even if no particular outcome is inevitable.[119] Still, even when Gould is mistaken he remains well worth reading.

The Dialectical Biologist,[120] a collection of essays by two of Gould's Harvard colleagues, Richard Levins and Richard Lewontin, is the best examination of evolutionary ideas from an explicitly Marxist perspective. Levins and Lewontin dedicate their book to Engels, 'who got it wrong a lot of the time but who got it right where it counted'.[121] The volume includes discussion of the historical and social background to Darwinism, arguments against the 'anti-ideological technocratic ideology'[122] that dominates capitalist society, reflections on the nature of dialectics, and specific examples of how a dialectical approach can lead to new insights in evolutionary biology (particularly in a chapter on 'The Organism as the Subject and Object of Evolution'). This is essential reading for anyone with a serious interest in Marxism and science.

Perhaps the biggest weakness in Darwin's work on evolution was the fact that he lacked a satisfactory theory of the mechanisms of heredity. How are characteristics passed on from parents to offspring, and why aren't favourable traits diluted by less favourable ones over successive generations? The work of the Czech monk Gregor Mendel in the 1860s marked the beginning of a satisfactory theory of heredity, but Mendel's work on the distribution of traits among successive generations of pea plants was unknown to Darwin, and was not rediscovered until the turn of the century when a new generation of biologists independently rediscovered his results. Mendel noticed that some traits appear to be dominant and others recessive, and he speculated that there were causal 'factors' in the plants that somehow governed such features as height and seed colour. In the early 20th century biologists gave these factors the name 'genes'.

Mayr's book mentioned above includes an excellent history of 'Variation and Its Inheritance' from the earliest ideas, through the emergence of Mendelian genetics, to the work of T H Morgan on fruit flies at Columbia University in the early 20th century which led to the first maps of the 'genome', and the development of modern molecular biology. Clark's biography of Darwin covers much of the same ground, including the development of the mathematical theory of population genetics in the 1930s by R A Fisher, Haldane and Sewall Wright, and the subsequent construction of the 'modern synthesis' of genetics and Darwinian evolution. The French geneticist and Nobel Prize winner François Jacob has also written a readable history of ideas about heredity called *The Logic of Life*.[123] Be warned, though, that Jacob writes from a reductionist standpoint that can get irritating.

The major breakthrough in understanding why variation exists and how inheritance takes place came in 1953 with Francis Crick and James Watson's discovery of the double helical structure of DNA (deoxyribonucleic acid), the substance in the nuclei of cells which carries genetic information from parent to offspring. The story of the discovery and the subsequent history of molecular biology is told in Horace Freeland Judson's *The Eighth Day of Creation*,[124] a book which could have done with a good editor. Watson's own account of the discovery can be found in his infamous memoir *The Double Helix*,[125] which demonstrates that his reputation as an obnoxious sexist egomaniac is well earned. On the other hand, Watson's book does effectively demolish the myth of the impartial scientist whose only concern is discovering the truth. Another molecular biologist, Gunther Stent, has edited a critical edition of Watson's book which includes reviews and other interesting commentary, as well as the original texts of many of the key scientific papers.[126] The person most slighted in Watson's account is Rosalind

Franklin, a brilliant researcher at the University of London whose X-ray diffraction photographs of DNA were crucial to determining its structure. Franklin died of cancer in 1958 and was thus deprived of sharing in the Nobel Prize awarded to Crick, Watson and her colleague Maurice Wilkins in 1962. Her role in the discovery is told in Ann Sayre's book *Rosalind Franklin and DNA*[127] which, as one reviewer put it, 'should be required reading for all aspiring scientists—especially women'.[128]

In Search of the Double Helix[129] by John Gribbin is much more than an account of how the structure of DNA was uncovered. Gribbin starts with Darwin, Mendel and the development of genetics, links molecular biology to quantum theory, and traces the history of molecular biology since Crick and Watson's discovery. Another generally reliable overview of the state of modern genetics is provided by *The Language of the Genes*[130] by Steve Jones. But perhaps most useful for busy socialists, facing the growing onslaught of arguments which claim that virtually every aspect of human behaviour can be explained genetically, are a number of recent books which mount powerful critiques of genetic determinism. The shortest and most accessible is *The Doctrine of DNA: Biology as Ideology*[131] by Lewontin. More wide ranging is *Exploding the Gene Myth*[132] by Ruth Hubbard (another Harvard biologist) and Elijah Wald. The most sophisticated response is in *Lifelines: Biology, Freedom, Determinism*, the latest book by the Marxist biologist Steven Rose.[133]

Genetic determinism (the idea that our behaviour is determined by our genes) and the closely related doctrine of genetic reductionism (the claim that all biological explanations can ultimately be replaced by explanations at the level of the gene), are just two examples of how biological ideas have been twisted to buttress ruling class ideology. Darwin's ideas were initially seen as posing a threat to the status quo, but were soon being used by the 'social Darwinists' as the basis for fallacious arguments supporting laissez-faire capitalism, social hierarchy, racism and women's oppression. Similar arguments were used in the early 20th century by the 'eugenics' movement which aimed to solve social problems by preventing those deemed biologically 'defective' from reproducing, and which eventually helped pave the way for the Nazi Holocaust.

Despite the fact that such claims have been repeatedly shown to lack scientific justification, they have reappeared whenever it has been necessary to deflect criticism from the capitalist system itself. Thus it is no surprise that biological determinism has re-emerged in various forms during the past 25 years as capitalist economies have staggered from one crisis to the next. Sociobiologists (like E O Wilson and Richard Dawkins) have argued that human beings are naturally selfish, aggressive and xenophobic, and that social inequality is ultimately a consequence of our biology—claims that have recently been revived by many working in the new field of evolutionary psychology.[134] Genetic reductionists have claimed that there are specific genes for everything from alcoholism to criminality. Racists, like Richard Herrnstein and Charles Murray in their odious book *The Bell Curve*,[135] have taken up these claims to resurrect the argument that intelligence is genetically based and that white people tend to be smarter than black ones.

Several books already mentioned, particularly those by Gould, Lewontin and Rose, take up and demolish many of these arguments. Lewontin, Rose and Leon Kamin's *Not In Our Genes*[136] is a comprehensive critique in one volume. Another good overview of many of these arguments is *From Genesis to Genocide*[137] by Stephan Chorover. A third is Martin Barker's *The New Racism*.[138] All of these books provide excellent discussion of the social and political background to the resurgence of biological determinism in the course of exploding its scientific pretensions. Probably the most comprehensive refutation of the sociobiologists' scientific arguments is in Philip Kitcher's *Vaulting Ambition*.[139] The long and sordid history of scientific racism from the early 19th century to the 1970s is told in Allan Chase's masterful study, *The Legacy of Malthus*.[140] Stephen Jay Gould covers some of the same ground in *The Mismeasure of Man*,[141] which is a first rate study of science in its social context. In its new revised edition, Gould's book includes a response to *The Bell Curve*. *In the Name of Eugenics*[142] by Daniel Kelves tells the history of the eugenics movement, while Troy Duster's *Backdoor to Eugenics*[143] shows how the misuse of new genetic technologies is bringing these old ideas back.

Conclusion

There is a fine tradition of Marxist thought about science, from the writings of Marx and Engels themselves, to the contributions of Lenin, Trotsky, Bukharin and Hessen, to the work of contemporary writers such as Richard Lewontin and Steven Rose. Marxism provides essential insights into the nature of modern science unavailable from any other perspective, and it provides the basis for both admiring its successes and critically analysing its weaknesses. But this by itself is not enough. Marxism is not simply a theory for contemplating the world. It is a revolutionary weapon which aims at the overthrow of the capitalist system. The Marxist critique of science as it currently exists is simultaneously a call for its transformation—a call to free it from the material and ideological constraints of a society based on profits for the few. 'The philosophers have only interpreted the world, in various ways; the point is to change it'.[144]

Notes

My thanks to Anthony Arnove, Judy Cox, Rob Hoveman, Kim Rabuck, John Rees, Eric Ruder and David Whitehouse for comments on an earlier version of this article.

1   'Marx and the Objectivity of Science' in R Boyd et al (eds), *The Philosophy of Science* (London, 1991), p769.

2   The terms internalism and externalism sometimes have other meanings. I am using them strictly as defined in the text. In 20th century philosophy of science, the archetypal internalists were the logical positivists of the Vienna Circle in the 1920s and 1930s, who offered highly abstract accounts of the nature of scientific theories, confirmation and explanation. By the late 1950s the positivists' attempt to explain actual scientific practice had effectively self destructed, but the decisive death blow is often seen as Thomas Kuhn's highly influential book *The Structure of Scientific Revolutions* (Chicago, 1962; 2nd edn 1970). Kuhn shows how scientific practice and methodology have undergone radical historical changes with the adoption of new 'paradigms' (roughly, major scientific theories which settle fundamental issues and provide working scientists with a steady stream of research puzzles to solve), and implies that shifts from one paradigm to another (the scientific revolutions of his book's title) are heavily influenced—perhaps even decided—by extra-scientific considerations. Kuhn's important contribution was to place science back in its historical context, and there is much to learn from his book. But the historical context in which he places science is defined so narrowly (and certainly without reference to the influence and interests of the ruling class) that he is almost inevitably led to relativist and idealist conclusions. On Kuhn's view, rival paradigms are incommensurable, which means that their adherents cannot fully understand each other and thus cannot rationally resolve their disagreements, so that science cannot be said to be approaching closer to the truth when one paradigm replaces another. Indeed, Kuhn sometimes says that supporters of different paradigms effectively inhabit different worlds, because theory constructs reality. Kuhn was reluctant to explicitly endorse the more radical consequences of his views, but many historians and sociologists of science influenced by him have not been so coy. There are several accessible surveys of these ideas, including A Chalmers, *What Is This Thing Called Science?* (Milton Keynes, 1982), W Newton-Smith, *The Rationality of Science* (London, 1981) and R Klee, *Introduction to the Philosophy of Science* (Oxford, 1997).

3   Atlantic Highlands, New Jersey, 1985. Sheehan's study begins with the writings of Marx and Engels, and ends with the dissolution of the Comintern in 1943. The author is a former member of the Communist Party who has remained sympathetic to much of what is best in the Marxist tradition, but who is not 'a Marxist in any unambiguous sense' (pxi), and who writes from the perspective of someone who wants to preserve the tradition's insights before moving on, not from the perspective of someone who is engaging with a living set of ideas. Nevertheless, I learned a lot from Sheehan's book.

4   *Capital* vol 1 (New York, 1967), ch XII, p316.

5   2nd edn Brighton, 1979. Ruben discusses how Marx's views about knowledge and reality emerged from, and help solve, problems left by his philosophical predecessors, and he attempts to articulate a Marxist theory of knowledge in greater detail. By calling his account a 'reflection theory', however, Ruben encourages a confusion between a theory of truth and a theory of knowledge which, as we shall see, it is important to avoid. The book's final chapter is a sympathetic discussion of Lenin's *Materialism and Empirio-Criticism*. Ruben is also the co-editor (with John Mepham) of the multi-volume series *Issues in Marxist Philosophy* (Atlantic Highlands, New Jersey, 1979) which contains a number of essays on dialectics, materialism and science.

6   Atlantic Highlands, New Jersey, 1988. Murray shows how Marx's own scientific method emerged from an internal critique of Hegel, and examines Marx's critique of political economy in the light of this. I have discussed Murray's interpretation in a review of his book in the *Radical Philosophy Review of Books*, no 2 (1990).

7   *The Holy Family* and *The German Ideology* are, of course, joint works written with Engels, but precisely because they are joint works they reflect Marx's views at the time as well.

8   Oxford, 1975.

9   *Economic and Philosophical Manuscripts*, in D McLellan (ed), *Karl Marx: Selected Writings* (Oxford, 1977), p94.

10   *Karl Marx* (London, 1981), p162. Wood's book is a very clear discussion of various aspects of Marx's philosophical thought. The sections on 'Philosophical Materialism' and 'The Dialectical Method' are particularly relevant to the topic of this article.

11   It is no coincidence that many recent defenders of scientific realism have been influenced by Marx. In the US these have included Hilary Putnam (in the late 1960s and early 1970s), Richard Boyd, Richard W Miller, Peter Railton and Michael Devitt. In Britain the best known figure is Roy Bhaskar. Essays by Putnam, Boyd, Miller and Railton can be found in R Boyd et al (eds), *The Philosophy of Science*, op cit.

12   *Capital* vol 3 (New York, 1967), ch XLVIII, p817.

13   *Theses on Feuerbach*, in D McLellan (ed), op cit, p156.

14   *The German Ideology*, in D McLellan (ed), op cit, p175.

15   Ibid, p160.

16   *History and Class Consciousness* (London, 1971), p204. Lukács is led to this claim because he rejects the view that human consciousness passively reflects existing reality. He is right to reject the latter view, but wrong to think that it is implied by realism or a correspondence theory of truth.

17   Ibid, pxvii.

18   *Toward a Marxist Humanism* (New York, 1968).

19   D McLellan (ed), op cit, p156.

20   *Capital* vol 1, p19.

21   P Murray, op cit, pxiv.

22   *Capital* vol 1, p20.

23   Letter to Engels, June 22 1867, *Selected Correspondence* (Moscow, 1975), p177.

24   A Wood, op cit, p219.

25   For a nice historical illustration, see the discussion of the 17th-century revolution in physics in A Einstein and L Infeld, *The Evolution of Physics* (New York, 1966), ch 1.

26   D McLellan (ed), op cit, p175.

27   Vol 1, ch XIV, section 5, p361.

28   Ibid, ch XV, section 2, p390n.

29   This argument is laid out in greater detail in P Railton, 'Marx and the Objectivity of Science', op cit.

30   The mechanical outlook was spelled out clearly by the German physicist Hermann von Helmholtz in the mid-19th century: 'Finally, therefore, we discover the problem of physical material science to be to refer natural phenomena back to unchangeable attractive and repulsive forces whose intensity depends wholly upon distance. The solubility of this problem is the condition of the complete comprehensibility of nature. Helmholtz argued that science will be ended as soon as the reduction of natural phenomena to simple forces is complete and the proof given that this is the only reduction of which the phenomena are capable.' Quoted in A Einstein and L Infeld, op cit, p54.

31   *Friedrich Engels* (New York, 1977), p91.

32   See, for instance, J D Hunley, *The Life and Thought of Friedrich Engels* (London, 1991).

33   Preface to *Dialectics of Nature* (New York, 1940), p xiv.

34   'The Philosophy of Science', in B Magee (ed), *Men of Ideas* (Oxford, 1982), p206. In the late 1960s and early 1970s Putnam developed a version of scientific realism strongly influenced by Marxist ideas, but by the time of this interview he had abandoned both realism and Marxism. Putnam goes on to claim that, while Engels' views on science are largely sensible, they are not original, but then immediately undermines this judgment by noting that Marxism 'might have made a contribution [to mainstream philosophy of science] if people had been less ideologically divided, because I think non-Marxists could have learned something from it.'

35   For the political background to these debates see P Le Blanc, *Lenin and the Revolutionary Party* (Atlantic Highlands, New Jersey, 1990), ch 8.

36   See in particular *The Analysis of Sensations* (Chicago, 1914), originally published in 1886. Mach's views are critically examined in R S Cohen and R J Seeger (eds), *Ernst Mach: Physicist and Philosopher* (Dordrecht, 1970).

37   For discussion, see G Holton, 'Mach, Einstein and the Search for Reality', in *Thematic Origins of Scientific Thought* (London, 1988).

38   Dubious social, political and philosophical ideas have led to important scientific insights on more than one occasion. Darwin claimed to have hit upon the theory of natural selection after reading the reactionary views of Thomas Malthus. For more on Darwin's case, see below.

39   Monism is the view that reality is composed of one fundamental kind of substance. Idealism (which claims that the world is composed of mental phenomena) and materialism are both varieties of monism. Some versions of the doctrine claim that the fundamental substance is neither mind nor matter, and that mind and matter are themselves composed of some underlying 'neutral' substance. Bogdanov may have believed that he was advocating some kind of neutral monism, but since he claims that the world is ultimately constructed from experience, and since experience is a mental phenomenon, his position collapses into a variety of idealism.

40   V I Lenin, *Materialism and Empirio-Criticism* (New York, 1927), pp63-64, 72.

41   This is the same mistake that Lukács was later to make—but whereas Lukács assimilates truth to knowledge, Lenin seems to assimilate knowledge to truth.

42   V I Lenin, op cit, p99.

43   London, 1975.

44   L Trotsky, *Literature and Revolution* (London, 1991), pp226-228.

45   Cited in Sheehan, op cit, p172.

46   New York, 1973.

47   Guildford, 1986.

48   New Jersey, 1998.

49   London, 1971.

50   New York, 1935. The one weak point in this collection is A M Deborin's essay on 'Karl Marx and the Present', which is a defence of the Stalinist theory of fascism and social-fascism.

51   See G Werskey, *The Visible College* (London, 1978). In this context, the writings of another Communist Party member at the time, Christopher Caudwell, should also be mentioned. Caudwell was not a professional scientist but a self taught and independently minded Marxist intellectual of broad interests, who produced original work on everything from poetry to physics, and who died at the tragically young age of 29, fighting in the Spanish Civil War. See in particular *The Crisis in Physics* (London, 1939). H Sheehan, op cit, contains a helpful exposition of Caudwell's views, and further references.

52   Oxford, 1985.
53   London, 1939.
54   Cambridge, 1954-84.
55   Cambridge, Massachusetts, 1971.
56   London, 1956.
57   'Marxism and the History of Science' in R C Olby et al (eds), *Companion to the History of Modern Science* (London, 1990), p82.
58   J D Bernal, *The Extension of Man*, (London, 1972).
59   Harmondsworth, 1964. (Originally published in 1942.)
60   Harmondsworth, 1961. (Originally published in 1944.)
61   New York, 1965.
62   Cambridge, 1977.
63   London, 1957.
64   Revised edn (London, 1985).
65   Cambridge, 1977.
66   London, 1953.
67   Oxford, 1991.
68   London, 1987.
69   New York, 1952. (Originally published 1908) p75.
70   New York, 1961. (Originally published 1916.)
71   New York, 1966. (Originally published 1938.)
72   Oxford, 1986.
73   Second edn (New York, 1993).
74   London, 1988.
75   New York, 1984.
76   'On the Intuitive Understanding of Non-locality as Implied by Quantum Theory', *Foundations of Physics* 5 (1975), pp95-96.
77   New York, 1987.
78   London, 1984.
79   London, 1995. Gribbin has also recently published *Companion to the Cosmos* (London, 1996), a useful dictionary-style guide to modern physics.
80   D Albert, *Quantum Mechanics and Experience* (London, 1992).
81   Cambridge, 1986.
82   Cambridge, 1986.
83   London, 1984.
84   London, 1988.
85   London, 1986.
86   London, 1977.
87   London, 1986.
88   New York, 1994.
89   Cambridge, 1988.
90   Harmondsworth, 1987.
91   Oxford, 1989.
92   New York, 1995.
93   This is actually the title of a short article by Dobzhansky published in the *American Biology Teacher* 35 (1973).
94   C Darwin, *The Origin of Species* (London, 1964). This is a facsimile of the first edition.
95   David Whitehouse has pointed out to me that Darwin never offers any examples of actual natural selection at work in the world. Instead he relies on imaginary examples and indirect evidence. At least one example of real natural selection was observed during Darwin's lifetime, the well known phenomenon of industrial melanism in moths, in which changes in the environment due to pollution led light

coloured moths to be replaced by dark coloured ones. Since Darwin's time, of course, numerous real cases have been observed.

96   See *Origin*, op cit, p63. Darwin's theory is often portrayed as being based on the idea of direct competition between individuals, but as the final sentence of this quotation shows, this is at best an oversimplification. On the previous page Darwin notes that 'I use the term Struggle for Existence in a large and metaphorical sense' which permits us to say, for example, that 'a plant on the edge of a desert…struggle[s] for life against the drought' (p62).

97   See S J Gould, 'Darwin's Middle Road', in *The Panda's Thumb* (London, 1980), pp65-66, for discussion and references.

98   Ibid, p68.

99   In light of the fact that evolutionary theories of mind are often portrayed as essentially reductionist, it is perhaps worth emphasising here that this is not so.

100   'Objections to Mr Darwin's Theory of the Origin of Species', in P Appleman (ed), *Darwin*, 2nd edn (London, 1979), p222. Sedgwick's review originally appeared anonymously in *The Spectator*, March 24 1860.

101   See S J Gould, 'Darwin's Delay', in *Ever Since Darwin* (London, 1977).

102   Both letters cited in *Marxism and Modern Thought*, p193.

103   All of these books are available in numerous editions.

104   Chicago, 1980.

105   Oxford, 1983.

106   Harmondsworth, 1992.

107   (Chicago, 1990).

108   (London, 1994 and 1997).

109   New York, 1984.

110   London, 1982.

111   *Los Angeles Times*, 2 May 1992.

112   London, 1982.

113   Stanford, California, 1990.

114   Boston, 1982.

115   London, 1977.

116   London, 1980.

117   London, 1989.

118   London, 1996.

119   The philosopher of biology Elliott Sober provides a sophisticated recent discussion of this issue in 'Progress and Direction in Evolution', in J Campbell and J Schopf (eds), *Creative Evolution* (London, 1994). Sober concludes that 'evolution is not, of necessity, a directional process. In this respect it fails to resemble thermodynamic processes, which seem to have an intrinsic directionality. Yet, in contingent circumstances, evolution can give rise to directional trends. The challenge to current biology is to document these trends and to explain them.'

120   London, 1985.

121   Levin & Lewontin, pv.

122   Ibid, p165.

123   New York, 1982.

124   New York, 1979.

125   (London, 1968). A thirtieth anniversary edition of Watson's book is due to be published this year.

126   London, 1980.

127   New York, 1975,

128   Quoted on the book's back cover.

129   London, 1985.

130   London, 1994.

131   R Lewontin, *The Doctrine of DNA: Biology as Ideology* (London, 1993).

132   Boston, 1993.
133   Oxford, 1997. See John Parrington's review in *International Socialism* 78.
134   See, for example, S Pinker, *How the Mind Works* (London, 1997).
135   New York, 1994.
136   New York, 1984.
137   London, 1979.
138   London, 1981.
139   London, 1985.
140   New York, 1980.
141   Revised edn (London, 1996).
142   Berkeley, California, 1985.
143   London, 1990.
144   K Marx, 'Eleventh Thesis on Feuerbach', in D McLellan (ed), op cit, p158.

The Socialist Workers Party is one of an international grouping of socialist organisations:

AUSTRALIA:	International Socialists, PO Box A338, Sydney South
BELGIUM	Socialisme International, 80, Rue Bois Gotha, 4000 Liége
BRITAIN:	Socialist Workers Party, PO Box 82, London E3
CANADA:	International Socialists, PO Box 339, Station E, Toronto, Ontario M6H 4E3
CYPRUS:	Ergatiki Demokratia, PO Box 7280, Nicosia
DENMARK:	Internationale Socialister, Postboks 642, 2200 København N
GREECE:	Sosialistiko Ergatiko Komma, c/o Workers Solidarity, PO Box 8161, Athens 100 10
HOLLAND:	Internationale Socialisten, PO Box 92052, 1090 AA Amsterdam
IRELAND:	Socialist Workers Party, PO Box 1648, Dublin 8
NEW ZEALAND:	Socialist Workers Organization, PO Box 8851, Auckland
NORWAY:	Internasjonale Socialisterr, Postboks 5370, Majorstua, 0304 Oslo 3
POLAND:	Solidarność Socjalistyczna, PO Box 12, 01-900 Warszawa 118
SOUTH AFRICA:	Socialist Workers Organisation, PO Box 18530, Hillbrow 2038, Johannesberg
SPAIN:	Socialismo Internacional, Apartado 563, 08080, Barcelona
UNITED STATES:	International Socialist Organisation, PO Box 16085, Chicago, Illinois 60616
ZIMBABWE:	International Socialist Organisation, PO Box 6758, Harare

The following issues of *International Socialism* (second series) are available price £3 (including postage) from IS Journal, PO Box 82, London E3 3LH. *International Socialism* 2:58 and 2:65 are available on cassette from the Royal National Institute for the Blind (Peterborough Library Unit). Phone 01733 370777.

International Socialism 2:78 Spring 1998
Colin Sparks: The eye of the storm ★ Shin Gyoung-hee: The crisis and the workers' movement in South Korea ★ Rob Hoveman: Financial crises and the real economy ★ Peter Morgan: Class divisions in the gay community ★ Alex Callinicos: The secret of the dialectic ★ John Parrington: It's life, Jim, but not as we know it ★ Judy Cox: Robin Hood: earl, outlaw or rebel? ★ Ian Birchall: The vice-like hold of nationalism? A comment on Megan Trudell's 'Prelude to revolution' ★ William Keach: In perspective: Alexander Cockburn and Christopher Hitchens ★

International Socialism 2:77 Winter 1997
Audrey Farrell: Addicted to profit—capitalism and drugs ★ Mike Gonzalez: The resurrections of Che Guevara ★ Sam Ashman: India: imperialism, partition and resistance ★ Henry Maitles: Never Again! ★ John Baxter: The return of political science ★ Dave Renton: Past its peak ★

International Socialism 2:76 Autumn 1997
Mike Haynes: Was there a parliamentary alternative in 1917? ★ Megan Trudell: Prelude to revolution: class consciousness and the First World War ★ Judy Cox: A light in the darkness ★ Pete Glatter: Victor Serge: writing for the future ★ Gill Hubbard: A guide to action ★ Chris Bambery: Review article: Labour's history of hope and despair ★

International Socialism 2:75 Summer 1997
John Rees: The class struggle under New Labour ★ Alex Callinicos: Europe: the mounting crisis ★ Lance Selfa: Mexico after the Zapatista uprising ★ William Keach: Rise like lions? Shelley and the revolutionary left ★ Judy Cox: What state are we really in? ★ John Parrington: In perspective: Valentin Voloshinov ★

International Socialism 2:74 Spring 1997
Colin Sparks: Tories, Labour and the crisis in education ★ Colin Wilson: The politics of information technology ★ Mike Gonzalez: No more heroes: Nicaragua 1996 ★ Christopher Hill: Tulmults and commotions: turning the world upside down ★ Peter Morgan: Capitalism without frontiers? ★ Alex Callinicos: Minds, machines and evolution ★ Anthony Arnove: In perspective: Noam Chomsky★

International Socialism 2:73 Winter 1996
Chris Harman: Globalisation: a critique of a new orthodoxy ★ Chris Bambery: Marxism and sport ★ John Parrington: Computers and consciousness: a reply to Alex Callinicos ★ Joe Faith: Dennett, materialism and empiricism ★ Megan Trudell: Who made the American Revolution? ★ Mark O'Brien: The class conflicts which shaped British history ★ John Newsinger: From class war to Cold War ★ Alex Callinicos: The state in debate ★ Charlie Kimber: Review article: coming to terms with barbarism in Rwanda in Burundi★

International Socialism 2:72 Autumn 1996
Alex Callinicos: Betrayal and discontent: Labour under Blair ★ Sue Cockerill and Colin Sparks: Japan in crisis ★ Richard Levins: When science fails us ★ Ian Birchall: The Babeuf bicentenary: conspiracy or revolutionary party? ★ Brian Manning: A voice for the poor ★ Paul O'Flinn: From the kingdom of necessity to the kingdom of freedom: Morris's *News from Nowhere* ★ Clare Fermont: Bookwatch: Palestine and the Middle East 'peace process'★

International Socialism 2:71 Summer 1996
Chris Harman: The crisis of bourgeois economics ★ Hassan Mahamdallie: William Morris and revolutionary Marxism ★ Alex Callinicos: Darwin, materialism and revolution ★ Chris Nineham: Raymond Williams: revitalising the left? ★ Paul Foot: A passionate prophet of liberation ★ Gill Hubbard: Why has feminism failed women? ★ Lee Sustar: Bookwatch: fighting to unite black and white★

International Socialism 2:70 Spring 1996
Alex Callinicos: South Africa after apartheid ★ Chris Harman: France's hot December ★ Brian Richardson: The making of a revolutionary ★ Gareth Jenkins: Why Lucky Jim turned right—an obituary of Kingsley Amis ★ Mark O'Brien: The bloody birth of capitalism ★ Lee Humber: Studies in revolution ★ Adrian Budd: A new life for Lenin ★ Martin Smith: Bookwatch: the General Strike★

International Socialism 2:69 Winter 1995
Lindsey German: The Balkan war: can there be peace? ★ Duncan Blackie: The left and the Balkan war ★ Nicolai Gentchev: The myth of welfare dependency ★ Judy Cox: Wealth, poverty and class in Britain today ★ Peter Morgan: Trade unions and strikes ★ Julie Waterson: The party at its peak ★ Megan Trudell: Living to some purpose ★ Nick Howard: The rise and fall of socialism in one city ★ Andy Durgan: Bookwatch: Civil war and revolution in Spain ★

International Socialism 2:68 Autumn 1995
Ruth Brown: Racism and immigration in Britain ★ John Molyneux: Is Marxism deterministic? ★ Stuart Hood: News from nowhere? ★ Lee Sustar: Communism in the heart of the beast ★ Peter Linebaugh: To the teeth and forehead of our faults ★ George Paizis: Back to the future ★ Phil Marshall: The children of stalinism ★ Paul D'Amato: Bookwatch: 100 years of cinema ★

International Socialism 2:67 Summer 1995
Paul Foot: When will the Blair bubble burst? ★ Chris Harman: From Bernstein to Blair—100 years of revisionism ★ Chris Bambery: Was the Second World War a war for democracy? ★ Alex Callinicos: Hope against the Holocaust ★Chris Nineham: Is the media all powerful? ★ Peter Morgan: How the West was won ★ Charlie Hore: Bookwatch: China since Mao ★

International Socialism 2:66 Spring 1995
Dave Crouch: The crisis in Russia and the rise of the right ★ Phil Gasper: Cruel and unusual punishment: the politics of crime in the United States ★ Alex Callinicos: Backwards to liberalism ★ John Newsinger: Matewan: film and working class struggle ★ John Rees: The light and the dark ★ Judy Cox: How to make the Tories disappear ★ Charlie Hore: Jazz: a reply to the critics ★ Pat Riordan: Bookwatch: Ireland ★

International Socialism 2:65 Special issue
Lindsey German: Frederick Engels: life of a revolutionary ★ John Rees: Engels' Marxism ★ Chris Harman: Engels and the origins of human society ★ Paul McGarr: Engels and natural science ★

International Socialism 2:64 Autumn 1994
Chris Harman: The prophet and the proletariat ★ Kieran Allen: What is changing in Ireland ★ Mike Haynes: The wrong road on Russia ★ Rob Ferguson: Hero and villain ★ Jane Elderton: Suffragette style ★ Chris Nineham: Two faces of modernism ★ Mike Hobart, Dave Harker and Matt Kelly: Three replies to 'Jazz—a people's music?' ★ Charlie Kimber: Bookwatch: South Africa— the struggle continues ★

International Socialism 2:63 Summer 1994
Alex Callinicos: Crisis and class struggle in Europe today ★ Duncan Blackie: The United Nations and the politics of imperialism ★ Brian Manning: The English Revolution and the transition from feudalism to capitalism ★ Lee Sustar: The roots of multi-racial labour unity in the United States ★ Peter Linebaugh: Days of villainy: a reply to two critics ★ Dave Sherry: Trotsky's last, greatest struggle ★ Peter Morgan: Geronimo and the end of the Indian wars ★ Dave Beecham: Ignazio Silone and *Fontamara* ★ Chris Bambery: Bookwatch: understanding fascism ★

International Socialism 2:62 Spring 1994
Sharon Smith: Mistaken identity—or can identity politics liberate the oppressed? ★ Iain Ferguson: Containing the crisis—crime and the Tories ★ John Newsinger: Orwell and the Spanish Revolution ★ Chris Harman: Change at the first millenium ★ Adrian Budd: Nation and empire—Labour's foreign policy 1945-51 ★ Gareth Jenkins: Novel questions ★ Judy Cox: Blake's revolution ★ Derek Howl: Bookwatch: the Russian Revolution ★

International Socialism 2:61 Winter 1994
Lindsey German: Before the flood? ★ John Molyneux: The 'politically correct' controversy ★ David McNally: E P Thompson—class struggle and historical materialism ★ Charlie Hore: Jazz— a people's music ★ Donny Gluckstein: Revolution and the challenge of labour ★ Charlie Kimber: Bookwatch: the Labour Party in decline ★

International Socialism 2:59 Summer 1993
Ann Rogers: Back to the workhouse ★ Kevin Corr and Andy Brown: The labour aristocracy and the roots of reformism ★ Brian Manning: God, Hill and Marx ★ Henry Maitles: Cutting the wire: a criticial appraisal of Primo Levi ★ Hazel Croft: Bookwatch: women and work ★

International Socialism 2:58 Spring 1993
Chris Harman: Where is capitalism going? (part one) ★ Ruth Brown and Peter Morgan: Politics and the class struggle today: a roundtable discussion ★ Richard Greeman: The return of Com-

rade Tulayev: Victor Serge and the tragic vision of Stalinism ★ Norah Carlin: A new English revolution ★ John Charlton: Building a new world ★ Colin Barker: A reply to Dave McNally ★

International Socialism 2:56 Autumn 1992
Chris Harman: The Return of the National Question ★ Dave Treece: Why the Earth Summit failed ★ Mike Gonzalez: Can Castro survive? ★ Lee Humber and John Rees: The good old cause—an interview with Christopher Hill ★ Ernest Mandel: The Impasse of Schematic Dogmatism ★
International Socialism 2:55 Summer 1992
Alex Callinicos: Race and class ★ Lee Sustar: Racism and class struggle in the American Civil War era ★ Lindsey German and Peter Morgan: Prospects for socialists—an interview with Tony Cliff ★ Robert Service: Did Lenin lead to Stalin? ★ Samuel Farber: In defence of democratic revolutionary socialism ★ David Finkel: Defending 'October' or sectarian dogmatism? ★ Robin Blackburn: Reply to John Rees ★ John Rees: Dedicated followers of fashion ★ Colin Barker: In praise of custom ★ Sheila McGregor: Revolutionary witness ★

International Socialism 2:54 Spring 1992
Sharon Smith: Twilight of the American dream ★ Mike Haynes: Class and crisis—the transition in eastern Europe ★ Costas Kossis: A miracle without end? Japanese capitalism and the world economy ★ Alex Callinicos: Capitalism and the state system: A reply to Nigel Harris ★ Steven Rose: Do animals have rights? ★ John Charlton: Crime and class in the 18th century ★ John Rees: Revolution, reform and working class culture ★ Chris Harman: Blood simple ★

International Socialism 2:51 Summer 1991
Chris Harman: The state and capitalism today ★ Alex Callinicos: The end of nationalism? ★ Sharon Smith: Feminists for a strong state? ★ Colin Sparks and Sue Cockerill: Goodbye to the Swedish miracle ★ Simon Phillips: The South African Communist Party and the South African working class ★ John Brown: Class conflict and the crisis of feudalism ★

International Socialism 2:49 Winter 1990
Chris Bambery: The decline of the Western Communist Parties ★ Ernest Mandel: A theory which has not withstood the test of time ★ Chris Harman: Criticism which does not withstand the test of logic ★ Derek Howl: The law of value In the USSR ★ Terry Eagleton: Shakespeare and the class struggle ★ Lionel Sims: Rape and pre-state societies ★ Sheila McGregor: A reply to Lionel Sims ★

International Socialism 2:48 Autumn 1990
Lindsey German: The last days of Thatcher ★ John Rees: The new imperialism ★ Neil Davidson and Donny Gluckstein: Nationalism and the class struggle in Scotland ★ Paul McGarr: Order out of chaos ★

International Socialism 2:46 Winter 1989
Chris Harman: The storm breaks ★ Alex Callinicos: Can South Africa be reformed? ★ John Saville: Britain, the Marshall Plan and the Cold War ★ Sue Clegg: Against the stream ★ John Rees: The rising bourgeoisie ★

International Socialism 2:44 Autumn 1989
Charlie Hore: China: Tiananmen Square and after ★ Sue Clegg: Thatcher and the welfare state ★ John Molyneux: *Animal Farm* revisited ★ David Finkel: After Arias, is the revolution over? ★ John Rose: Jews in Poland ★

International Socialism 2:41 Winter 1988
Polish socialists speak out: Solidarity at the Crossroads ★ Mike Haynes: Nightmares of the market ★ Jack Robertson: Socialists and the unions ★ Andy Strouthous: Are the unions in decline? ★ Richard Bradbury: What is Post-Structuralism? ★ Colin Sparks: George Bernard Shaw ★

International Socialism 2:39 Summer 1988
Chris Harman and Andy Zebrowski: Glasnost, before the storm ★ Chanie Rosenberg: Labour and the fight against fascism ★ Mike Gonzalez: Central America after the Peace Plan ★ Ian Birchall: Raymond Williams ★ Alex Callinicos: Reply to John Rees ★

International Socialism 2:35 Summer 1987
Pete Green: Capitalism and the Thatcher years ★ Alex Callinicos: Imperialism, capitalism and the state today ★ Ian Birchall: Five years of *New Socialist* ★ Callinicos and Wood debate 'Looking for alternatives to reformism' ★ David Widgery replies on 'Beating Time' ★

International Socialism 2:30 Autumn 1985
Gareth Jenkins: Where is the Labour Party heading? ★ David McNally: Debt, inflation and the rate of profit ★ Ian Birchall: The terminal crisis in the British Communist Party ★ replies on Women's oppression and *Marxism Today* ★

International Socialism 2:29 Summer 1985
Special issue on the class struggle and the left in the aftermath of the miners' defeat ★ Tony Cliff: Patterns of mass strike ★ Chris Harman: 1984 and the shape of things to come ★ Alex Callinicos: The politics of *Marxism Today* ★

International Socialism 2:26 Spring 1985
Pete Green: Contradictions of the American boom ★ Colin Sparks: Labour and imperialism ★ Chris Bambery: Marx and Engels and the unions ★ Sue Cockerill: The municipal road to socialism ★ Norah Carlin: Is the family part of the superstructure? ★ Kieran Allen: James Connolly and the 1916 rebellion ★

International Socialism 2:25 Autumn 1984
John Newsinger: Jim Larkin, Syndicalism and the 1913 Dublin Lockout ★ Pete Binns: Revolution and state capitalism in the Third World ★ Colin Sparks: Towards a police state? ★ Dave Lyddon: Demystifying the downturn ★ John Molyneux: Do working class men benefit from women's oppression? ★

International Socialism 2:18 Winter 1983
Donny Gluckstein: Workers' councils in Western Europe ★ Jane Ure Smith: The early Communist press in Britain ★ John Newsinger: The Bolivian Revolution ★ Andy Durgan: Largo Caballero and Spanish socialism ★ M Barker and A Beezer: Scarman and the language of racism ★

International Socialism 2:14 Winter 1981
Chris Harman: The riots of 1981 ★ Dave Beecham: Class struggle under the Tories ★ Tony Cliff: Alexandra Kollontai ★ L James and A Paczuska: Socialism needs feminism ★ reply to Cliff on Zetkin ★ Feminists In the labour movement ★

International Socialism 2:13 Summer 1981
Chris Harman: The crisis last time ★ Tony Cliff: Clara Zetkin ★ Ian Birchall: Left Social Democracy In the French Popular Front ★ Pete Green: Alternative Economic Strategy ★ Tim Potter: The death of Eurocommunism ★